Kent Cynewulf, Charles William

Elene

An Old English Poem

Kent Cynewulf, Charles William

Elene
An Old English Poem

ISBN/EAN: 9783744710886

Printed in Europe, USA, Canada, Australia, Japan

Cover: Foto ©Thomas Meinert / pixelio.de

More available books at **www.hansebooks.com**

AN OLD ENGLISH POEM

EDITED WITH INTRODUCTION, LATIN ORIGINAL, NOTES, AND
COMPLETE GLOSSARY

BY

CHARLES W. KENT, M.A.(*U. of Va.*), PH.D.(*Leipsic*)

PROFESSOR OF ENGLISH AND MODERN LANGUAGES
IN THE UNIVERSITY OF TENNESSEE

BOSTON, U.S.A., AND LONDON
PUBLISHED BY GINN & COMPANY
1889

TYPOGRAPHY BY J. S. CUSHING & CO., BOSTON.

PRESSWORK BY GINN & CO., BOSTON.

TO

THOSE SCHOLARS

TO WHOM AMERICA OWES THE REVIVAL OF THE
STUDY OF

Old English

THIS LITTLE VOLUME IS DEDICATED

AS A MARK OF THE AUTHOR'S HIGH ESTEEM, AND A
PLEDGE OF HIS HUMBLE SUPPORT

PREFACE.

⎯⎯◆⎯⎯

It was at first intended that this edition should be the joint work of Dr. Henry Johnson, of Bowdoin College, Maine, and the present editor. Those who miss the scholarly criticism and excellent taste of Dr. Johnson cannot more sincerely regret that his duties and engagements threw the burden of editing upon me, than I have regretted the loss of his aid and advice. His sympathy and interest, I am fortunate in being able to say, I have retained.

Because I do not know how to divide my knowledge in order to ascribe to its proper source each of its parts, I gratefully and cheerfully acknowledge my general indebtedness to my esteemed instructors, Drs. Napier, Zupitza, and Wülker. Without their influence and encouragement my study of Old English would have been meagre indeed, and without their instruction perhaps this work would never have been attempted.

In attributing, then, all that is good in this edition to them, I assume all responsibility for its errors and deficiencies.

To Professor Wülker I am furthermore indebted for renewed expressions of interest in this edition, and to Professor Garnett, of the University of Virginia, and Dr.

Baskervill, of Vanderbilt University, I owe sincere thanks for appreciated kindnesses.

The text of this edition is that of· Zupitza's Second Edition, carefully compared with Wülker's Edition and Zupitza's Third Edition, in which the results of Napier's collation are contained.

The introduction and the notes have been prepared as helps for students, and in nowise to furnish scholars with an *apparatus criticus.* The glossary has been made more complete than is usual in English editions of Old English poems, and it is hoped that it may prove of especial use to students.

I do not deprecate unfavorable criticism; if the book deserve it, in the interest of scholarship, let it not be withheld; but I do beg those to whom the errors seem too numerous, to attribute them not to carelessness, but to my inexperience in text-editing, and the necessity I have been under of being my own proof-reader.

CHARLES W. KENT.

UNIVERSITY OF TENNESSEE,
June 3, 1889.

INTRODUCTION.

MANUSCRIPT.

THAT a manuscript in letters that resembled the Latin letters, but in a language unknown to the Italian scholars, was preserved in the Cathedral Library in Vercelli, was known early in this century. It was even conjectured that this was an Old English manuscript; but this was not ascertained with certainty until 1822, when Dr. Fr. Blume visited, among others, the library of Vercelli, and not only called the attention of scholars to it, but also made a copy of the poetical parts. Blume published the results of this famous visit to Vercelli, in 1824.

Kemble intended to examine the manuscript for himself (1834) and publish the results, but was prevented by a protracted stay in Germany and the obstruction of the mountain passes. He returned to England to find that the Record-Commission had employed Dr. Blume to copy the manuscript, and engaged Mr. Thorpe to extract and print the poems.

The poems were first published in Appendix B to Mr. Cooper's Report for 1836. From one of the few copies of this Report issued, Jacob Grimm published his "Andreas und Elene," 1840, and later (1843 and 1856) Kemble published "The Poetry of the Codex Vercellensis."

The manuscript, according to Wülker, who has twice examined the Codex carefully, consists of twenty *lagen* ("quires"), with one added folio. Each one of these *lagen* is marked with numbers and with letters in this wise. For example: Lage II. begins 10ᵃ, which is marked at the top II.; it closes on 18ᵇ where at the bottom B stands. Lage III. ends 24ᵇ; here we find C at the bottom, etc. This system of marking shows us at once that the manuscript exists to-day very much as it left the copyist's hands. There are some leaves missing which were clearly cut out before the copying was completed, because they cause no break; other leaves have been cut out since.

Wülker is of the opinion that the copy was made by two, probably three, copyists. This copy was probably made about the beginning of the eleventh century.

The most puzzling question connected with the Codex Vercellensis is this, — How comes it to be in Vercelli? There are several theories to account for this. The Italian scholar Gazzera was of the opinion [1] that Johannes Scotus Erigena, who sojourned a while in Vercelli, was the medium through which it reached Vercelli. Scotus died in 875. The manuscript cannot be so old. Wülker says (*Grundriss*, p. 237): "Ich kann nur *eine* Erklärung, die mir aber auch genügend zu sein scheint, finden. Wie mir in Vercelli mitgeteilt wurde, befand sich dort ziemlich frühe ein Hospiz für angelsächische Pilger, welche nach Rom wollten. Vercelli liegt ja auch für jeden, der über den Mont Cenis, den kleinen oder grossen St. Bernard wollte (dies waren im frühern Mittelalter die Strassen, welche für einen Angelsachsen in Betracht kamen), geradezu auf dem Wege nach Rom. Hier mag bei dem Hospiz auch eine kleine Bibliothek gewesen sein und aus dieser dann später die Handschrift in den Besitz der Dombibliothek übergegangen sein."

This is a reasonable conjecture; but it is based upon no direct, or even strong, circumstantial evidence. Wülker mentions, in a foot-note on pp. 485, 486, of the *Grundriss*, the opinion of a certain critic in the *Quarterly Review*, vol. lxxv. (December, 1844, and March, 1845), that Guala Bicchiere gave this manuscript, along with other collections, to this library.

Pauli in his "History of England," iii. 512, accepts this as true, and in 1866 (in the *Gött. Gel. Anz.*, p. 1412), says: "Es ist längst bekannt dass das Buch erst im Jahre 1218 mit dem Kardinal Guala nach Sant Andrea zu Vercelli kam." Wülker characterizes this opinion as a supposition which has much to oppose it.

In the University of California Library Bulletin No. 10, Cook has examined with acumen and pains this question. After quoting the words of the critic and Pauli, he says: —

"The facts upon which the Quarterly Reviewer and Pauli seem to have based their inferences are these, —

---

[1] This view of Gazzera is found in No. 12 of the *Serapeum*, published by Naumann, Leipzig, 1857.

"1. Cardinal Guala was in England from 1216 to 1218.

"2. While in England he had in his possession the priory of St. Andrew at Chester (*Quarterly Review*) or at Chesterton in Cambridgeshire (Pauli).

"3. After his return to Italy he founded the Collegiate Church of St. Andrew, at Vercelli, and bestowed upon it relics of English saints.

"4. The income from his English benefices perhaps enabled him to establish and endow the church at Vercelli.

"5. The plan and many of the details of the church are Early English.

"6. One of the chief poems of the Vercelli book is 'St. Andrew.'"

After a careful examination of these and other grounds of inferences, Cook says:—

"The facts not hitherto adduced in support of the hypothesis, and which seem to be as conclusive as circumstantial evidence can well be, are: Guala was a learned man, zealous for learning and religion, and the owner of perhaps the finest private library possessed at that time in Western Europe. The funds for the establishment of the monastery and the purchase of his books must have come largely from England — and why not certain books, also? He must have been open-minded, and appreciative of the good he found in foreign parts, and especially anxious to testify his appreciation of English art; then why not of English letters? His spirit of good-will toward England was to some extent reciprocated there, and he sought to perpetuate it by selecting as Abbot an ecclesiastic who, though French, should have English connections and sympathies and a stake in English prosperity. The wisdom of his course is attested by the renown of the monastery school, and the fact that it immediately attracted one of the greatest Englishmen of the Middle Ages, who remained a firm friend after his departure and perhaps gained other friends for its head. Guala must have thought oftenest of St. Martin and St. Andrew, patrons of France and North Britain respectively, especially revered by the two foreign nations in which his lot was cast, and which he afterwards honored on his return to his native country and his native town. Several circumstances must have conspired to deepen the impression thus made, particularly with reference to St. Andrew. We need not be surprised, then, at his immediate commemoration of that saint (by founding the monastery of St. Andrew in 1219), nor should we be surprised if a book once belonging to him commemorated both St. Martin and St. Andrew. By evincing a special interest in the Vercelli book, he would have been honoring another saint (St. Helena) peculiarly dear to the English heart. Finally, his library did contain one or more books in English chirography, was bequeathed to this monastery, and, with whatever augmentations it had received, was a notable one at the beginning of the fifteenth century."

This chain of circumstances, constructed upon evidence adduced and compared by Cook, may not be flawless, but it represents at present not only the most plausible, but by far the best substantiated theory to account for the presence of this famous book in Vercelli.

"Elene" is found in the Vercelli book in folios 121ᵃ–133ᵇ, and is complete.

AUTHOR.

KEMBLE first discovered that the runes in " The Riddles," " Crist," " Juliana," and " Elene," gave the name *Cynewulf* [ᚳᚤᚾᛖᚹᚢᛚᚠ], and recognized in this the name of the author of these poems.

Much has been written about this author, and, upon small foundations of fact, many imposing structures of his life have been erected. As a matter of fact, very little is known about him except that the authorship of the works already mentioned — which bear, as it were, his signature — entitle him to our respect and grateful memory. It is generally agreed that he lived in the eighth century. Ten Brink puts the date of his birth between 720 and 730. Ten Brink and Rieger have attempted to show that he was by birth a Northumbrian. This they will establish by proving that the proper form of the name is *Cænewulf*, not *Cynewulf*. Their proof is in no wise conclusive; and, as the manuscript is West-Saxon, and there is no linguistic testimony to a Northumbrian origin, the presumption is that he was a West-Saxon. His youth was hopeful and full of joy (1264), and hunting was one of its greatest pleasures (1266); the bow and his caparisoned horse were his beloved companions (1260). To him, too,

were well known the festive mead-halls, where the assembled lis-
teners had applauded his song and rewarded him with golden
gifts (1259ᵗ); but even in the midst of these distractions, frequent
thoughts of the cross and all it portended had entered his mind ·
(1252); but it was not until he became an old man (1247) that,
after much study of books, he fathomed its real mystery (1255).
Scholars once thought that there was evidence in the words "þurh
léohtne hâd" (1246) that he entered the ranks of the clericals;
but there seems no justification of this interpretation, and no evidence, except an austere monastic asceticism, that he was in any
way connected with the church.   He complains of the burdens of
his life in his old age, and asserts that all the joy of living has
passed out of his life with the vanishing days.

"The Riddles" belong, no doubt, to the youthful period of his
life; and it is altogether probable that the "unwise words formerly
spoken" (1285) may refer to these worldly poems.   "Elene," from
internal evidence as well as by poetical worth, is no doubt his last
work, while "Crist" and "Juliana" belong between "The Riddles"
and "Elene."   These are the only works that can be declared to
be Cynewulf's.

Among others ascribed to him, *very probable* seem the last part
of "Guðlac," and "Phœnix"; *possible*, "The Harrowing of Hell,"
"Andreas" and "Ruthwell Cross"; *very improbable*, "Bi manna
cræftum," "Bi manna wyrdum," "Bi manna mode," "Bi manna
lease," "Old English Physiology" (designated a Fragment by
Thorpe), "The Wanderer," "The Seafarer," "The Ruin."

THEME, PLAN, AND LITERARY MERIT OF
THE POEM.

CYNEWULF tells us that this work of his was the joint result of
his reading and reflection, that the material was collected, and that
its present shape cost him much thought — perhaps many a sleep-
less night (1237 ff.).   The question arises, at once, Where had he
found his material?

Source. — It has been generally accepted that the source of this
poem is the "Vita Quiriaci" in the *Acta Sanctorum* of the 4th of

May. It has been thought by some that Cynewulf may have used the Greek original direct, and not through a Latin medium; while Glöde, in "Anglia," ix.,[2] attempts to show that the source of "Elene" must have possessed some other form than that given in this work. Glöde's argument, while ingenious and suggestive, is by no means convincing.

Treatment of Original. — Comparing in outline the text of this poem with its source, we find these peculiarities: —

The few lines relating to Constantine's fear of the opposing hosts, and the appearance of the angel to allay this terror, are expanded to some forty odd (57–98). The vivid description of the battle is the author's work (110 ff.). Constantine's return home and his inquiry about the cross are described much more fully (148 ff). There is no notice in the text of the visit of Eusebius, from whom Constantine is said to have received baptism; but, on the other hand, Silvester is said to have performed this act (198 ff.). We have no mention, in this part of the poem, that Constantine built churches and destroyed idols' temples (193 ff.).

The simple mention, in the original, that Helena was sent to seek the cross is expanded into a description of Constantine's investigation of the Scriptures and consequent command (195 ff.); while no mention is made in the poem of Helena's careful study of the Scriptures. The splendid description of the journey of Helena is the poet's own conception (220 ff.).

After Helena arrives in Jerusalem and begins to hold assemblies of the learned Jews, there is a marked parallelism between text and original; so in divisions IIII., V., VI., VII., VIII., IX., X., *i.e.* 277–894. In these, however, Judas's prayer — a most remarkable production — is greatly expanded (726 ff.). A like expansion is found in the Devil's speech (899–934) and Judas's rejoinder (940–953), as well as in Helena's gratification (953–967).

The description of the spread of the news concerning the discovery of the cross, and the effect of this news, the announcement of this discovery to Constantine, his order to erect a church upon the site, and Helena's execution of this order, as well as the ark in which the cross was to be kept, are barely mentioned in the original (968–1033).

The baptism of Judas, his elevation to the bishopric, and Helena's delight, are drawn from the original (1033–1067), as are also the discovery of the nails (1067–1147), the use made of the nails (1147–1197), Helena's injunction, etc. (1197–1236). From 1237 to the end is, of course, independent of any basis.

In general it may be said, that, though Cynewulf has followed his source with fidelity, he has rarely limited himself to a literal translation — and never, except for a few clauses or sentences. Now and then there is a striking parallelism between the text and the original, though freedom in expression, and, more frequently, expansion of the thought, are characteristics of the poem. In several places there have been noted interpolations; and these belong to the chief beauties of the poem. Perhaps the appreciative reader would most praise the description of the battle and the description of Helena's journey, both of which Cynewulf himself draws.

The *motif* of this Christian legend is the discovery of the cross; and the whole action of the poem proper leads to this end. The *dramatis personæ* are chiefly Helena and Cyriacus; in less important rôles, Constantine, the Devil, and the wise men among the Jews, and Constantine's counsellors. The Huns, Goths and Franks, Jews and Romans, complete the list of personages.

Constantine's vision of the cross, after having experienced the terrors of imminent danger, is the type of Helena's vision of the true cross, after braving the dangers of the deep, hostile peoples, and conspiring enemies. From one vision to another we are led without much clogging of dramatic action, save that due to the peculiarities of Old English style, in describing effects of events by corresponding states of mind, in adding predicate after predicate to personalities, etc. On the whole, however, little time is lost, few words wasted, in picturing fully Helena's journeyings, her pleadings, her stratagem, and her success. One cannot help feeling that the climax has been reached with the discovery of the cross.

The historical account of Judas sounds like an author's postscript to tell the reader what became of a certain character; while Helena's anxiety about the nails may contribute to the perfection of her saintly character, but in nowise to the unity and harmony of the poem.

Division XV., the most entertaining portion for some reasons, is a kind of author's appendix, filled with autobiographical notes and a salutary "exhortation in conclusion," and forms no part of the poem proper.

METRICAL INTRODUCTION.

THE essential element of Old English verse is the regular recur-
rence of accented syllables.   The marked characteristics of Old
English verse are that it is stichic and alliterative.   The so-called
" long-verse " consists of two hemistichs, which are separated by
cæsura and united by alliteration.   In each of these hemistichs
there are two accented syllables; and at least one of these accented
syllables in the first hemistich must be used in alliteration with
one of the accented syllables in the second hemistich.   All words
beginning with vowels may be used in alliteration, as may all words
with the same initial consonants;   except that *sc*, *sp*, and *st* are
always taken together, — and hence may be used only with *sc*, *sp*,
st, respectively, — and that *j* and *g* may be so used.

Of the *four* accented syllables in a long-verse, 1, 2, and 3 may
show alliteration.

> *w*intra for *w*orulde, þæs þe *w*ealdend god   4

So may 1, 2, and 4, —

> *r*incas under *r*oderum, wǽron *R*ômware   46

So may 2, 3, and 4, —

> heht þâ *w*igena *w*eard þâ *w*îsestan   153

So may 1 and 3, —

> sô∂ fæstra lêoht; þâ wæs *s*yxte geâr   7

So may 2 and 3, —

> þâ wear∂ on *s*lǽpe *s*ylfum ætŷwed   69

So may 1 and 3, 2 and 4, —

> âcenned *w*ear∂, cyninga *w*uldor   5

It was once thought that 1, 2, 3, and 4 might all be used in alliteration; but this is questionable.   Compare

> (·)
> sǽgdon *s*ígerôfum, swâ fram *S*iluéstre   190

There are, then, in each long-verse, two or three alliterative
syllables.   As a rule, in Old English the first hemistich contained two, and the second one, such syllables.   The twofold

alliteration is, however, more used in "Elene." The proportion is as follows : [1] —

In every hundred verses there are, —

Verses with two alliterative syllables	52.
Verses with three alliterative syllables	48.

Where there is a relative diminution of the threefold alliteration, as in "Elene," "Juliana," etc., there seems to be a corresponding increase in the number of cases in which the hemistichs, either of the same long-verse or of successive long-verses, are bound together by assonance or rime.

In "Elene" the vowels are naturally much used in alliteration. The consonants are used in the following order of frequency : —

$$w, \ s, \ h, \ f, \ g, \ l, \ m.$$

The anacrusis of the first hemistich consists of from one to three syllables, generally of one only; the anacrusis of the second hemistich is most frequently dissyllabic.

The first hemistich closes generally with a syllable or with syllables (from one to five) unstressed; and the second hemistich closes generally with one unstressed syllable, but occasionally with two or three. Now and then an accumulation of syllables occurs, giving us such unwieldy verses as "Elene," 582–585.

Rime. — It is very difficult — indeed, well-nigh impossible — to determine just when we are dealing with intended rime and when this rime is purely accidental. It is true that in some cases — as, for instance, in the 114th and 115th lines, and in 1237 ff. — there can be little doubt that the author purposely used rime; but there are other cases, and these are numerous, where this seems doubtful or improbable. There has been no attempt made to determine this question in the examples of rime given below. While these results have been obtained by a careful investigation of the text, it is not unlikely that there are other occurrences which the independent investigator would desire to see included, and some here recorded he would probably reject.

---

[1] These figures are taken from Fritzsche, "Andreas und Cynewulf." (See Bibliography.)

Masculine[1] rimes are perfect when the riming vowels are identical, and are followed by the same consonants or consonant combinations.

Perfect Masculine Rimes. —

lixtan : wælhlencan   23ᵇ 24ᵃ
hornboran : friccan   54
ende : sammode   60
gebrec : geþrec   114
handgeswing : hergagring   115
hildenædran : onsendan   119ᵇ 120ᵇ
bordhrêðan : dufan   122
flugon : burgon   134
stênan : nêosan   151ᵇ 152ᵇ
ôðȳwde : generede   163
meahton : cûðon   166ᵇ 167ᵇ
gefrugnon : wǽron   172ᵃ 173ᵃ
wǽron : môston   174ᵇ 175ᵇ
hergum : witum   180
dryhtnes : nihtes   198
weorðan : gehyrwan   220ᵇ 221ᵇ
stôdon : wrǽcon   232
ordum : byrnwîgendum   235
scrîþan : brimþissan   237ᵇ 238ᵃ
snyrgan : plegean   244ᵇ 245ᵇ
plegean : wǽgflotan   245ᵇ 246ᵃ
bliðe : collenferhðe   246ᵇ 247ᵃ
bôcum : geârdagum   290
unclǽnum : gâstum   301ᵃ 302ᵃ
þȳstrum : inwitþancum   307ᵇ 308ᵇ
ongunnon : lifdon   311
ord : word   393ᵃ 394ᵃ
cûðon : cunnon   398ᵇ 399ᵇ
gangað : âsêcað   406ᵇ 407ᵃ
frignan : rǽran   443
hâlgan : sendan   457
bisǽton : sôhton   473ᵇ 474ᵃ
ealra : bearna   475ᵇ 476ᵇ
ǽlǽrendra : betera   506
gefremmað : geswîcaþ   515ᵇ 516ᵇ

[1] See Introduction to Cook's " Judith," pp. xlix. ff.

friccan : bodan   550ᵇ 551ᵃ

wǽron : éodon   556ᵇ 557ᵇ

ongan : négan   558ᵇ 559ᵇ

lufan : heardran   564ᵇ 565ᵇ

geséðan : beníðan : wênan   582ᵃ 583ᵇ 584ᵇ

âreccan : rîm ne can   635

dareðlâcendra : byrgenna   651ᵃ 652ᵇ

can : cann   683ᵇ 684ᵇ

sceolu : heolstorhofu   763ᵇ 764ᵃ

þrôwian : þolian   769ᵇ 770ᵃ

mêðum : mânweorcum   812

delfan : turfhagan   829ᵇ 830ᵃ

sceoldon : hŷrdon   838ᵇ 839ᵇ

fêðegestas : æðelingas   845ᵇ 846ᵃ

ferhðsefan : ongan   850

feorhnere : cynne   898

wyrdeð : strûdeð   904ᵇ 905ᵇ

can : siððan   925ᵇ 926ᵇ

halfa : glædra   955ᵇ 956ᵇ

hellesceaþan : bryttan   957ᵇ 958ᵇ

gehwæðres : sigebêames   964ᵇ 965ᵇ

gefrêge : folcsceare   968

wealdend : nergend   1085ᵃ 1086ᵃ

fêollon : gespon   1134ᵇ 1135ᵃ

gêoce : þancode   1139

ongan : sêcan :   1156ᵇ 1157ᵇ

sêlost : déorlîcost   1158ᵇ 1159ᵃ

cûðe : ferhðe   1168ᵇ 1169ᵃ

sêcað : winnað   1180ᵇ 1181ᵇ

geweorðod : god   1193ᵇ 1194ᵇ

fûs : hûs   1237

riht : miht   1241ᵃ 1242ᵃ

onwrâh : fâh   1243

færeð : gewurðeþ   1274ᵇ 1275ᵇ

When the first riming syllables are perfect masculine rimes, and the following syllables are identical, we have perfect feminine rimes.

Perfect feminine rimes are the following : —

ymbsittendra : burgwîgendra   34

dynede : clynede   50

 wǣre : nǣre 171
 andsweredon : leornedon 396[b] 397[b]
 healdan : wealdan 449[b] 450[a]
 sweartestan : wyrrestan 931[b] 932[a]
 nearwe : gearwe 1240
 geþeaht : þeaht 1241[b] 1242[b]
 âsǣled : gewǣled 1244

Rimes that vary from these are called "imperfect." These may be of various kinds, —

 1. The consonants of the riming syllables may be identical, and the preceding vowels similar but not identical.

 gescyrded : lindwered 141[b] 142[a]
 þus : ûs 400
 wîs : is 592[a] 593[b]
 sefa : wâ 627[b] 628[b]
 hyge : geswerige 685[b] 686[a]
 gode : ânmôde 1117[b] 1118[a]
 sêleste : wiste 1202[b] 1203[b]

 2. The consonants of the riming syllables may be identical, and the preceding vowels dissimilar.

 âgêfon : gecýðan 587[b] 588[b]
 dêað : bið 606
 brâd : geswiðrod 917[b] 918[b]
 þreodude : reodode 1239
 âmæt : begeat 1248

 3. The vowels may be identical, and the following consonants dissimilar. This is "assonance."

 fôr : gôl 51[b] 52[b]
 boda : þingode 77
 ǣrdæge : wǣpenþræce 105[b] 106[b]
 sungon : hergum 109[b] 110[a]
 âhôf : stôd 112[b] 113[b]
 geolorand : gemang 118
 hafen : galen 123[b] 124[b]
 ôð : forð 139
 þræce : dæge 185
 lagofæsten : hæfdon 249
 ŝclêawe : geþrêade 321

þǣre : getǣhte 601
cwicne : scyldigne 091ᵃ 092ᵃ
séaðð : léas 693
fæst : wæs 883ᵃ 884ᵇ
gode : sceolde 1048ᵇ 1049ᵇ
wæf : læs 1238
gebunden : geððrungen 1245
onlâg : hâd 1246
ontŷnde : gerŷmde 1249

4. Two syllables may rime, perfectly or imperfectly, but one of them be followed by another syllable while the other is not.

god : scêawode 345
þîn : þîne 928ᵇ 929ᵇ
stânhleoððum : some 653
gâst : fæste 936ᵇ 937ᵃ
onfêng : swengas 238ᵇ 239ᵇ

Besides these, attention must be called to

cræftige : cræftige 314ᵇ 315ᵇ

and to the imperfect feminine rime, —

boden : samnodân 18ᵇ 19ᵇ

Moreover, there are several cases of rime within a single hemistich. This occurs usually in formulas or fixed expressions.

mǣrððum ond nihtum 15
wordum ond bordum 25
beorhte ond lêohte 92
yldra oððe gingra 159
bordum ond ordum 235
werum ond wîfum 236 1222
sîde ond wîde 272
engla ond elda 476
sume hyder, sume þyder 548
ôðð ende forðð 590
frôdra ond gôdra 637
heofon ond eorððan 728
nu ic wât, þæt ððû eart 815
bord ond ord 1187

BIBLIOGRAPHY.

EDITIONS.

1836. Appendix B to Mr. Cooper's Report (on Rymer's Fœdera. Edited by Benjamin Thorpe).

1840. Andreas und Eleue herausgegeben von Jacob Grimm. Cassel.

1856. The Poetry of the Codex Vercellensis, with an English Translation. Part II. By J. M. Kemble. London.

1858. Bibliothek der angelsächischen Poesie herausgegeben von Christ. Grein. II. Band. Göttingen.

1877. Cynewulf's Elene. Mit einem Glossar herausgegeben von Julius Zupitza. Berlin.

1883. Second edition of the same.

1888. Bibliothek der angelsächischen Poesie begründet von Christ. Grein. Neubearbeitet, etc., von Richard Paul Wülker, Bd. ii. Leipzig.

1888. Third edition of Zupitza's " Elene."

TRANSLATIONS.

1856. Translation into English in Kemble's Edition of the Codex Vercellensis. (See aboye.)

1859. Dichtungen der Angelsachsen stabreimend übersetzt von C. W. M. Grein. Zweiter Band. Göttingen, 1859.

1863. (Zweite Ausgabe, Cassel und Göttingen, 1863, pp. 104 ff.)

1888. A Literal Translation of Cynewulf's Elene by Richard Francis Weymouth. London.

MANUSCRIPT, COLLATIONS, TEXTUAL CRITICISM, AND REVIEWS.

The results of Prof. P. Knöll's manuscript collation are incorporated in Zupitza's first, second, and third editions.

The results of Professor Wülker's examinations, in 1881 and 1884, are embodied in Wülker's edition of Grein's " Bibliothek " (see above). Zupitza's second edition contains the fruit of the 1881 collation; and the third edition, those of both 1881 and 1884. Napier's recent collation has been used by Zupitza in his third edition.

Christ. Grien: Zur Textkritik der angelsächsischen Dichter, in Pfeiffer's *Germania*. Bd. x., S. 424 f.

Einleitung in das Studium des Angelsächsischen, von K. Körner. ii. Heilbronn, 1880.

Sievers in den Gött. gel. anz: vom 9ten aug. 1880. S. 997 ff.

The following reviews of Zupitza's editions of " Elene ": —

Sievers, in *d. Anglia*, i., 573 ff.

Körner, in *d. Englischen Studien*, ii., 252 ff.

Ten Brink, in *Anzeiger für Deutsches Altertum*, v.

Varnhagen, in *d. Deutschen Litteraturzeitung*, 1884, 426 ff.

Kluge, in *Litteraturblatt*, 1884, S. 138 f.

Cardinal Guala and the Vercelli Book. University of California Library Bulletin, No. 10. By A. S. Cook. Sacramento, 1888.

Zöpfl. Forschungen über das Recht der salischen Franken. Berlin, 1876.

Anglosaxonum poetae atque scriptores prosaici, quorum partim integra opera, partim loca selecta collegit, correxit, edidit Ludovicus Ettmüllerus. Quedlinburgii et Lipsiae, 1850. pp. 156 ff.

LANGUAGE.

1884. Joseph Schürman: Darstellung der Syntax in Cynewulf's Elene. (Münster Diss.) Paderborn.

1885. R. Rössger: Über den syntaktischen Gebrauch des Genitivs in Cynewulf's Elene, Crist, und Juliana. *Anglia*, Bd. viii., Heft. 3.

1888. Hermann Leiding: Die Sprache der Cynewulfschen dichtungen Crist, Juliana, und Elene. Marburg.

1888. F. Holthausen: Deutsche Litteraturzeitung sp. 1114 ff.

METRE.

E. Sievers: Zur Rhytmik des germanischen alliterations verses in d. Beiträgen von Paul und Braune. x., 209 ff., 453 ff.; xii., 454 ff.

Philipp Frucht: Metrisches und sprachliches zu Cynewulf's Elene, Juliana, und Crist. (Greiswald. Diss.) 1887.

G. Jansen: Beiträge zur Synonymik und Poetik allgemein als echt anerkannter Dichtungen Cynewulf's. (Münster Doktorschrift.) 1883.

Source.

Otto Glöde: Cynewulf's Elene und ihre quelle (Rostocker Diss.),
1885; und dessen Untersuchungen über die quelle von Cynewulf's
Elene in *der Anglia*, ix., 271 ff.

Wolfgang Golther, im *Litteraturblatt*, 1887, sp. 261 ff.

Acta sanctorum maii collecta, digesta, illustrata a G. Henschenio
et D. Papebrochio. Tomus i. Antverpiae, 1680. pp. 445[b] ff.

Mombritii: Vitae sanctorum. Mediolani, 1479. Tomus i., fol.
ccxii.

Jacobi Gretseri: Opera omnia. Tomus ii. Ratisbonae, 1734.
pp. 417 ff.

Legends of the Holy Rood. Edited by R. Morris. London,
1871. E. E. Text Society, No. 46.

Heilagra manna sǫgur. Edited by C. R. Unger. Christiania,
1877. i., pp. 301 ff.

Author.

1840. Kemble: On Anglo-Saxon Runes, in *Archæologia*, vol. xxviii.,
pp. 360–363.
   Grimm's Andreas und Elene, S. l., lii., and S. 167–170.
1842. Wright: Biographia Brittanica Literaria, i., pp. 501 ff.
   Thorpe's Codex Exoniensis, pp. v.–xi., 501–502.
1843. Kemble's Codex Vercellensis, pp. vii.–x.
1844. Thorpe: The Homilies of the Anglo-Saxon Church, vol. i.,
   p. 622.
1847. Ettmüller's Handbuch, pp. 132 f.
1850. Ettmüller's Scopas and Boceras p. x. f.
1853. Dietrich: Über Crist, in Haupt's *Zeitschrift*, ix., S. 193–214.
1857. Henrici Leonis, Quae de se ipso Cynewulfus, sive Cenevulfus,
   sive Cœnevulfus, poeta Anglo-Saxonicus tradiderit. Hal-
   lesches Universitäts Programm.
1859. Dietrich, in Ebert's *Jahrbuch*, vol. i., pp. 241–246.
   Dietrich: Die Rätsel des Exeterbuches. In Haupt's *Zeitschrift*, ii., S. 448–490, 232–252.
1859. Francisci Dietrichi: Commentatio de Kynewulfi poetae
   aetate, aenigmatum fragmento e codice Lugdunensi edito
   illustrata. Marburg.
1865. Francisci Dietrich: Disputatio de Cruce Ruthwellensi. Marburg.

1865. Christ. Grein: Das Reimlied des Exeterbuches. In Pfeiffer's *Germania*, Bd. x., S. 305–307.

1867. Morley: English Writers, i., pp. 323 and 325.

1869. Rieger: Über Cynewulf. In Zacher's *Zeitschrift für deutsche
Philologie*, i., 215–220, 313–334.

1871. Henry Sweet: Sketch of the History of Anglo-Saxon Poetry.
In "Warton's History," vol. ii., pp. 16–19.

1873. Hammerich's Epick-Kristelige Oldquad und die deutsche
Übersetzung. 1874. pp. 75–104.

1877. Ten Brink's Geschichte der englischen Litteratur, i., S. 64–75.

1878. Richard Wülker, in der *Anglia*, i., S. 483–507.
Charitius: Die angelsächsischen Gedichte von Guðlac, in *der
Anglia*, ii., S. 265–308.

1879. Fritzsche: Das angelsächsische Gedicht Andreas und Cynewulf, in der *Anglia*, ii., S. 441–500.
Ten Brink, in Haupt's *Zeitschrift*, xxiv., und *Anzeiger*, S.
53–70.

1880. Christ. Grein, in seiner kurzgefassten angelsächsischen Grammatik, S. 11–15.

1883. Ten Brink's Early English Literature, pp. 386–389.
Theodor Müller: Angelsächische Grammatik, pp. 16, 26 ff.
Lefevre: Das altenglische Gedicht von Guðlac. In *der
Anglia*, vi., S. 181–240.
Otto D'Ham: Der gegenwärtige Stand der Cynewulf-Frage.
(Tübinger Doktorschrift.)

1884. J. Earle: Anglo-Saxon Literature, chap. xi.

1885. Friedrich Ramhorst: Das altenglische Gedicht vom Heiligen
Andreas. (Berliner Doktorschrift.)

1887. Sarrazin: Beowulf und Kynewulf. *Anglia*, ix., 3.

1888. H. Morley: English Writers, ii., chaps. viii. and ix.

BIBLIOGRAPHICAL.[1]

1885. Wülker: Grundriss zur Geschichte der Angelsächischen Lite-
ratur, pp. 147, 148, 174, 175, 514.

1888. Zupitza: Cynewulf's Elene, third edition, pp. vii., viii.

---

[1] From these sources most of the bibliography of this edition has been
compiled.

ELENE.

I.

Þa wæs ágangen gêara hwyrftum
tuhund ond þrêo geteled rímes,
swylce .xxx. êac, þinggemearces,
wintra for worulde, þæs þe wealdend god
5   ácenned wearð, cyninga wuldor,
in middangeard þurh mennisc hêo,
sôðfæstra lêoht ; þâ wæs syxte gêar
Constantînes câserdômes,
þæt hê Rômwara in rîce wearð
10 âhæfen, hildfruma, tô heretêman.
Wæs se lindhwata lêodgebyrga
eorlum ârfæst. Æðelinges wêox
rîce under roderum. Hê wæs riht cyning
gûðweard gumena. Hine god trymede
15 mêrðum ond mihtum, þæt he manegum wearð
geond middangeard mannum tô hrôðer,
werþeodum tô wræce, syððan wêpen âhôf
wið hettendum. Him wæs hild boden,
wîges wôma. Werod samnodan,
20 Hûna lêode ond Hrêðgotan,
fôron fyrdhwate Francan ond Hûgas
wêron hwate weras . . . . .

(1–41ª) Anno ducentesimo tricesimo tertio post passionem domini
nostri Jesu Christi regnante venerabili dei cultore, magno viro, Con-

gearwe tô gûðe : gâras lîxtan
wriðene wælblencan : wordum ond bordum
25　hôfon herecumbol.　Þa wǽron heardingas
sweotole gesamnod † ond eal geador.
　. Fôr folca gedryht.　Fyrdlęoð âgôl
wulf on wealde, wælrûne ne mâð :
ûrigfeðera earn sang âhôf
30　lâðum on lâste.　Lung.ɔ scynde
ofer burgenta beaduþrêata mǽst
hergum tô hilde, swylce Hûna cyning
ymbsittendra âwer meahte
âbannan tô beadwe burgwîgendra.
35　Fôr fyrda mǽst, fêðan trymedon
éoredcestum, þæt on ælfylce
deareðlâcende on Dânûbie
stærcedfyrhðe stæðe wîcedon,
ymb þæs wæteres wylm, werodes breahtme.
40　woldon Rômwara rîce geþringan, ,
hergum âhÿðan.　Þǽr wearð Hûna cyme
cûð ceasterwarum.　Þâ se câsere heht
ongeân gramum gûðgelǽcan
under earhfære ofstum myclum
45　bannan tô beadwe, beran ût þrǽce
rincas under roderum.　Wǽron Rômware
secgas sigerôfe, sôna gegearwod
wǽpnum tô wîgge, þêah hie werod lǽsse
hæfdon tô hilde, þonne Huna cining
50　ridon ymb rôfne.　Þonne rand dynede
campwudu clynede ; cyning þrêate fôr,
herge, tô hilde.　Hrefen uppe gôl

---

stantino in sexto anno regni eius gens multa barbarorum congregata
est super Danubium parati ad bellum contra Romaniam.

　　(41ᵇ–56) Nunciatum est autem regi Constantino, tunc congregans et
ipse multitudinem exercitus profectus est obviam et invenit eos, qui
vindicaverunt Romaniae partes et erant secus Danubium.

wan ond wælfel. Werod wæs on tyhte,
hlêopon hornboran, hrêopan friccan.

55 Mearh moldan træd. Mægen samnode,
cåfe, tô cêase.⸰ Cyning wæs âfyrhted,
egsan geâclad, siððan elþêodige,
Hûna ond Hrêða here, scêawedon,
ðæt þe on Rômwara rîces ende

60 ymb þæs wæteres stæð werod samnode,
mægen unrîme. Môdsorge wæg
Rômwara cyning, rîces ne wênde
for werodlêste : hæfde wîgena tô lŷt,
eaxlgestealna, wið ofermægene

65 hrôrra tô hilde. Here wîcode,
eorlas, ymb æðeling êgstrêame nêah
on nêaweste nihtlangne fyrst,
þæs þe hîe fêonda gefær fyrmest gesêgon.
Þâ wearð on slæpe sylfum ætŷwed

70 þâm câsere, þær hê on corðre swæf,
sigerôfum gesegen swefnes wôma.
Þûhte him wlitescŷne on weres hâde
hwît ond hîwbeorht hæleða nâthwylc
geŷwed ænlicra, þonne hê ær oððe sîð

75 gesêge under swegle. Hê of slæpe onbrægd
eofurcumble beþeaht. Him se âr hraðe,
wlitig wuldres boda, wið þingode
ond be naman nemde (nihthelm tôglâd):
‘Constantînus, heht þê cyning engla,

80 wyrda wealdend, wære bêodan,
duguða dryhten. Ne ondræd þû ðê,
ðêah þe elþêodige egesan hwôpan,
heardre hilde. Þû tô heofenum beseoh

on wuldres weard : þǽr ðû wraðe findest,
85 sigores tâcen'.   Hê wæs sôna gearu
þurh þæs hâlgan hǽs, hreðerlocan onspêon,
ûp lôcade, swâ him se âr âbêad,
fǽle friðowebba.   Geseah hê frætwum beorht
wliti wuldres trêo ofer wolcna hrôf
90 golde geglenged : gimmas lîxtan.
Wæs se blâca bêam bôcstafum âwriten
beorhte and lêohte : ' mid þŷs bêacne ðû
on þâm frêcnan fǽre fêond oferswîðesð,
geletest lâð werod'.   þâ þæt lêoht gewât,
95 ûp sîðode ond se âr somed
on clǽnra gemang.   Cyning wæs þŷ blîðra
ond þê sorglêasra, secga aldor,
on fyrhðsefan þurh þâ fǽgeran gesyhð.

II.

Heht þâ onlîce æðelinga hlêo,
100 beorna bêaggifa, swâ hê þæt bêacen geseah,
heria hildfruma, þæt him on heofonum ǽr
gelewed wearð, ofstum myclum,
Constantînus, Crîstes rôde,
tîrêadig cyning, tâcen gewyrcan.
105 Heht þâ on ûhtan mid ǽrdæge
wîgend wreccan ond wǽpenþræce,
hebban heorucumbul ond þæt hâlige trêo
him beforan ferian, on fêonda gemang

sursum in coelum, et vide;" et intendens in coelum vidit signum Crucis
Christi, ex lumine claro constitutum, et desuper litteris scriptum titu-
lum; 'IN HOC VINCE.' (99) Viso autem signo hoc Rex Constantinus
fecit similitudinem Crucis quam viderat in coelo : et surgens impe-
tum fecit contra Barbaros, et fecit antecedere signum Crucis; et veniens cum suo exercitu super barbaros, coepit caedere eos proxima luce;

beran bêacen godes.　Bŷman sungon

110　hlûde for hergum.　hrefn weorces gefeah,

ûrigfeðra earn sîð behôold,

wælhrêowra wîg, wulf sang âhôf,

holtes gehlêða.　Hildegesa stôd.

þæir wæs borda gebrec ond beorna geþrec,

115　heard handgeswing ond herga gring,

syððan hêo earhfære ærest mêtton.

On þæt fæge folc flâna scûras,

gâras ofer geolorand on gramra gemang

hetend heorugrimme, hildenædran

120　þurh fingra geweald forð onsendan.

Stôpon stîðhîdige, stundum wræcon,

bræcon bordhrêðan, bil in dufan,

þrungon præchearde.　Þâ wæs þûf hafen,

segn, for sweotum, sigelêoð galen.

125　Gylden grîma, gâras lîxtan

on herefelda.　Hæðene grungon,

fêollon friðelêase.　Flugon instæpes

Hûna lêode, swâ þæt hâlige trêo

âræran heht Rômwara cyning

130　heaðofremmende.　Wurdon heardingas

wîde tôwrecene.　Sume wîg fornam,

sume unsôfte aldor generedon

on þâm herestîðe, sume healfcwice

flugon on fæsten ond feore burgon

135　æfter stânclifum, stede weardedon

ymb Danûbie, sume drenc fornam

on lagostrêame lîfes æt ende.

Ðâ wæs môdigra mægen on luste,

êhton elþeoda óð þæt æfen forð

140　fram dæges orde : daroðæsc flugon,

hildenædran.　Hêap wæs gescyrded,

---

et timuerunt barbari, et dederunt fugam per ripas Danubii, et mortua

láðra lindwered. Lýthwón becwom
Húna herges hám eft þauon.

þá wæs gesýne, þæt sige forgeaf
145 Constantíno cyning ælmihtig
     æt þám dægweorce, dómweorðunga,
     ríce under roderum, þurh his róde tréo.

Gewát þá heriga helm hám eft þanon
  húðe hrêmig (hild wæs gesceáðen),
150 wígge geweorðod. Cóm þá wígena hléo
     þegna þreate þrýðbord stenan,
     beaduróf cyning, burga neoþan.

Heht þá wigena weard þá wísestan
snúde tó sionoðe, þá þe snyttro cræft
155 þurh fyrngewrito gefrigen hæfdon, ⸵
     héoldón higeþancum hæleða rædas.

Ðá þæs fricggan ongan folces aldor,
sigeróf cyning, ofer síd weorod,
wære þær ænig yldra oððe gingra,
160 þê him tó sóðe secggan meahte,
     galdrum cýðan, hwæt se god wære,
     blædes brytta, ' þe þis his béacen wæs,
     þê mê swá léoht óðýwde ond míne léode generede,
     tácna torhtost, ond mê tír forgeaf,
165 wígspéd wið wráðum, þurh þæt wlitige tréo '.
     hío him andsware ænige ne meahton
     ágifan tógênes nê ful geare cúðon
     sweotole gesecggan be þám sigebéacne.

þá þá wísestan wordum cwædon
170 for þám heremægene, þæt hit heofoncyninges

est non minima multitudo: et dedit Deus in illa die victoriam Regi
Constantino per virtutem sanctae Crucis. (148) 2. Veniens autem Rex
Constantinus in suam civitatem, convocavit omnes Sacerdotes omnium
deorum vel idolorum: et quaerebat ab eis cujus vel quid esset hoc
signum Crucis, et not poterant dicere ei. Responderunt autem quidam
ex ipsis et dixerunt: "Hoc signum coelestis Dei est." (172ᵇ) Audi-

tâcen wǽre ond þæs twêo nǽre.
Þâ þæt gefrugnon, þâ þurh fulwihte
lærde wǽron, him wæs leoht sefa,
ferhð gefêonde, þêah hira fêa wǽron,
175 ðæt hîe for þâm câsere cŷðan môston
godspelles gife, hû se gâsta helm
in þrŷnesse þrymme geweorðad
âcenned wearð, cyninga wuldor,
ond hû on galgan wearð godes âgen bearn
180 âhangen for hergum heardum wîtum,
âlŷsde lêoda bearn of locan dêofla,
geômre gâstas, ond him gife sealde
þurh þâ ilcan gesceaft, þê him geŷwed wearð
sylfum on gesyhðe sigores tâcne
185 wið þêoda þræce, ond hû ðŷ þriddan dæge
of byrgenne beorna wuldor,
of dêaðe, ârâs, dryhten ealra
hæleða cynnes, ond tô heofonum âstâh.
Ðus glêawlîce gâstgerŷnum
190 sægdon sigerôfum, swâ fram Siluestre
lǽrde wǽron. Æt þâm se lêodfruma
fulwihte onfêng ond þæt forð gehêold
on his dagana tîd dryhtne tô willan.

---

entes autem hoc pauci Christiani, qui erant eodem tempore, venerunt
ad Regem, et evangelizaverunt ei mysterium Trinitatis et adventum
Filii Dei, quemadmodum natus est et crucifixus et tertia die resurrexit.
Mittens autem Rex Constantinus ad Eusebium Episcopum urbis Romae,
fecit eum venire ad se, et catechizavit eum fidem Christianorum et
omnia ministeria, et baptizavit eum in nomine Domini nostri Jesu
Christi, et confirmatus est in fide Christi. Jussit autem aedificari
ubique ecclesias, templa vero idolorum destrui.

III.

Ða wæs on sǽlum sinðes brytta,
195 niðheard cyning. Wæs him niwe gefêa
     befolen in fyrhðe. Wæs him frôfra mǽst
     ond hyhta hîhst heofonrîces weard.
     Ongan þâ dryhtnes ǽ dæges ond nihtes
     þurh gâstes gife georne cŷðan
200 ond hine, sôðlîce, sylfne getengde
     goldwine gumena in godes þêowdôm
     æscrôf, unslâw. Þâ se æðeling fand,
     lêodgebyrga, þurh lârsmiðas
     gûðheard, gârþrîst on godes bôcum,
205 hwǽr âhangen wæs heriges beorhtme
     on rôde trêo rodora waldend
     æfstum þurh inwit, swâ se ealda fêond
     forlǽrde ligesearwum lêode, fortyhte   •
     Iûdêa cyn, þæt hîe god sylfne
210 âhêngon, herga fruman : þæs hîe in hŷnðum sculon
     tô wîdan feore wergðu drêogan.
     Þâ wæs Crîstes lof þâm câsere
     on firhðsefan † forð gemyndig
     ymb þæt mǽre trêo ond þâ his môdor hêt
215 fêran foldwege folca þrêate
     tô Iûdêum, georne sêcan
     wigena þrêate, hwǽr se wuldres bêam
     hâlig under hrûsan hŷded wǽre,
     æðelcyninges rôd. Elene ne wolde
220 þæs sîðfates sǽne weorðan

(194 ff.) Erat autem beatus Constantinus perfectus in fide, et fervens
Spiritu sancto exercebatur in sanctis Evangeliis Christi. Cum didi-
cisset autem a sanctis Evangeliis ubi esset Dominus crucifixus, misit
suam matrem Helenam ut exquireret sanctum lignum Crucis Domini,
et in eodem loco aedificaret ecclesiam. Gratia autem Spiritus sancti

né ðæs wilgifan word gehyrwan,
hiere sylfre suna, ac wæs sóna gearu
wíf on willsíð, swâ hire weoruda helm,
byrnwîggendra, beboden hæfde.

225　Ongan þâ ófstlíce eorla mengu
tô flote fýsan.　Fearoðhengestas
ymb geofenes stæð gearwe stódon,
sælde sæmearas, sunde getenge.
Dâ wæs orcnæwe idese síðfæt,

230　siððan wæges welm werode gesóhte.
þær wlanc manig æt wendelsæ
on stæðe stódon.　Stundum wræcon
ofer mearcpaðu, mægen æfter óðrum,
ond þâ gehlódon hildesercum,

235　bordum ond ordum, byrnwîgendum,
werum ond wífum wæghengestas.
Lêton þâ ofer fífelwæg fâmige scríðan
bronte brimþisan.　Bord oft onfêng
ofer earhgeblond ýða swengas.

240　Sæ swinsade.　Ne hýrde ic síð nê ær
on êgstrêame idese lædan,
on merestræte, mægen fægerre.
þær meahte gesîon, sê ðone síð behêold,
brecan ofer bæðweg brimwudu, snyrgan

245　under swellingum, sæmearh plegean,
wadan wægflotan.　Wigan wæron blîðe
collenferhðe: cwên síðes gefeah.
Syþþan tô hýðe hringedstefnan
ofer lagofæsten geliden hæfdon

250　on Crêca land, cêolas lêton

---

requievit in beatissima matre Constantini Imperatoris Helena; haec
autem in omnibus Scripturis se exercebat, et nimiam in Domino nostro
Jesu Christo possedit dilectionem : postmodum et salutare sanctae Crucis lignum exquisivit.　Cum legisset autem intente adventum humani-
tatis Salvatoris nostri Jesu Christi et crucis ejus assumptionem et a

æt sǽfearoðe sunde bewrecene,
ald ýðhofu, oncrum fæste
on brime bídan beorna geþinges,
hwonne hêo sîo gúðcwên gumena þrêate
255 ofer ĉastwegas eft gesôhte.
Ðǽr wæs on eorle êðgesýne
brogden byrne ond bill gecost,
geatolîc gúðscrûd, grîmhelm manig,
ĉnlîc eoforcumbul. Wǽron æscwigan,
260 secggas ymb sigecwên, sîðes gefýsde.
Fyrdrincas frome fôron on luste
on Crêca land, câseres bodan,
hilderincas hyrstum gewerede.
Þǽr wæs gesýne sincgim locen
265 on þâm hereþrêate, hlâfordes gifu.
Wæs sêo êadhrêðige Elene gemyndig
þrîste on geþance þêodnes willan,
georn on môde, þæt hîo Iûdêa
ofer herefeldas hêape gecoste
270 lindwîgendra land gesôhte,
secga þrêate; swâ hit siððan gelamp
ymb lýtel fæc, þæt ðæt lêodmægen,
gúðrôfe hæleþ, tô Hierusalem
cwômon in þâ ceastre corðra mǽste,
275 eorlas æscrôfe, mid þâ æðelan cwên.

---

mortuis resurrectionem non est moras passa donec victoriae Christi
invenit lignum, ubi dominicum et sanctum fixum est corpus. Invenit
autem illud hoc modo. Vicesima et octava die secundi mensis in
sanctam civitatem Hierusalem introivit una cum exercitu magno,

IIII.

HEHT ðá gebêodan burgsittendum
þâm snoterestum sîde ond wîde
geond Iûdêas, gumena gehwylcum,
meðelhêgende on gemôt cuman,
280 þâ ðe dêoplîcost dryhtnes gerŷno
law þurh rihte ǽ reccan cûðon.
·Ðâ wæs gesamnod of sîdwegum
mægen unlŷtel, þâ ðe Moyses ǽ
reccan cûðon. þǽr on rîme wæs
285 þrêo .m̅. þǽra lêoda
âlesen tô lâre. Ongan þâ lêoflic wîf
weras Ebrêa wordum nêgan :
' ic þæt gearolîce ongiten hæbbe
þurg wîtgena wordgerŷno
290 on godes bôcum, þæt gê geârdagum
wyrðe wǽron wuldorcyninge,
dryhtne dŷre ond dǽdhwǽte.
Hwæt, gê þǽre snyttro † unwîslîce,
wrâðe, wiðwurpon, þâ gê wergdon þane,
295 þe êow of wergðe þurh his wuldres miht,
fram lîgcwale, lŷsan þôhte,
of hæftnêde. Gê mid horu spêowdon
on þæs andwlitan, þe êow êagena lêoht,

et congregavit in ea congregationem magnam de impiissima gente
Judaeorum. Non solum autem eos qui in ea erant civitate, sed et eos
qui in circuitu erant castellis, possessionibus vel civitatibus Judaeos
congregari praecepit. Erat autem Hierosolyma deserta tempore illo,
ut vix invenirentur omnes Judaei tria millia virorum. . . . [1](Post haec
congregavit multitudinem magnam de impiissima Judaeorum gente,)
quos convocans beatissima Helena dixit ad eos. Cognovi de sanctis
libris propheticis, quia fuistis dilecti Dei ; sed quia repellentes omnem
sapientiam, eum qui volebat de maledicto vos redimere maledixistis,
et eum qui per sputum oculos vestros illuminavit immundis potius

[1] An interpolation from Rufinus.

fram blindnesse bóte gefremede
300 edníowunga þurh þæt æðele spáld
ond fram unclénum oft generede
dêofla gâstum. Gê tô dĉaþe þone
dêman ongunnon, sê ðe of dêaðe sylf
worn âwehte on wcra corþre
305 in þæt ærre líf êowres cynnes.
Swâ gê môdblinde mengan ongunnon
ligê wið sôðe, lêoht wið þýstrum,
æfst wið âre, inwitþancum
wrôht webbedan. Éow sêo wergðu forðan
310 sceôþeð scyldfullum. Gê þâ sciran miht
dêman ongunnon ond gedwolan lífdon,
þêostrum geþancum, ôð þýsne dæg.
Gangaþ nû snûde, snyttro geþencaþ
weras wîsfæste, wordes cræftige,
315 þâ ðe êowre ĉ æðelum † cræftige
on ferhðsefan fyrmest hæbben,
þâ mĉ sôðlîce secgan cunnon,
andsware cýðan for êowic forð
tâcna gehwylces, þe ic him tô sêce '.
320 Éodan þâ on gerûm rêonigmôde
eorlas ĉclêawe, egesan geþrêade,
gehðum geômre, georne sôhton
þâ wîsestan wordgerýno,
þæt hîo þ̂ére cwêne oncweðan meahton
325 swâ tiles, swâ trâges, swâ hîo him tô sôhte.
Hîo þâ on þrêate .m̄. manna

sputis injuriastis, et eum qui mortuos vestros vivificabat in mortem
tradidistis, et lucem tenebras existimastis et veritatem mendacium,
pervenit in vos maledictum quod est in lege vestra scriptum. Nunc
autem eligite ex vobis viros, qui diligenter sciunt legem vestram, ut
respondeant mihi de quibus interrogavero eos. Qui abeuntes cum
timore, et multas quaestiones inter semetipsos facientes, invenerunt
legis doctores numero mille, et adduxerunt eos ad Helenam, testi-

fundon ferhþglêawra, þâ þe fyrngemynd
mid Iûdêum gearwast cûðon.
Þrungon þâ on þrêate, þæͤr on þrymme bâd
330 in cynestôle câseres mæͤg,
geatolĭc gûðcwên golde gehyr̨sted.✸
Elene maþelode ond for eorlum spræc:
' gehŷrað, higeglêawe, hâlige rûne,
word ond wîsdôm. Hwæt, gê wîtgena
335 lâre onfêngon, hû se lĭffruma
in cildes hâd cenned wurde,
mihta wealdend. Be þâm Moyses sang
ond þæͤt *word* gecwæð, weard Israhêla:
" êow âcenned bĭð cniht on dêgle
340 mihtum mæͤre, swâ þæs môdor ne bið
wæstmum gêacnod þurh weres frige".
Be ðâm Dâuid cyning dryhtlêoð âgôl,
frôd fyrnweota, fæder Salomônes,
ond þæt word gecwæþ, wigona baldor:
345 " ic frymþa god fore scêawode,
sigora dryhten. Hê on gesyhðe wæs,
mægena wealdend, mĭn on þâ swĭðran,
þrymmes hyrde. Þanon ic ne wen*de*
æͤfre tô aldre onsĭon mĭne ".
350 Swâ hit eft be êow Essâias
wîtga for weorodum wordum mæͤlde
dêophycggende þurh dryhtnes gâst:
" ic ûp âhof eaforan ging*e*
ond bearn cende, þâm ic blæͤd forgeaf,
355 hâlige higefrôfre: ac hĭe hyrwdon *mê*,

monium perhibentes eis, quod legis scientiam multam haberent.
Helena autem dixit ad eos, Audite mea verba, auribus percipite meos
sermones. Non enim intellexerunt patres vestri neque vos in ser-
monibus Prophetarum, quemadmodum de adventu Christi propheta-
verunt, quia prius dictum est, "Puer nascetur et mater ejus virum non
agnoscet:" et Isaias vobis dixit, "Filios genui et exaltavi, ipsi autem

fêodon þurh fêondscipe, náhton foreþancas,
wîsdômes gewitt, ond þâ wêregan nêat,
þê man daga gehwâm drîfeð ond þirsceð,
ongitaþ hira gôddênd, nales gnyrnwrêcum
360 feogað frŷnd hiera, þê him fôdder gifeð.
Ond mê Israhêla sêfre ne woldon
folc oncnâwan, þêah ic feala for him
æfter woruldstundum wundra gefremede ".

V.

Hwæt, wê þæt gehŷrdon þurh hâlige bêc,
365 þæt êow dryhten geaf dôm unscyndne,
meotod, mihta spêd, Moyse sægde,
hû gê heofoncyninge hŷran sceoldon,
lâre lêstan.   Êow þæs lungre âþrêat,
ond gê þâm ryhte wiðroten hæfdon,
370 onscunedon þone scîran scippend eallra,
dryhtna dryhten, ond gedwolan fylgdon
ofer riht godes.   Nû gê raþe gangaþ
ond findaþ gên, þâ þe fyrngewritu
þurh snyttro cræft sêlest cunnen,
375 êriht êower, þæt mê andsware
þurh sîdne sefan secgan cunnen '.
Êodan ðâ mid mengo môdcwânige
collenferhðe, swâ him sîo cwên bêad,

spreverunt me : cognovit bos possessorem suum et asinus praesepe
Domini sui, Israel autem me non cognovit, et populus meus me non
intellexit:" et omnis Scriptura de ipso locuta est. Qui sciebatis legem
errastis, nunc autem eligite ex vobis qui diligenter noverint scientiam
legis, ut ad interrogationes meas dent responsum : et militibus jussit
ut custodirent eos cum summa diligentia.
    Consilio autem facto inter se elegerunt optimos legis doctores viros
numero quingentos, et venientes steterunt in conspectu Helenae: quae

fundon þâ .d.　Forþsnotterra
380　âlesen lêodmâga, þâ ðe leornungcræft
þurh môdgemynd, mâste hæfdon
on sefan snyttro.　Hêo tô salore eft
ymb lŷtel fæc laðode wâron,
ceastre weardas.　Hîo sîo cwên ongan
385　wordum genêgan (wlât ofer ealle):
' oft gê dyslîce dâd gefremedon,
wêrge wræcmæcggas, ond gewritu herwdon,
fædera lâre, nâfre furður, þonne nû,
ðâ gê blindnesse bôte forsêgon
390　ond gê wiðsôcon sôðe ond rihte,
þæt in Bethleme bearn wealdendes,
cyning ânboren, cenned wâre,
æðelinga ord.　Þêah gê þâ â cûðon,
wîtgena word, gê ne woldon þâ,
395　synwyrcende, sôð oncnâwan '.
Hîe þâ ânmôde andsweredon:
' hwæt, wê ebrêisce â leornedon,
þâ on fyrndagum fæderas cûðon,
æt godes earce, nê wê geare cunnon,
400　þurh hwæt ðû ðus hearde, hlâfdige, ûs
eorre wurde.　Wê ðæt âbylgð nyton,
þê wê gefremedon on þysse folcscere,
þêoden bealwa wið þec âfre '.
Elene maðelade ond for eorlum spræc
405　undearninga, ides reordode

---

dixit: "Qui sunt hi?" At illi dixerunt: "Hi sunt qui optime noverunt
legem." Et coepit iterum dicere ad eos: "Vos quam stulti estis filii
Israel secundum Scripturas, qui patrum vestrorum caecitatem secuti
estis, qui dicitis Jesum non esse filium Dei, qui legistis legem et Pro-
phetas et non intellexistis." Illi autem dixerunt: Nos quidem et
legimus et intelligimus, pro qua causa talia nobis dicis, Domina,
manifesta nobis, ut et nos cognoscentes respondeamus de his quae a
te dicuntur. Ipsa autem dixit iterum ad eos: Adhuc euntes eligite

hlûde for herigum : ' gê nû hraðe gangað,
sundor âsêcaþ, þâ ðe snyttro mid êow
mægn ond môdcræft mæste hæbben,
þæt mê þinga gehwylc þrîste gecŷðan
410 untrâglîce, þê ic him tô sêce '.
Êodon þâ fram rûne, swâ him sîo rîce cwên
bald in burgum beboden hæfde,
geômormôde georne smêadon,
sôhton searoþancum, hwæt sîo syn wêre,
415 þê hîe on þâm folce gefremed hæfdon
wið þâm câsere, þê him sîo cwên wite.∕
þâ þær for eorlum ân reordode
gidda gearosnotor (ðâm wæs Iûdas nama),
wordes cræftig : ' ic wât geare,
420 þæt hîo wile sêcan be ðâm sigebêame,
on ðâm þrôwode þêoda waldend
eallra gnyrna lêas, godes âgen bearn,
þone † unscyld*igne* eofota gehwylces
þurh hete hêngon on hêanne bêam
425 in fyrndagum fæderas ûsse.
þæt wæs þrêalic geþôht. Nû is þearf mycel,
þæt wê fæstlîce ferhð staðelien,
þæt wê ðæs morðres meldan ne weorðen,
hwær þæt hâlige trîo beheled wurde
430 æfter wîgþræce, þŷ lǽs tôworpen sîen
frôd fyrngewritu ond þâ fæderlîcan
lâre forlêten. Ne bið lang ofer ðæt,
þæt Israhêla æðelu môten

---

meliores legis doctores. Qui cum irent dicebant intra se, pro qua causa
putas hunc laborem facit nobis Regina.∕Unus ex eis, nomine Judas,
dixit : "Ego scio, quia quaestionem vult facere ligni, in quod Christum
suspenderunt patres nostri : videte ergo nemo ei confiteatur : nam vere
destruentur paternae traditiones, et lex ad nihilum redigetur. Zach-
aeus autem avus meus praenunciavit patri meo, et pater meus cum
moreretur adnuntiavit mihi, dicens :

      ofer middangeard mâ rîcsian,

435   ŝcræft eorla, gif ðis ŝppe bið ;

      swâ þâ þæt ilce gið mîn yldra fæder

      sigerôf sægde (þâm wæs Sachîus nama),

      frôd fyrnwiota, fædere mînum,

      . . . . eaferan

440   (wende hine of worulde) ond þæt word gecwæð :

      '' gif þê þæt gelimpe on lífdagum,

      þæt ðû gehŝre ymb þæt hâlige trêo

      frôde frignan ond geflitu rêeran

      be ðâm sigebêame, on þâm sôðcyning

445   âhangen wæs, heofonrîces weard,

      eallre sybbe bearn, þonne þû snûde gecŷð,

      mîn swês sunu, êr þec swylt nime.

      Ne mæg êfre ofer þæt Ebrêa þêod,

      rêdþeahtende, rîce healdan,

450   duguðum wealdan, ac þâra dôm leofað

      ond hira dryhtscipe . . . .

      in woruld weorulda willum gefylled,

      ðê þone âhangnan cyning heriaþ ond lofiað ''. /

VI.

      Þa ic fromlîce fædere mînum,

455   ealdum ŝwitan, âgeaf andsware :

      '' hû wolde þæt geweorðan on woruldrîce,

      þæt on þone hâlgan handa sendan

      tô feorhlege fæderas ûsse

      þurh wrâð gewitt, gif hîe wiston êr,

''Vide, fili, cum quaestio facta fuerit de ligno, in quod Christum suspenderunt patres nostri, manifesta illud antequam crucieris: jam enim amplius Hebraeorum genus non regnabit, sed regnum eorum erit qui adorant Crucifixum, ipse autem regnabit in seculum seculi.''/
Ego vero dixi ei; '' Pater, si ergo sciebant patres nostri quia ipse esset

460 þæt hê Crîst wǽre, cyning on roderum,
sôð sunu meotudes, sâwla nergend?"
ðâ mê yldra mîn âgeaf andsware,
frôd on fyrhðe fæder reordode :
" ongit, guma ginga, godes hêahmægen,
465 nergendes naman. Sê is niða gehwâm
unâsecgendlic. þone sylf ne mæg
on moldwege man âspyrigean.
Nǽfre ic þâ geþeahte, þe þêos þêod ongan,
sêcan wolde, ac ic symle mec
470 âscêd þâra scylda, nales sceame worhte
gâste mînum. Ic him georne oft
þæs unrihtes andsæc fremede,
| onne ûðweotan æht bisǽton,
on sefan sôhton, hû hîe sunu meotudes
475 âhêngon, helm wera, hlâford eallra,
engla ond elda, æðelust bearna.
Ne meahton him swâ disige dêað ôðfæstan
weras wonsǽlige, swâ hîe wêndon ǽr,
sârum settan, þêah hê sume hwîle
480 on galgan his gâst onsende,
sigebearn godes. þâ siððan wæs
of rôde âhæfen rodera wealdend,
eallra þrymma þrym, þrêo niht siððan
in byrgenne bîdende wæs
485 under þêosterlocan ond þâ þŷ þriddan dæg,
ealles lêohtes lêoht, lifgende ârâs,

Christus, quare manus suas injecerunt in eum?" Dixit autem mihi:
"Audi me, fili, et cognosce ejus inenarrabile nomen, quia numquam
consiliatus sum neque conveni cum eis, sed multoties contradicebam
illis; sed quia arguebat seniores et Pontifices nostros, ideo condemnaverunt eum crucifigi, putantes mortificare immortalem: quem et de-
ponentes de ligno sepelierunt. Ipse autem sepultus post tertium
diem surrexit, et manifestavit se suis discipulis: unde credidit
Stephanus frater tuus, et coepit docere in nomine ejus: et consilio

ðêoden engla, ond his þegnum hine,
sôð sigora frêa, seolfne geŷwde
beorht on blǽde. Þonne brôðor þîn
490 onfêng æfter fyrste fulwihtes bæð,
lêohtne gelêafan. Þâ for lufan dryhtnes
Stephanus wæs stânum worpod,
ne geald hê yfel yfele, ac his ealdfêondum
þingode þrohtherd, bæd þrymcyning,
495 þæt hê him þâ wêadǽd tô wræce ne sette,
þæt hîe for æfstum unscyldigne,
synna lêasne, Sawles lârum
feore berǽddon, swâ hê þurh fêondscipe
tô cwale monige Crîstes folces
500 dêmde, tô dêaþe. ⁄ Swâ þêah him dryhten eft
miltse gefremede, þæt hê manegum wearð
folca tô frôfre, syððan him frymða god,
niða nergend, naman oncyrde,
ond hê syððan wæs sanctus Paulus
505 be naman hâten, ond him nǽnig wæs
ǽlǽrendra ôðer betera
under swegles hlêo syðþan ǽfre,
þâra þe wîf oððe wer on woruld cendan,
þêah hê Stephanus stânum hehte
510 âbrêotan on beorge, brôðor þînne.
nû ðû meaht gehŷran, hæleð mîn se lêofa,
hû ârfæst is ealles wealdend,
þêah wê ǽbylgð wið hine oft gewyrcen,

<hr>

facto Pharisaei cum Saducaeis condemnaverunt eum ut lapidaretur; et tollens eum multitudo lapidaverunt eum.   Sed beatus ille cum traderet animam, expandit manus suas ad coelum, et orabat dicens: "Domine ne statuas illis hoc peccatum." ⁄ Audi me, fili, et doceo te de Christo et de pietate ejus : quia et Paulus, qui ante templum sedebat et exercebat artem scenographiae; erat persequens eos qui in Christo credebant, qui concitavit populum adversus fratrem suum Stephanum; et pietate ductus super eum Dominus, unum de sanctis suis fecit eum.

synna wunde, gif wê sôna eft
515 þâra bealudǽda bôte gefremmaþ
ond þæs unrihtes eft geswîcaþ.
Forðan ic, sôðlîce, ond mîn swǽs fæder
syðþan gelŷfdon . . . . ,
þæt geþrôwade eallra þrymma god,
520 lífes láttîow, lâðlic wîte
for oferþearfe ilda cynnes.
Forðan ic þê lǽre þurh lêoðrûne,
hyse lêofesta, þæt ðû hospcwide,
æfst nê eofulsæc ǽfre ne fremme,
525 grimne geagncwide, wið godes bearne.
Þonne ðû geearnast, þæt þê bið êce lîf,
sêlust sigelêana, seald in heofonum ".
Ðus mec fæder mîn on fyrndagum
unweaxenne wordum lǽrde,
530 septe sôðcwidum (þâm wæs Sŷmon nama),
guma gehðum frôd.   Nû gê geare cunnon,
hwæt êow þæs on sefan sêlest þince
tô gecŷðanne, gif ðêos cwên ûsic
frigneð ymb ðæt trêo, nû gê fyrhðsefan
535 ond môdgeþanc mînne cunnon '.
Him þâ tôgênes þâ glêawestan
on wera þrêate wordum mǽldon :
' nǽfre wê hŷrdon hæleð ǽnigne
on þysse þêode, bûtan þec nûðâ,
540 þegn ôðerne, þyslic cŷðan
ymb swâ dŷgle wyrd.   Dô, swâ þê þynce,
fyrngidda frôd, gif ðû frugnen sîe
on wera corðre.   Wîsdômes beðearf,

Propter quod ego et patres mei credidimus in eum, quia vere filius Dei
est.   Et nunc, fili, noli blasphemare eum, neque eos qui in eum credunt :
et habebis vitam aeternam.
Haec mihi contestatus est pater meus Simon, Ecce omnia audistis :
quid vobis placet, si interrogaverit nos de ligno Crucis ? "   Ceteri autem

      worda wærlicra ond witan snyttro,
545 sê ôðre æðelan sceal andwyrde âgifan
      for þyslicne þrêat on meþle '.

VII.

      WEoxan word cwidum : weras þeahtedon
      on healfa gehwæne, sume hyder, sume þyder,
      þrydedon ond þôhton. Þâ cwom þegna hêap
550 tô þâm heremeðle. Hrêopon friccan,
      câseres bodan : ' êow þêos cwên laþaþ,
      secgas, tô salore, þæt gê seonoðdômas
      rihte reccen. Is êow rædes þearf
      on meðelstede, môdes snyttro '.
555 Hêo wæron gearwe, geômormôde
      lêodgebyrgean, þâ hie laðod wæron
      þurh heard gebann, tô hofe êodon
      cýðan cræftes miht. Þâ sîo cwên ongan
      weras ebresce wordum nêgan
560 friccggan fyrhðwêrige ymb fyrngewritu,
      hû on worulde ær wîtgan sungon,
      gâsthâlige guman, be godes bearne,
      hwær se þêoden geþrôwade,
      sôð sunu meotudes, for sâwla lufan.
565 Hêo wæron stearce, stâne heardran,
      noldon þæt gerýne rihte cýðan
      nê hire andsware ænige secgan,
      torngenîðlan, þæs hîo him tô sôhte,
      ac hîo worda gehwæs wiðersæc fremedon

---

dixerunt, " Nos talia numquam audivimus, qualia a te hodie dicta sunt.
Si ergo inquisitio facta fuerit de hoc, vide ne ostendas. Manifeste
autem qui haec dicis et locum nosti." Haec eis dicentibus, ecce veni-
unt milites ad eos dicentes, " Venite, vocat vos Regina." Illi autem
dum venissent judicabantur ab ea ; et nihil verum volebant dicere de hoc

570 fæste on fyrhðe, þæt hêo frignan ongan,
cwædon, þæt hîo on aldre ôwiht swylces
nê ær nê sîð æfre hŷrdon.
Elene maþelade ond him yrre oncwæð:
' ic êow tô sôðe secgan wille,
575 ond þæs in lîfe lige ne wyrðeð,
gif gê þissum lêase leng gefylgað
mid fæcne gefice, þê mê fore standaþ,
þæt êow in beorge bælfŷr fornimeð,
hâttost heaðowelma, ond êower hrâ bryttað,
580 lâcende lîg, þæt êow þæt lêas *sceal*
âwended weorðan tô woruldgedâle.
Ne magon gê ðâ word gesêðan, † þe gê hwîle nû on unriht
wrigon under womma scêatum.   Ne magon gê þâ wyrd bemîðan,
bedyrnan þâ dêopan mihte'.   Ðâ wurdon hîe dêaðes on wênan,
585 âdes ond endelîfes, ond þær þâ ænne betæhton
giddum gearusnottorne (þâm wæs Iûdas nama
cenned for cnêomâgum)—þone hîe þære cwêne âgêfon,
sægdon hine sundorwîsne: ' hê þê mæg sôð gecŷðan,
onwrêon wyrda gerŷno, swâ ðû hine wordum frignest,
590 æriht from orde ôð ende forð.
Hê is for eorðan æðeles cynnes,
wordcræftes wîs ond wîtgan sunu,
bald on meðle.   Him gebyrde is,
þæt hê gêncwidas glêawe hæbbe,
595 cræft in brêostum.   Hê gecŷðeð þê
for wera mengo wîsdômes gife

þurh þá myclan miht, swá þín mód lufaþ'.
Hío on sybbe forlêt sêcan gehwylcne
ágenne eard ond þone ǽnne genam
600 Iúdas tô gísle ond þá georne bæd,
þæt hê be ðǽre rôde riht getǽhte,
þá ǽr in legere wæs lange bedyrned,
ond hine seolfne sundor ácígde.
Elene maþelode tô þám ánhagan,
605 tîrêadig cwên : ' þê synt tû gearu,
. swá líf, swá déað, swá þê lêofre bið
tô gecêosanne. Cýð ricene nû,
hwæt ðû þæs tô þinge þafían wille'.
Iúdas hire ongên þingode (ne meahte hê þá gehðu
   bebúgan,
610 oncyrran † rex geníðlan. Hê wæs on þǽre cwêne
   gewealdum) : ̄
' hû mæg þǽm geweorðan, þe on wêstenne
mêðe ond metelêas môrland trydeð,
hungre gehæfted, ond him hláf ond stân
on gesihðe bú samod geweorðað
615 streac ond hnesce, þæt hê þone stân nime
wið hungres hlêo, hláfes ne gíme,
gewende tô wǽdle ond þá wiste wiðsæce,
beteran wiðhyccge, þonne hê bêga beneah ? '

VIII.

   Him þá sêo êadige andwyrde ágeaf
620 Elene for eorlum undearnunga :

Judam solum.   Et convocans eum, dixit ad illum : "Vita et mors
propositae sunt tibi : elige tibi quod vis, vitam an mortem." Judas
dixit : "Et quis in solitudine constitutus, panibus sibi appositis, lapides
manducat ?" Beata autem Helena dixit : "Si ergo in coelo et in terra
vis vivere, dic mihi ubi absconditum est lignum pretiosae Crucis."

'gif ðû in heofonrîce habban wille
eard mid englum ond on eorðan lîf,
sigorlêan in swegle, saga ricene mê,
hwǽr sêo rôd wunige radorcyninges
625 hâlig under hrûsan, þê gê hwîle nû
þurh morðres mân mannum dyrndun'.
Jûdas maðelade (him wæs geômor sefa,
hât æt heortan ond gehwæðres wâ,
gê hê heofonrîces *hyht* swâ môde
630 ond þis andwearde ânforlête
rîce under roderum, gê hê ðâ rôde *tǽhte*):
'hû mæg ic þæt findan, þæt swâ fyrn gewearð
wintra gangum? Is nû worn sceacen,
.cc. oððe mâ geteled rîme.
635 Ic ne mæg âreccan, nû ic þæt rîm ne can.
Is nû feale sîðþan forðgewitenra
frôdra ond gôdra, þê ûs fore wǽron,
glêawra gumena. Ic on geogoðe wearð
on sîðdagum syððan âcenned,
640 cnihtgeong hæleð. Ic ne can, þæt ic nât,
findan on fyrhðe, þæt swâ fyrn gewearð'.
Elene maðelade him on andsware:
'hû is þæt geworden on þysse werþêode,
þæt gê swâ monigfeald on gemynd witon,
645 alra tâcna gehwylc, swâ Trôiâna
þurh gefeoht fremedon? Þæt wæs fær mycel,
open ealdgewin, þonne þêos æðele gewyrd,
geâra gongum. Gê þæt geare cunnon
êdre gereccan, hwæt þær eallra wæs

Judas dixit: "Quemadmodum habetur in gestis, sunt jam anni
ducenti plus minusve: et nos, cum simus juniores, quomodo possumus
haec nosse?" Beata Helena dixit: "Quomodo ante tantas generationes in Ilio et Troade factum est bellum, et omnes nunc commemorantur
qui ibi sunt mortui: et monumenta eorum et loca scriptura tradit."
Judas dixit: Vere, Domina: quia conscripta sunt: nos autem non

650 on maurîme morðorslehtes,
dareðlâcendra dêadra gefeallen
under bordhagan. Gê þâ byrgenna
under stânhleoðum ond þâ stôwe swâ some
ond þâ wintergerîm on gewritu settou'.
655 Iûdas maðelade (gnornsorge wæg):
'wê þæs hereweorces, hlæfdige mîn,
for nŷdþearfe nean myndgiaþ
ond þâ wîggþræce on gewritu setton,
]ôoda gebæru, ond þis næfre
660 þurh æniges mannes mûð gehŷrdon
hæleðum cŷðan, bûtan hêr nûðâ'.
Him sêo æðele cwên âgeaf andsware:
'wiðsæcest ðû tô swîðc sôðe ond rihte
ymb þæt lîfes trêow ond nû lŷtle ær
665 sægdest sôðlîce be þâm sigebêame
lêodum þînum ond nû on lige cyrrest'.
Iûdas hire ongên þingode, cwæð, þæt hê þæt on gehðu
gespræce
ond twêon swîðost, wênde him trâge hnâgre.
Him oncwæð hraðe câseres mæg:
670 'hwæt, wê ðæt hŷrdon þurh hâlige bêc
hæleðum cŷðan, þæt âhangen wæs
on Caluarie cyninges frêobearn,
godes gâstsunu. þû scealt geagninga
wîsdôm onwrêon, swâ gewritu secgaþ,
675 æfter stedewange hwær sêo stôw sîe
Caluarie, ær þec cwealm nime, ·
swilt, for synnum, þæt ic hîc syððan mæge

geclǽnsian Crîste tô willan,
hæleðum tô helpe, þæt mê hâlig god
680　gefylle, frêa mihtig, feores ingeþanc,
weoruda wuldorgeofa, willan mînne,
gâsta gêocend'.　Hire Iûdas oncwæð
stîðhycgende : 'ic þâ stôwe ne can
nê þæs wanges wiht nê þâ wîsan cann'.

685　Elene maðelode þurh eorne hyge :
'ic þæt geswerige þurh sunu incotodes,
þone âhangnan god, þæt ðû hungre scealt
for cnêomâgum cwylmed weorðan,
bûtan þû forlǽte þâ lêasunga
690　ond mê sweotollîce sôð gecýðe'.
Heht þâ swâ cwicne corðre lǽdan,
scûfan scyldigne (scealcas ne gǽldon)
in drŷgne sêað, þǽr hê duguða lêas
sîomode in sorgum .vii. nihta fyrst
695　under hearmlocan hungre geþrêatod,
clommum beclungen, ond þâ cleopigan ongan
sârum besylced on þone seofeðan dæg
mêðe ond metelêas (mægen wæs geswiðrod):
'ic êow healsie þurh heofona god,
700　þæt gê mê of ðyssum earfeðum ûp forlǽten
hêanne fram hungres genîðlan.　Ic þæt hâlige trêo
lustum cýðe, nû ic hit leng ne mæg
helan for hungre.　Is þes hæft tô ðan strang,
þrêanŷd þæs þearl ond þes þroht tô ðæs heard
705　dôgorrîmum.　Ic âdrêogan ne mæg
nê leng helan be ðâm lîfes trêo,
þêah ic ǽr mid dysige þurhdrifen wǽre
ond ðæt sôð tô late seolf gecnêowe'.

locum novi; quia nec eram tunc."　Beata Helena dixit: " Per Crucifixum fame te interficiam, nisi dixeris veritatem."　Et cum haec dixisset, jussit eum mitti in lacum siccum, usque in septem dies, sic
ut custodiretur a custodibus.　Cum transissent autem septem dies,

VIIII.

Þâ ðæt gehŷrde, sîo þảr hæleðum scêad,

710 beornes gebǽro, hîo bebêad hraðe,

þæt hine man of nearwe ond of nŷdcleofan,

fram þâm engan hofe, ûp forlête.

Hîe ðæt ofstlîce efnedon sôna

ond hine mid ârum ûp gelǽddon

715 of carcerne, swâ him sêo cwên bebêad.

Stôpon þâ tô þǽre stôwe stîðhycgende

on þâ dûne ûp, ðê dryhten ǽr

âhangen wæs, heofonrîces weard,

godbearn, on galgan, ond hwæðre geare nyste

720 hungre gehŷned, hwǽr sîo hâlige rôd

721.2 þurh *fêondes* searu foldan getŷned

lange legere fæst lêodum dyrne

wunode wælreste. Word stunde âhôf

725 elnes oncŷðig ond on ebrisc spræc:

'dryhten hǽlend, þû ðe âhst dôma geweald

ond þû geworhtest þurh þînes wuldres miht

heofon ond eorðan ond holmþræce,

sǽs sîdne fæðm, samod ealle gesceaft

730 ond þû âmǽte mundum þînum

ealne ymbhwyrft ond ûprador

ond þû sylf sitest, sigora waldend,

ofer þâm æðelestan engelcynne,

þe geond lyft farao lêohte bewundene,

---

clamavit Judas de lacu, dicens, "Obsecro vos, educite me, et ego osten-
dam vobis crucem Christi."

Cum ascendisset autem de lacu, perrexit usque ad locum, nesciens
certius ubi jacebat Crux Christi, levavitque vocem suam ad Dominum
Hebraica lingua et dixit: "Deus, Deus, qui fecisti coelum et terram,
qui palmo metisti coelum et pugno terram mensurasti; qui sedes super
currum Cherubin, et ipsa sunt volantia in aeris cursibus luce immensa,

735 mycle mægenþrymme. Ne mæg þǽr manna gecynd
      of eorðwegum úp gefêran
      in lîchoman mid þâ lêohtan gedryht,
      wuldres âras.   Þû geworhtest þâ
      ond tô þegnunge þînre gesettest,   .
740 hâlig ond heofonlic.   Þâra on hâde sint
      in sindrêame syx genemned,
      þâ ymbsealde synt mid syxum êac
      fiðrum, gefrætwad, fǽgere scînaþ.
      Þâra sint .iiii., þe on flihte â
745 þâ þegnunge þrymme beweotigaþ
      fore onsŷne êces dôman,
      singallîce singaþ in wuldre
      hǽdrum stefnum heofoncininges lof,
      wôða wlitegaste, ond þâs word cweðaþ
750 clǽnum stefnum (þâm is ceruphîn nama):
      'hâlig is se hâlga hêahengla god,
      weoroda wealdend.   Is ðæs wuldres ful
      heofun ond corðe ond eall hêahmægen
      tîre getâcnod'.   Syndon tû on þâm,
755 sigorcynn, on swegle, þe man sêraphîn
      be naman hâteð. Hîe sceolon neorxnawang
      ond lîfes trêo lêgene sweorde
      hâlig healdan.   Heardecg cwacaþ,
      beofaþ, brogdenmǽl ond blêom wrixleð
760 grâpum gryrefæst.   Þæs ðû, god dryhten,
      wealdest wîdan fyrhð, ond þû womfulle
      scyldwyrcende sceaðan of radorum

---

ubi humana natura transire non potest; quia tu es qui fecisti ea ad
ministerium tuum : sex animalia, quae habent senas alas ; quattuor
quidem ex ipsis quae volant, ministrantia et incessabili voce claman-
tia, "Sanctus, Sanctus, Sanctus," Cherubin vocantur ; duo autem
ex his posuisti in Paradiso custodire lignum vitae, quae vocantur
Seraphin. Tu autem dominaris omnium, quia tua factura sumus,
qui incredibiles Angelos profundo tartaro tradidisti; et ipsi sunt sub

âwurpe wonhŷdige. Þâ sio wêrge sceolu
under heolstorhofu hrêosan sceolde
765 iu wîta forwyrd. Þǽr hîe in wylme nû
drêogaÞ dêaðcwale in dracan fæðme
Þêostrum forÞylmed. Hê Þînum wiðsôc
aldordôme, Þæs hê in ermðum sccal,
ealra fûla fûl, fâh Þrôwian,
770]·êownǫd Þolian. Þǽr hê Þîn ne mæg
word âweorpan, is iu wîtum fæst,
ealre synne fruma, sûsle gebunden.
Gif Þîn willa sie, wealdend engla,
Þæt rîcsie, sê ðe on rôde wæs
775 ond Þurh Mârian in middangeard
âcenned wearð in cildes hâd,
Þêoden engla (gif hê Þîn nǽre
sunu synna lêas, nǽfre hê sôðra swâ feala
iu woruldrîce wundra gefremede
780 dôgorgerîmum. Nô ðû of dêaðe hine
swâ Þrymlîce, Þêoda wealdend,
âweahte for weorodum, gif hê in wuldre Þîn
Þurh ðâ beorhtan bearn ne wǽre),
gedô nû, fæder engla, forð bêacen Þîn.
785 swâ ðû gehŷrdest Þone hâlgan wer,
Moyses, on meðle, Þâ ðû, mihta' god,
geȝwdest Þâm eorle on Þâ æðelan tîd
under beorhhlîðe bân Iosephes,
swâ ic Þê, weroda *wealdend*, gif hit sie willa Þîn,
790 Þurg Þæt beorhte gesceap biddan wille,

---

fundo abyssi a draconum foetore cruciandi, et tuo praecepto contra-
dicere non possunt. Et nunc, Domine, si tua voluntas est regnare
filium Mariae, qui missus est a te (nisi autem fuisset ex te, non
tantas virtutes fecisset; nisi vero tuus puer esset, non suscitares eum ·
a mortuis) fac nobis, Domine, prodigium hoc; et sicut exaudisti
famulum tuum Moysen, et ostendisti ei ossa patris nostri Joseph;
ita et nunc, si est voluntas tua, ostende nobis occultum thesaurum:

þæt mê þæt goldhord, gâsta scyppend,
geopenie, þæt yldum wæs
lange behŷded. ForlÍt nû, lîfes fruma,
of ðâm wangstede wynsumne ûp
795   under radores ryne rêc âstîgan
lyftlâcende. Ic gelŷfe þê sêl
ond þŷ fæstlîcor ferhð staðelige,
hyht untwêondne, on þone âhangnan Crîst,
þæt hê sîe sôðlîce sâwla nergend,
800   êce, ælmihtig, Israhela cining,
walde wîdan ferhð wuldres on heofenum,
â bûtan ende, êcra gestealda'. /

X.

Ða of ðÍre stôwe stêam ûp ârâs,
swylce rêc, under radorum. Þâr ârÍred wearð
805   beornes brêostsefa. Hê mid bÍm handum
êadig ond Íglêaw ûpweard plegade.
Iûdas maþelode glêaw in geþance :
' nû ic þurh sôð hafu seolf gecnâwen
on heardum hige, þæt ðu hÍlend eart
810   middangeardes. Sîe ðê, mægena god,
þrymsittendum þanc bûtan ende,
þæs ðû mê swâ mêðum ond swâ mânweorcum
þurh þîn wuldor inwrige wyrda gerŷno.
Nû ic þê, bearn godes, biddan wille,
815   weoroda willgifa, nû ic wât, þæt ðû eart

---

et fac ab eodem loco fumum odoris aromatum et suavitatis ascendere :
ut et ego credam crucifixo Christo, quia ipse est Rex Israel, et nunc
et in secula seculorum." /
    Haec cum orasset Judas, statim commotus est locus, et multitudo
fumi et aromatum odoris suavitatis ascendit de loco : ita ut admira-
tus Judas plauderet ambabus manibus suis, et diceret : " In veritate,

gecŷðed ond âcenned allra cyninga þrym,
þæt ðû mâ ne sîe mînra gylta,
þâra þe ic gefremede nalles fêam sîðum,
metud, gemyndig.   Lǽt mec, mihta god,
820   on rîmtale rîces þînes
mid hâligra hlŷte wunigan
in þǽre beorhtan byrig, þǽr is brôðor mîn
geweorðod in wuldre, þæs hê wǽre wið þec,
Stephanus, hêold, þeah hê stângreopum
825   worpod wǽre. Hê hafað wîgges lêan,
blǽd bûtan blinne. Sint in bôcum his
wundor, þâ hê worhte, on gewritum, cŷðed
Ongan þâ wilfægen æfter þâm wuldres trêo
elnes ânhŷdig eorðan delfan
830   under turfhagan, þæt hê on .xx.
fôtmǽlum feor funde behelede,
under nêolum niðer næsse gehŷdde
in þêostorcofan — hê ðǽr .iii. mêtte
in þâm rêonian hofe rôda ætsomne
835   grêote begrauene, swâ hîo geârdagum
ârlêasra sceolu eorðan bepeahton,
Iûdêa *cynn*. Hîe wið godes bearne
nîð âhôfun, swâ hîe nô sceoldon,
þǽr hîe leahtra fruman lârum ne hŷrdon.
840   Þâ wæs môdgemynd myclum geblîssod,
hige onhyrded þurh þæt hâlige trêo,
inbryrded brêostsefa, syððan bêacen geseh
hâlig under hrûsan. Hê mid handum befêng
wuldres wynbêam ond mid weorode âhôf

Christe, tu es Salvator mundi; gratias tibi ago, Domine, qui cum sim indignus, non me fraudasti dono gratiae tuae. Deprecor te, Domine Jesu Christe, memor esto mei et dele peccata mea, et adnumera me cum fratre meo Stephano, qui scriptus est in Actibus duodecim Apostolorum tuorum." ⁄Haec cum dixisset, accipiens fossorium praecinxit se viriliter, et coepit fodere. Cum autem fodisset passus viginti,

845 of foldgræfe. Fêðcgestas
     êodon, æðelingas, in on þâ ceastre.
     Âsetton þâ on gesyhðe sigebêamas .iii.
     eorlas ânhŷdige fore Elenan cnêo
     collenferhðe. Cwên weorces gefeah
850 on ferhðsefan ond þâ frignan ongan,
     on hwylcum þâra bêama bearn wealdendes,
     hæleða byhtgifa, hangen wære.
     ' Hwæt, wê þæt hŷrdon þurh hâlige bêc
     tâcnum cŷðan, þæt twêgen mid him
855 geþrôwedon, ond hê wæs þridda sylf
     on rôde trêo. Rodor eal geswearc
     on þâ slîðan tîd. Saga, gif ðû cunne,
     on hwylcre þyssa þrêora þêoden engla
     geþrôwode, þrymmes hyrde '.
860 Ne meahte hire Iûdas (nê ful gere wiste)
     sweotole gecŷþan be ðâm sigebêame,
     on hwylcne se hælend âhafen wære,
     sigebearn godes, ær hê âsettan heht
     on þone middel þære mæran byrig
865 bêamas mid bearhtme ond gebîdan þær,
     ôð ðæt him gecŷðde cyning ælmihtig
     wundor fôr weorodum be ðâm wuldres trêo.
     Gesæton sigerôfe, sang âhôfon,
     rædþeahtende, ymb þâ rôda þrêo
870 ôð þâ nigoðan tîd, hæfdon nêowne gefêan
     mærðum gemêted. Þâ þær menigo cwom,
     folc unlŷtel, ond gefærenne man
     brôhton on þære beorna þrêate

---

invenit tres cruces absconditas, quas ejiciens attulit in civitatem.
Interrogabat autem beatissima Helena, quae esset crux Christi : " sci-
mus autem quia ceterae duae latronum sunt, qui cum eo crucifixi
sunt." Et ponentes eas in media civitate expectabant gloriam Christi.
Et circa horam nonam ferebatur mortuus juvenis in grabato : Judas
autem gaudio repletus dixit : "Nunc cognosces, Domina, dilectissimum

on nêaweste (wæs þâ nigoðc tid),
875　gingne gâstlêasne.　Þâ ðæ̂r Iûdas wæs
on môdsefan miclum geblissod.
Heht þâ âsettan sâwllêasne,
lîfe belidenes lîc, on eorðan,
unlifgendes, ond ûp âhôf,
880　rihtes wêmend, þâra rôda twâ
fyrhôglêaw on fæðme ofer þæ̂t fæ̂ge hûs,
dêophycgende.　Hit wæs dêad, swâ æ̂r,
lîc legere fæ̂st : leomu côlodon
þrêanêdum beþeaht.　Þâ sîo þridde wæs
885　âhafen hâlig.　Hrâ wæs on anbîde,
ôð ðæt him uppan æðelinges wæs
rôd âræ̂red, rodorcyninges bêam,
sigebêacen sôð.　Hê sôna ârâs
gâste gegearwod, geador bû samod
890　lîc ond sâwl.　Þæ̂r wæs lof hafen
fæger mid þŷ folce.　Fæder weorðodon
ond þone sôðan sunu wealdendes
wordum heredon.　Sîe him wuldor ond þanc
â bûtan ende eallrâ gesceafta.

XI.

895　Đa wæs þâm folce on ferhðsefan
ingemynde, swâ him â scyle,
wundor, þâ þe worhte weoroda dryhten
tô feorhnere fira cynne,

---

lignum et virtutem ejus."　Et tenens grabatum Judas, fecit deponi
mortuum, et posuit super eum singulas cruces, et non surrexit : im-
posita autem tertia cruce Dominica super mortuum, statim surrexit
qui mortuus fuerat juvenis, et omnes, qui aderant, glorificabant
Dominum.
Sed omnium bonorum semper invidus diabolus cum furore voci-

lífes láttíow. þá þér ligesynnig
900   on lyft ástáh lácende féond.
Ongan þá hléoðrian helledéofol,
eatol éclǽca, yfela gemyndig :
'hwæt is þis, lá, manna, þe mínne eft
þurh fyrngeflit folgaþ wyrdeð,
905   íceð ealdne níð, éhta strúdeð?
þis is singal sacu. Sáwla ne móton
mánfremmende in mínum leng
éhtum wunigan, nú cwom elþéodig,
þone ic ér on firenum fæstne talde,
910   hafað mec beréafod rihta gehwylces,
feohgestréona. Nis ðæt fǽger síð.
Feala mê se hélend hearma gefremede,
níða nearolicra, sé ðe in Nazareð
áféded wæs. Syððan furþum wéox
915   of cildháde, symle cirde tó him
éhte míne. Ne mót énige nú
rihte spówan. Is his ríce brád
ofer middangeard, mín is geswiðrod
réd under roderum. Ic þá róde ne þearf
920   hleahtre herigean. Hwæt, se hélend mê
in þám engan hám eft getýnde
geómrum tó sorge. Ic þurh Iúdas ér
hyhtful gewearð ond nú gehýned éom,
góda geásne, þurh Iúdas eft,
925   fáh ond fréondléas. Gén ic findan can
þurh wróhtstafas wiðercyr síððan
of ðám wearhtreafum. Ic áwecce wið ðê
óðerne cyning, sé éhteð þín,

ferabatur in aere, dicens: "Quis iterum hic est, qui non permittet me
suscipere animas meorum? O Jesu Nazarene, omnes traxisti ad te :
ecce et lignum tuum manifestasti adversum me. O Juda! quid hoc
fecisti? Nonne prius ego per Judam traditionem perfeci, et populum
concitavi impie agere? Ecce nunc per Judam ego hinc ejicior.

ond hê forlǽteð lâre þîne
930 ond mânþêawum mínum folgaþ
ond þec þonne sendeð in þâ sweartestan
ond þâ wyrrestan wîtebrôgan,
þæt ðû sârum forsôht wiðsæcest fæste
þone âhangnan cyning, þâm ðû hýrdest ǽr '
935 Him ðâ glêawhýdig Iûdas oncwæð,
hæleð hildedêor (him wæs hâlig gâst
befolen fæste, fýrhât lufu,
weallende gewitt þurh wîgan snyttro),
ond þæt word gecwæð wîsdômes ful :
940 'ne þearft ðû swâ swîðe, synna gemyndig,
sâr nîwigan ond sæce ræran,
morðres mânfrêa, þæt þê se mihtiga cyning
in nêolnesse nyðer bescûfeð,
synwyrcende, in sûsla grund
945 dômes lêasne, sê ðe dêadra feala
worde âwehte. Wite ðû þê gearwor,
þæt ðû unsnyttrum ânforlête
lêohta beorhtost ond lufan dryhtnes,
þone fǽgran gefêan, ond on fýrbæðe
950 sûslum beþrungen syððan wunodest,
âde onǽled, ond þǽr âwa scealt,
wiðerhycgende, wergðu drêogan,
yrmðu, bûtan ende '. Elene gehýrde,
hû se fêond ond se frêond geflitu rǽrdon,
955 tîrêadig ond trâg, on twâ halfa,
synnig ond gesǽlig. Sefa wæs þê glædra,
þæs þe hêo gehýrde þone hellesceaþan
oferswîðedne, synna bryttan,

Inveniam et ego quid faciam adversum te : suscitabo alium Regem,
qui derelinquet Crucifixum, et mea exequetur consilia, et immittet in
te iniqua tormenta : et tunc cruciatus negabis Crucifixum."—Judas
autem, fremens in spiritu sancto, dixit : "Qui mortuos suscitavit
Christus, ipse te damnet in abyssum ignis aeterni." Haec audiens

ond þâ wundrade ymb þæs weres snyttro,
960 hû hê swâ gelêafful on swâ lýtlum fæce
ond swâ uncýðig ǣfre wurde
glêawnesse þurgoten. Gode þancode,
wuldorcyninge, þæs hire se willa gelamp
þurh bearn godes bêga gehwæðres,
965 gê æt þǣre gesyhðe þæs sigebêames
gê ðæs gelêafan, þe hio swâ lêohte oncnêow
wuldorfæste gife in þæs weres brêostum.

XII.

Ðâ wæs gefrêge in þǣre folcsceare,
geond þâ werþêode wîde lǣded,
970 mǣre morgenspel manigum on andan,
þâra þe dryhtnes ǣ dyrnan wéldon, o
boden æfter burgum, swâ brimo fæðmað,
in ceastra gehwǣre, þæt Crîstes *rôd*
fyrn foldan begræfen funden wǣre,
975 sêlest sigebêacna, þâra þe sîð oððe ǣr
hâlig under heofenum âhafen wurde,
ond wæs Iûdêum gnornsorga mǣst,
werum wansǣligum, wyrda lâðost,
þæt hîe hit for worulde wendan *ne* meahton,
980 cristenra gefêan. Ðâ sîo cwên bebêad
ofer eorlmægen âras fýsan
ricene tô râde, sceoldon Rômwarena
ofer hêanne holm hlâford sêcean
ond þâm wîggende wilspella mǣst
985 seolfum gesecgan, þe ðæt sigorbêacen
þurh meotodes êst mêted wǣre,

beata Helena admirabatur fidem Judae: cum magno autem studio
collocans praetiosam Crucem, auro et lapidibus pretiosis, faciens
loculum argenteum, in ipso collocavit Crucem Christi et ecclesiam

funden in foldan, þæt ǽr fcala mǽla
behŷdcd wæs hálgum tó téonan,
cristenum folce.   þá ðám cininge wearð
990 þurh þá mæran wórd mód geblissod,
ferhð gefêonde.   Næs þá fricgendra
·   under goldhoman gád in burgum
feorran gefêrede.   Wæs him frófra mǽst
geworden in worlde æt ðám willspelle,
995 hlihſende hyge, þe him hererǽswan
ofer êastwegas, áras, bróhton,
hú gesundne sîð ofer swonráde
secgas mid sigecwên áseted hæfdon
on Crêca land.   Hîe se cásere hcht
1000 ófstum myclum eft gearwian
sylfe tó sîðe.   Secgas ne gǽldon,
syððan andsware ǽdre gehŷrdon,
æðclinges word.   Hcht hê Elenan hǽl
ábêodan beadurófre, gif hîe brim † nescn
1005 ond gesundne sîð settan mósten,
hæleð hwætmóde, tó þǽre hálgan byrig.
Hcht hire | á áras éac gebêodan
Constantînus, |æt hîo cirican þǽr
on þám beorhhlîðe bêgra rǽdum
1010 getimbrede, tempel dryhtnes,
on Caluarie Crîste tó willan,
hæleðum tó helpe, þǽr sîo hálige ród
gemêted wæs, mǽrost bêama,
þára þe gefrugnen foldbûende
1015 on corðwege.   Hîo geefnde swá,
siððan winemagas westan bróhton
ofer lagufæsten lêofspell manig.
Dá sêo cwên bebêad cræftum getŷde

construxit in ipso Calvariae loco. Judas autem accipiens incorrup-
tionis baptismum in Christo Jesu, de praecedentibus signis ostensus
est fidelis, et commendavit eum Episcopo qui illo tempore erat adhuc

     sundor âsêcean, þâ sêlestan,
1020 þâ þe wrætlîcost wyrcan cûðon
     stângefôgum, on þâm stedewange
     girwan godes tempel. Swâ hire gâsta weard
     reord of roderum, hêo þâ rôde heht
     golde beweorcean ond gimcynnum,
1025 mid þâm æðelestum eorcnanstânum,
     besetton searocræftum ond þâ in seolfren fæt
     locum belûcan. þær þæt lîfes trêo,
     sêlest sigebêama, siððan wunode
     æðelum unbræce. þær bið â gearu
1030 wraðu wannhâlum wîta gehwylces,
     sæce ond sorge. Hîe sôna þær
     þurh þâ hâlgan gesceaft helpe findaþ,
     godcunde gife. Swylce Iûdas onfêng
     æfter fyrstmearce fulwihtes bæð
1035 ond geclênsod wearð Crîste getrŷwe,
     lîfwearde lêof. His gelêafa· wearð
     fæst on ferhðe, siððan frôfre gâst
     wic gewunode in þæs weres brêostum,
     bylde tô bôte. Hê þæt betere gecêas,
1040 wuldres wynne, ond þâm wyrsan wiðsôc,
     dêofulgildum, ond gedwolan fylde,
     unrihte æ. Him wearð êce rex,
     meotud, milde, god mihta wealdend.

XIII.

     Þâ wæs gefulwad, sê ðe ær feala tîda
1045 lêoht gearu . . . . ,
     inbryded brêostsefa on þæt betere lîf,

Jerosolymis, et baptizavit eum in Christo. Cum moraretur beata
Helena in Jerosolyma factum est Beatum Episcopum dormitionem

gewended tô wuldre.   Hûru, wyrd gescrêâf,
þæt hê swâ gelêaffull ond swâ lêof gode
in worldrîce weorðan sceolde,
1050 Crîste gecwême.   Þæt gecŷðed wearð,
siððan Elene heht Eusebium
on rǽdgeþeaht, Rôme bisceop,
gefetian on fultum forðsnotterne
hæleða gerǽdum tô þǽre hâlgan byrig,
1055 þæt hê gesette on sacerdhâd
in Ierusalem Iûdas þâm folce
tô bisceope burgum on innan
þurh gâstes gife tô godes temple
cræftum gecorenne, ond hine Cyriacus
1060 þurh snyttro geþeaht syððan nemde
nîwan stefne.   Nama wæs gecyrred
beornes in burgum on þæt betere forð
ǽ hǽlendes. / Þâ gên Elenan wæs
môd gemynde ymb þâ mǽran wyrd
1065 geneahhe for þâm næglum, þe ðæs nergendes
fêt þurhwodon ond his folme swâ some,
mid þâm on rôde wæs rodera wealdend
gefæstnod, frêa mihtig.   Be ðâm frignan ongan
cristenra cwên, Cyriacus bæd,
1070 þæt hire þâ gîna gâstes mihtum
ymb wundorwyrd willan gefylde,
onwrige wuldorgifum, ond þæt word âcwæð
tô þâm bisceope, bald reordode:

---

accipere in Christo.   Beata autem Helena accersivit Episcopum Eusebium urbis Romae, et ordinavit Judam Episcopum in Jerosolyma
Ecclesiae Christi: mutavit autem nomen ejus, et vocatus est Cyriacus. /
  Beata autem Helena, repleta Dei fide, et intelligens Scripturas per
vetus et novum Testamentum, instructa et repleta Spiritu sancto,
iterum coepit studiose requirere qui in cruce confixi fuerant clavi, in
quibus impii Judaei Salvatorem crucifixerunt: et convocans Judam,

'þû mê, eorla hlêo, þone æðelan bôam,

1075 rôde rodera ciuing*es*, ryhte getæhtesð,

on þa*m* âhangen wæs hæðenum folmum

gâsta gôocend, godes âgen bearn,

nerigend fira. Mec þæra nægla gên

on fyrhðsefan fyrwct myngaþ.

1080 Wolde ic, þæt ðû͡ funde, þâ ðe in foldan gên

dôope bedolfen dierne sindon,

heolstre behŷded. Â mîn hige sorgað,

rêonig rôoteð ond geresteð nô,

æ̂rþan mê gefylle fæder ælmihtig,

1085 wereda wealdend, willan mînne,

niða nergend, þurh þâra nægla cyme,

hâlig of hîehða. Nû ðû hrædlîce

eallum êaðmôdum, âr sôlesta,

þîne bêne onsend in ðâ beorhtan gesceaft

1090 on wuldres w*ealdend*, bide wigena þrym,

þæt þê gecŷðc cyning ælmihtig

hord under hrûsan, þæt gchŷded gôn,

duguðum dyrne, dêogol, bîdeð'.

þâ se hâlga ongan hyge staðolian

1095 brêostum onbryrded bisceop þæs folces,

glædmôd êode gumena þrôate

god hergendra ond þâ geornlîce

Cyriacus on Caluarie

hlêor onhylde, hygerûne ne mâð,

---

qui cognominatus est Cyriacus, dixit ei: "Quod circa lignum crucis erat, repletum est desiderium meum: sed de fixoriis qui infixi sunt imminet tristitia. Sed non requiescam et de hoc, donec Dominus compleat desiderium meum: sed accede adhuc, et de hoc precare Dominum."/Sanctus vero Episcopus Cyriacus, veniens ad Calvariae locum una cum multis Fratribus, qui in Domino Jesu Christo crediderunt per inventionem sanctae Crucis, et quod in mortuo factum est signum; elevans in coelum oculos suos et manibus simul percutiens pectus, exclamavit ex toto corde ad Dominum, confitens priorem ignorantiam, et beatificans omnes qui crediderunt in Christo

1100　gâstes mihtum tô gode cleopode
　　　eallum éaðmêdum, bæd him engla weard
　　　geopenigean uncûðe wyrd
　　　nîwan on nearwe, hwær hê þâra nægla swîðost
　　　on þâm wangstede wênan þorfte.
1105　Leorte ðâ tâcen forð, þær hîe tô sægon,
　　　fæder, frôfre gâst, ðurh fŷres blêo
　　　ûp ôðigean, þær þâ æðelestan
　　　hæleða gerædum hŷdde wæron
　　　þurh nearusearwe næglas on eorðan.
1110　Ðâ cwom semninga sunnan beorhtra
　　　lâcende lig. Lêode gesâwon
　　　hira willgifan wundor cŷðan,
　　　ðâ ðær of heolstre, swylce heofonsteorran
　ᶜ　oððe goldgimmus, grunde getenge
1115　næglas of nearwe neoðan scînende
　　　lêohte lîxton. Lêode gefægon,
　　　weorud willhrêðig, sægdon wuldor gode
　　　ealle ânmôde, þêah hîe ær wæron
　　　þurh dêofles spild in gedwolan lange,
1120　âcyrred fram Crîste. Hîe cwædon þus:
　　　‘ nû wê seolfe gesêoð sigores tâcen,
　　　sôðwundor godes, þæt wê wiðsôcun ær
　　　mid lêasingum. Nû is in lêoht cymen,
　　　onwrigen, wyrda bigang. Wuldor þæs âge
1125　on hêannesse heofonrîces god’.
　　　Ðâ wæs geblissod, sê ðe tô bôte gehwearf

---

et qui credituri sunt adhuc. Diu autem eo orante, ut manifestaretur illi signum aliquod, quemadmodum in cruce ita et in fixoriis, in fine orationis, cum diceret; “Amen,” factum est tale signum, quod omnes qui aderamus vidimus. Magna autem coruscatio de loco illuxit, ubi inventa est sancta Crux, clarior solis lumine; et statim apparuerunt clavi illi, qui in Dominico confixi fuerant corpore, tamquam aurum fulgens in terra; ita ut omnes sine dubio dicerent credentes, “Nunc cognoscimus in quem credimus.” Quos accipiens cum magno timore

þurh bearn godes, bisceop þâra lêoda,
nîwan stefne. Hê þâm næglum onfêng
egesan geâclod ond þære ârwyrðan
1130 cwêne brôhte. Hæfde Ciriacus
call gefylled, swâ him sôo æðelc bebêad,
wîfes willan. þâ wæs wôpes hring,
hât hêafodwylm ofer hlêor goten,
nalles for torne : têaras fêollon
1135 ofer wîra gespon. Wuldres gefylled
cwêne willa. Hêo hîe on cnêow sette
lêohte gelêafan, lâc weorðode
blissum hrêmig, þe hire brungen wæs
gnyrna tô gêoce. Gode þancode,
1140 sigora dryhtne, þæs þe hîo sôð gecnêow
andweardlîce, þæt wæs oft bodod
feor ær beforan fram fruman worulde
folcum tô frôfre. Hêo gefylled wæs
wîsdômes gife, ond þâ wîc behêold
1145 hâlig heofonlic gâst, hrêðer weardode,
æðelne innoð. Swâ hîe ælmihtig
sigebearn godes sioððan freoðode.

XIIII.

Ongan þâ geornlîce gâstgerŷnum
on sefan sêcean sôðfæstnesse
1150 weg tô wuldre. Hûru, weroda god
gefullæste, fæder on roderum,

---

obtulit Beatae Helenae. Quae figens genua et caput inclinans, ado-
ravit eos.
  Repleta autem sapientia et scientia multa valde, cogitabat quid de
his faceret. Quae cum in semetipsa posuisset omnem exquirere viam
veritatis ; Spiritus sancti gratia misit in sensum ejus tale quiddam

cining ælmihtig, þæt sêo cwên begeat
willan in worulde. Wæs se wîtedôm
þurh fyrnwitan beforan sungen
1155 eall æfter orde, swâ hit eft gelamp
ðinga gehwylces. Þêodcwên ongan
þurh gâstes gife georne sêcan
nearwe geneahhe, tô hwan hîo þâ næglas sêlost
ond dêorlîcost gedôn meahte
1160 dugoðum tô hrôðer, hwæt þæs wære dryhtnes willa.
Heht ðâ gefetigean forðsnotterne
ricene tô rûne, þone þe rædgeþeaht
þurh glêawe miht georne cûðe,
frôdne on ferhðe, ond hine frignan ongan,
1165 hwæt him þæs on sefan sêlost þûhte
tô gelæstenne, ond his lâre gecêas
þurh þêodscipe. Hê hire *þrîste* oncwæð :
' þæt is gedafenlic, þæt ðû dryhtnes word
on hyge healde, hâlige rûne,
1170 cwên sêlest, ond þæs cininges bebod
georne begange, nû þê god sealde
sâwle sigespêd ond snyttro cræft,
nerigend fira. Þû ðâs næglas hât
þâm æðelestan eorðcyninga
1175 burgâgendra on his brîdels dôn
mearc tô mîdlum. Þæt manigum sceall
geond middangeard mære weorðan,
þonne æt sæcce mid þŷ oferswîðan mæge
fêonda gehwylcne, þonne fyrdhwate
1180 on twâ healfe tohtan sêcaþ
sweordgenîðlan, þær hîe ymb *sige* winnað,

---

facere, ad commemorationem generationum quae venturae erant, quod
Prophetae pronuntiaverunt ante multas generationes. Convocans
autem virum fidelem et disciplinatum, cui testimonium perhibebant
multi, dixit ei: Regis mandata custodi et regale sacramentum exerce;
accipe hos clavos, et fac eos salivares in fraeno equi, qui Regis erit;

wrâð wið wrâðum. Hê âh æt wîgge spêd,
sigor æt sæcce ond sybbe gehwǽr,
æt gefeohte frið, sê þe foran lǽdeð
1185 brîdels on blancan, þonne beadurôfe
æt gârþrœce guman gecoste
beraô bord ond ord. Þis bið beorna gehwâm
wið æglǽce unoferswîðed
wǽpen æt wîgge. Be ôâm se wîtga sang
1190 snottor searuþancum. Sefa dêop gewôd,
. wîsdômes gewitt. Hê þǽt word gecwæð:
" cûþ þæt gewyrðeð, þæt þæs cyninges sceal
mearh under môdegum mîdlum geweorðod,
brîdelshringum./ Bið þæt bêacen gode
1195 hâlig nemned ond sê hwætðadig,
wîgge weorðod, sê þæt wicg byrð."
Þâ þæt ôfstlîce eall gelǽste
Elene for eorlum, æðelinges heht,
beorna bêaggifan, brîdels frætwan,
1200 hire selfre suna sende tô lâce
ofer geofenes strêam gife unscynde.
Heht þâ tôsomne, þâ hêo sêleste
mid Iûdêum gumena wiste,
hæleða cynnes, tô þǽre hâlgan byrig,
1205 cuman iu þâ ceastre. Þâ sêo cwên ongan
lǽran lêofra hôap, þæt hîe lufan dryhtnes
ond sybbe swâ same sylfra betwêonum,
frêondrǽddenne, fǽste gelǽston

---

erunt autem arma inexpugnabilia contra omnes adversarios, victoria
vero erit Regis et pax belli, ut id quod dictum est per Prophetam
impleatur. "Et erit in illo die quod est in fraeno equi sanctum Domini
vocabitur (Zac. 14, 20)."/ Beata autem Helena, qui in Jesu Christo
fide sunt confirmans in Hierosolymis, et omnia perficiens, persecu-
tionem Judaeis immisit, quia increduli facti sunt, et minavit eos a
Judaea. Tanta autem gratia secuta est Sanctum Cyriacum Episcopum, ut daemones per orationes ejus effugaret, et omnes hominum
sanaret infirmitates. / Beata autem Helena dona multa derelinquens

     leahtorlêase in hira lîfes tîd
1210 ond þæs lâttêowes lârum hŷrdon,
     cristenum þêawum, þê him Cyriacus
     bude bôca glêaw Wæs se bissceophâd
     fǽgere befæsted. Oft him feorran tô
     laman, limsêoce, lefe cwômon,
1215 healte, heorudrêorige, hrêofe ond blinde,
     hêane, hygegeômre, symle hǽlo þǽr
     æt þâm bisceope, bôte, fundon
     êce tô aldre. þâ gên him Elene forgeaf
     sincweorðunga, þâ hîo wæs sîðes fûs
1220 eft tô êðle, ond þâ eallum bebêad
     on þâm gumrîce god hergendum,
     werum ond wîfum, þæt hîe weorðeden
     môde ond mægene þone mǽran dæg,
     heortan gehigdum, in ðâm sîo hâlige rôd
1225 gemêted wæs, mærost bêama,
     þâra þe of eorðan ûp âwêoxe
     geloden under lêafum. Wæs þâ lencten âgân
     bûtan .vi. nihtum ǽr sumeres cyme
     on maias *kalendas*. Sîe þâra manna gehwâm
1230 behliden helle duru, heofones ontŷned,
     êce geopenad engla rîce,
     drêam unhwîlen, ond hira dǽl scired
     mid Mârian, þe on gemynd nime
     þǽre dêorestan dægweorðunga
1235 rôde under roderum, þâ se rîcesða
     ealles oferwealdend earme beþeahte. — Finit.

---

sancto Episcopo Cyriaco ad ministerium pauperum, dormivit in pace,
septimo decimo Kalendas Maji demandans omnibus qui Christum
diligunt, viris ac mulieribus, celebrare commemorationem diei, in qua
inventa est sancta Crux quinto nonarum Majarum. Quicumque vero
memoriam faciunt sanctae Crucis, accipiant partem cum Dei genitrice
sancta Maria, et cum Domino nostro Jesu Christo, qui cum Patre et
Spiritu sancto vivit et regnat, per infinita saecula seculorum.

wuldorcyninge, ac hîe worpene bêoð

1305 of ðâm heaðuwylme in hellegrund,
torngeniðlan. Bið þâm twâm dælum
ungelîce. Môton engla frêan
gesêon, sigora god. Hîe âsodene bêoð,
âsundrod fram synnum, swâ smæte gold,

1310 þæt in wylme bið womma gehwylces
þurh ofnes fŷr eall geclænsod,
âmered ond gemylted. Swâ bið þâra manna ælc
âscyred ond âsceâden scylda gehwylcre,
dêopra firena, þurh þæs dômes fŷr.

1315 Môton þonne siðþan sybbe brûcan,
êces êadwelan. Him bið engla weard
milde ond blîðe þæs ðe hîe mâna gehwylc
forsâwon, synna weorc, ond tô suna metudes
wordum cleopodon. Forðan hîe nû on wlite scînaþ

1320 englum gelîce, yrfes brûcaþ
wuldorcyninges tô wîdan feore. Amen.

NOTES.[1]

——◆——

1. **wæs**, 3d p. s. pret. from **wesan**.   Singular, notwithstanding plural subject.   Cf. N.E.

geâra, gen. pl., dependent upon **hwyrftum**.   The form is also used adverbially (= N.E. *yore*).

2. **geteled rîmes** = *the number told.*   Cf. Dickens, "He overmatched me five hundred times told."   **geteled** is p.p. from **tellan** (= *to count*), and **rîmes** is gen. sing. (cf. B. 2729).   The whole is an adverbial phrase, in which the instrumental is sometimes used instead of the genitive.

3. **þinggemearces**, gen. sg., used adverbially, *according to time,* — as one counts time.

4. **wintra**.   Winter, as a measure of time for year, was frequent in O.E.   Cf., also, usage of *winter* and *summer* in N.E.

6. **heo**, *form, shape, hue.*   Cf. *hue* in Shakespeare's "Sonnets" (22).

middangeard = the midearth lying between heaven and hell.   This word had this signification, no doubt, even before the introduction of Christianity; for the pagans placed their fiends and monsters under the ground, — whether at the bottom of lakes, as Grendel, or under the world, as Loki, — and Wælheal was above the earth, and between them lay the plain upon which mortal man moved.   Cf. Grimm's "Mythologie," 754; "Antiq. in A. & E.," 25.

9. **Rômwara.**   Cf. **Rômwarena**, 982.

10. **âhæfen**, p.p. from **ahebban**.   The word used in reference to the custom of raising a newly elected king upon a shield, in order to exhibit him to the people.   Cf. Grimm, "Rechtsalterthümer," 234.   Kemble ("Saxons in England," 154, foot-note) remarks that "levatus in regem = tô cyninge âhafen continued to be the words in use long after the custom of really chairing the king had, in all probability, ceased to be observed."

---

[1] A number of these notes are transcriptions from the author's "Teutonic Antiquities in Andreas and Elene" (abbreviated "Antiq. in A. & E.").

wuldorcyninge, ac hîe worpene bêoð
1305 of ðâm heaðuwylme in hellegrund,
torngenîðlan. Bið þâm twâm dǽlum
ungelîce. Môton engla frêan
gesêon, sigora god. Hîe âsodene bêoð,
âsundrod fram synnum, swâ smǽte gold,
1310 þæt in wylme bið womma gehwylces
þurh ofnes fŷr eall geclǽnsod,
âmered ond gemylted. Swâ bið þâra manna ǽlc
âscyred ond âsceâden scylda gehwylcre,
dêopra firena, þurh þæs dômes fŷr.
1315 Môton þonne siðþan sybbe brûcan,
êces êadwelan. Him bið engla weard
milde ond blîðe þæs ðe hîe mâna gehwylc
forsâwon, synna weorc, ond tô suna metudes
wordum cleopodon. Forðan hîe nû on wlite scînaþ
1320 englum gelîce, yrfes brûcaþ
wuldorcyninges tô wîdan feore. Amen.

NOTES.[1]

1. **wæs,** 3d p. s. pret. from **wesan.** Singular, notwithstanding plural subject. Cf. N.E.
geûra, gen. pl., dependent upon **hwyrftum.** The form is also used adverbially (= N.E. *yore*).
2. **geteled rîmes** = *the number told.* Cf. Dickens, "He over-matched me five hundred times told." **geteled** is p.p. from **tellan** (= *to count*), and **rîmes** is gen. sing. (cf. B. 2729). The whole is an adverbial phrase, in which the instrumental is sometimes used instead of the genitive.
3. **þinggemearces,** gen. sg., used adverbially, *according to time,* — as one counts time.
4. **wintra.** Winter, as a measure of time for year, was frequent in O.E. Cf., also, usage of *winter* and *summer* in N.E.
6. **heo,** *form, shape, hue.* Cf. *hue* in Shakespeare's "Sonnets" (22).
middangeard = the midearth lying between heaven and hell. This word had this signification, no doubt, even before the introduction of Christianity; for the pagans placed their fiends and monsters under the ground, — whether at the bottom of lakes, as Grendel, or under the world, as Loki, — and Wælheal was above the earth, and between them lay the plain upon which mortal man moved. Cf. Grimm's "Mythologie," 754; "Antiq. in A. & E.," 25.
9. **Rômwara.** Cf. **Rômwarena,** 982.
10. **âhæfen,** p.p. from **ahebban.** The word used in reference to the custom of raising a newly elected king upon a shield, in order to exhibit him to the people. Cf. Grimm, "Rechtsalterthümer," 234. Kemble ("Saxons in England," 154, foot-note) remarks that "levatus in regem = **tô cyninge âhafen** continued to be the words in use long after the custom of really chairing the king had, in all proba-bility, ceased to be observed."

---

[1] A number of these notes are transcriptions from the author's "Teutonic Antiquities in Andreas and Elene" (abbreviated "Antiq. in A. & E.").

14. **gumena**, gen. pl. from **guma** (Lat. *homo*, N.H.G. bräutigam, N.E. bride*groom*. The N.E. *groom*, save in this compound, has another etymon).

19. **wîges wôma**, *noise of war*. **wîg** is a designation of a heathen god (cf. Grimm's "Andreas und Elene," Preface). The god Tiw seems to have been the god of war, and identical with Mars of classical mythology, which is used in the Epinal Glosses as the rendering of Tiw (cf. Tuesday and Mardi); now **wîg** is rendered in the same glosses by Mars which seems to identify Tiw and Wîg (cf. "Antiq. in A. & E.," p. 5; Kemble, in "S. in E.," I. 351). **wôma**, according to Grimm ("A. u. E.") corresponds to *ómi* in Old Norse, which is a name of Oðin, and means *the noise-producing god;* hence **wôma** is in all probability a name of Woden (Oðin), which has lost all of its power except the quality of noise it then attributed. Cf. "Antiq. in A. & E.," pp. 5 ff.

20. **Hreðgotan** = *the renowned Goths* (Zupitza). Cf. Müllenhoff, Haupt's *Zeitschrift*, xii. This union of the Huns and Goths could not have occurred at this time; for the Huns did not appear until A.D. 375. See "Traveller's Song" for another allusion to this union.

21. **Francan.** Some aversion of the author to this people probably gave rise to the addition of their name.

Hugas (?). Grimm reads **Hunas**; Grein translates *Hunen*.

24. **wælhlencan**, pl. of **wælhlenc** (f.) = *coat-of-mail*. **wæl** is found in *Walkyr;* **hlenc** is M.E. *lenke*, N.E. *link*.

wordum ond bordum is a frequently recurring formula, signifying here the noise attending the raising of the battle standard. Cf. Tac., "Hist.," v. 17; "Germ.," XI.

26. **sweotole**, adv., *visibly, clearly*, etc. There exists, however, a substantive, **sweot** (= *crowd*), and this adverb may refer to that substantive. The heroes were assembled there in crowds (*schaarenweise*), and all together.

eal, strongly inflected adj., with loss of *l* in word-end. Cf. Sievers (Cook's edition), § 295. 2.

28. **wulf**, **earn** 29, and **hrefen** 52. The wolf, eagle, and raven were sacred to the highest god, Wodan, and the attendants of war over which he presided. Cf. Grimm, "A. u. E.," xxvi. f.; Kemble, "S. in E.," i. 343, note; "Antiq. in A. & E.," 7.

29. **ûrigfeðera** (cf. 111), *with moist feathers*, is a not uncommon predicate of the eagle. S., "Judith," 210.

31. **burgenta**, *burg, stadt* (??) (Zupitza). Grimm translates it *Riesenburg*, and makes it refer to some definite locality, but mentions that it may refer to some castle-crowned rock. Grein makes it the land of

the Burgundians. It seems to me to refer to some old castle-crowned rock, some giant's wall; and this view seems supported by analogy in such expressions as enta ærgewcorc (A. 1237), eald enta geweorc (A. 1497, Ruin 2), fyrngeweorc (A. 738). I take it that we have to do with two words here, — burg, the acc. dependent upon ofer, and enta, the gen. pl. of possession. Cf. "Antiq. in A. & E.," 9.

35. feðan trymedon eoredcestum. This is a dark passage. Cf. Zupitza, "Anz: deut. Alt.," v. 43 ff.; "Recension zu Zupitza's erster Ausgabe," in Haupt's *Zeitschrift.* Grimm translates eoredcestum by *electa legio;* Grein, by *turma, legio;* Körner, by *ausgewählte reiterschar.* According to Ten Brink it has the significance of *division, regiment (marschkolonne)* (cf. "Phœnix," 325; "Panther," 52; "Aeðelstan," 24). Wülker translates it by *schaar.* The infantry was strengthened by crowds.

42. cuð, *known.* Cf. uncouth. "Bound on a voyage uncouth." — *Milton.*

ceasterwarum. ceastre from *castra,* the Roman camps, then cities founded on their sites; and later, cities generally.

44. under earhfære, *by means of the circuit of the arrow.* An allusion to the custom, prevalent among Teutonic nations, of sending an arrow around, in any time of danger or sudden attack, to summon the people with despatch (Grimm, "Rechtsalthümer," 162). The word occurs twice in the "Codex Exonicus," and once later. Dietrich translates it *impetus saggitarum.*

49. hilde. *Hild,* goddess of war; = *Bellona.*

52. hrefen. S. 28, 29.

gôl, from galan, *to sing,* with which compare the M.E. *gale.* "In Chaucer's 'Court of Love' the Nightingale is said to cry and *gale;* hence its name nightegale or nightengale." — *Tyrwhitt.* In N.E., *gale (to sing)* is obsolete or rare.

54. Napier's collation, used in Zupitza's third edition, shows hlôopon.

56. câfe, as punctuated, an adj. Why not an adv.?

58. sceawedon, 3d p. pl. A change from the expected subject, *he* (the king), to *they* (the army, including the king).

59. þæt þe, which refers to army; he, hie (Ten Brink) would be a more intelligible construction.

64. eaxlgestealna, *shoulder-companions, trusted companions.* The word indicates the serried files of an army, and evidences the comradeship based upon a partnership in dangers and duties. B. 359, 2853.

68. gefær. "Phœnix," 426.

71. swefnes wôma, *vision,* lit. *the noise of a dream.* Cf. 19.

73. hwit. N.E. *white,* by metathesis.

73. **nathwylc,** *nescio quis.*

74. **þonne.** Before this word we expect a comparative, which for the translation must be supplied; but we find only a positive form here. Cf. B. 69; Orosius, 2d book, at the end, etc.

76. **eofurcumbol** means *the sign of the boar.* It has reference to the sign on the helmet, and is used, by synecdoche, for the helmet itself. Grimm ("A. u. E.," xxviii. f.) and Kemble (" S. in E.," i. 357) both connect this with the cult of Freyr, to whom this beast was sacred. It had probably lost its heathen significance.

78. **nihthelm tôglâd,** *the helmet of night fell apart,* i.e. darkness vanished. When night fell, earth was said to have put ou her helmet of darkness (cf. A. 1307 ff.). **tôglâd** expresses, with particular happiness, the breaking or splitting of this helmet (cf. B. 2488). Here the celestial brilliancy of the angel caused the helmet to split (cf. A. 126) and light to prevail.

80. Cf. 1047.

81. **þe,** ethical dative.

84. **findest,** with future significance.

90. **gimmas.** N.E. *gem* comes from Latin *gemma,* through French *gemme.*

91. **bôcstafum awrîten.** **bôcstæf** (N.H.G.) *beech stave, beech staff,* i.e. little pieces of beech, upon the ends of which characters were cut, hence a name for the characters themselves. **awrîtan** means *einritzen, eingraben,* i.e. *cut in,* and refers to the primitive mode of writing; for our word comes from the O.N. *wrîta,* through this word. Lat. *scribere,* N.H.G. *schreiben,* lives in N.E. *shrive.*

92. **mid þys bêacne ðû ... oferswîðesð,** *in hoc signo vinces.*

96. **þŷ ... þê.** Instrumental, and the explanation of N.E. *the, the* before comparatives; as, " the sooner, the better."

II.

97. **onlîce,** adv., with dat. regimen, **rôde.**

100. **beaggifa,** *ring-giver.* Alluding to the custom of the king to distribute rings of gold in the mead halls; hence, a name for a king.

114 ff. This is evidently a kind of formula describing the opening of battle. Note, for instance, the rhyme. It can hardly refer to a hand-to-hand combat, in which the hostile shields clash against each other; for the hurling of spears, in the next line, would have been futile, if not impossible, at such close quarters. Cf. "Antiq. in A. & E.," p. 47.

116. **earhfære**, *Anprall der Geschosse* (Grein), or *Kampf* (Zupitza). Cf., however, 44, and note the aptness of this explanation for this passage.

118. **geolorand** (cf. 50), *yellow border.* The border of the shield served, as we know from the Gnomic verses (" Menology," Grein, "Bibliothek der Agls. Poesie," ii. 346), as a protection or guard for the fingers. It is here used for the shield. Tac. "Germ.," vi.; "Ann.," ii. 14.

131. **sume wîg fornam**, a formula recalling **wyrd**. Cf. **sume drenc fornam** (136), **hine Wyrd fornam** (B. 1206) ("Antiq. in A. & E.," pp. 4 ff.).

141. **gescyrded**, p.p. from **gescyrdan**, *to destroy.* Cf. Sievers, *Anglia*, i. 578; "Wulfstan," 68. ii.; "Andreas," 1315. Grimm has **gescryded** by metathesis.

142. **lÿthwôn.** Cf. Murray, "Dialects of the Several Counties of Scotland."

143. **þanon, þannonne.** M.E. *þanne, þonne, þonnes, þennes;* N.E. *thence.*

151. **þrÿðbord stênan**, *bejewel the shield.* Was this a custom after the happy issue of battle? Cf. Grimm, "A. u. E.," 131. **scênan**, *to make shine.*

162 ff. Constantine had just won a most complete victory by virtue of the cross; and now he calls an assembly, to inquire about the unknown God, and asks, —

> " þe þis his bêacen wæs
> þe mê swâ lêoht ôðÿwde ond mîne lêode generede
> tâcna torhtost, ond mê tîr forgeaf
> wîgspêd wið wrâðum, þurh þæt wlitige trêo.

There can be no doubt that **tîr, gloria** is closely connected etymologically with Tiw (O.N. *Tyr*), and it was most probably at first another name for the same god. The rune for *t* (⟨rune⟩), which means Tir, recalls ♂, the sign of Mars, with whom Tiw was unmistakably connected. This sign of Mars is of great antiquity (cf. Grimm, "A. u. E.," 156).

It is striking, too, as Grimm further notices, that **tîr** so often occurs with **tacen**, or words from the same root. Thus here, and in E. 754 (**tîre getâcnod, decore insignitum**), B. 1654, and several times in "Juliana." The connection with **torht** is scarcely less noticeable (cf. "Judith," 93, 157). In a word, the Teutonic mind attached great importance to the signs and symbols of the gods; and that of this Tir

must have been bright, for that idea seems inseparably connected with
this symbol mentioned with Tir.

Now **wîgspêd**, in the next line, is formed of **wîg**, which has been
seen to be a name of Mars, and equivalent to Tiw, with which Tir is
closely related; and **spêd** is *success;* that is, the word means *the success
which Mars grants,* hence success in war. Now this passage denotes the
desire of a *heathen* king to find out who an unknown God is, — a God
unknown because his sign or emblem (a cross) was unknown; but, as
if this showed a lack of confidence in the god of war, upon whom he
was in the habit of relying, the heathen king ascribes his success to
the heathen God (**wîgspêd**). Indeed, though I am not bold enough
to propose a change in the usual rendering of this passage, I mention
that a capital *T* and Grein's punctuation — namely, the omission of the
comma after **forgeaf** — would give us a sentence entirely heathen, —
" And Tiw (Mars) granted me Wigspeed (cf. *Godspeed*) against the
inimical, through this shining tree "; thus uniting this brightest of
signs with the signs of Tiw, in whose martial character this new,
unknown God had revealed himself.

179. **on galgan.** Crucifixion was a form of punishment unknown
to the Anglo-Saxons; and hence they most frequently described it in
the vocabulary of hanging ("Antiq. in A. & E.," 42).

183. **îlcan,** Scotch *Ilk* (Murray, " Dialects," etc.). Not to be confounded with *ilk* (= *each, every*).

190. **fram,** agent. M.E. *of;* N.E. *by.*

191. **æt þâm,** *from this one.* Cf. B. 621, 2229.

192. **þæt** refers to Christianity.

193. **tîd,** *tide;* in Whitsuntide, Shrovetide, " time and tide wait for
no man," etc.

III.

194. **sælum,** cf. adj. **gesælig.** M.E. *seliga;* N.E. *silly* (not with its
present significance, but equivalent to *happy*).

197. **hyhta.** S. " Guthlac," 116.

198. **ongan . . . cŷðan = cŷðede.**

dæges ond nihtes, adv., *day and night.* **nihtes** is adv. gen., from
a feminine substantive.

203. **lâr (læran) + smiðas** (N.E. *smith), teaching-smiths, i.e.* teachers.

213. **gemyndig,** generally with gen. Cf. 1064; " Harrowing of
Hell," 29.

219. **Elene,** *Helena,* hence name of poem. This poem makes no
allusion to her English origin.

225. From this point to 272 is independent of original.

226. flote (M.E. *flote*; N.E. *flote*, *float*) = *wave* (Shaks. " Tempest," i. 2).

227. Geofon, which Müller (Haupt's *Zeitschrift*, i. 95) considers as connected with the sea-goddess Gefjon, occurs again, 1201. Merbach (" Das Meer in der Dichtung der Angelsachsen ") sees, in the fact that this word occurs only twice in composition, — geofonhus, "Gen." 1321; geofonflod, "Azar." 125, — further proof of the mythological origin of the word.

231. æt wendelsǽ seems capable of a twofold interpretation. Either the sea lying between Helen and the cross, *i.e.* separating two lands; or wendel may easily refer, and particularly in connection with on stæðe, to the varying line dividing land and water, *i.e.* the border of the sea; hence, *at shore, near the coast*.

233. ofer mearcpaðu. The divisions of land held in common by a tribe or band, or under the control of a lord or king, were called *Marks* (cf. "God save the mark!"). mearcpaðu refers to the roads running through these divisions.

235. bordum ond ordum : formula. Cf. wordum ond bordum (24).

236. werum ond wîfum : formula.

237. scrîðan suggests equine motion. Cf. 238.

238. brimþisan, *rusher over the sea*. Perhaps recalling the horse.

bord, spoken of as receiving the blows of the waves (ŷða swengas), is a figurative epithet drawn from the shield in battle, rather than simply the hull of a ship.

239. earhgeblond betrays as much familiarity with the battle as the sea.

241. idese lǽdan, acc. and inf., objective complement of hŷrde.

242. merestræte [from mere, *sea* (cf. N.E. *mer*maid), + stræt (N.E. *street*), *path*], *in the sea-path*.

244. snyrgan under swellingum, *glides along under swelling sails*, — like some bird, perchance a swan. Cf. fugole gelîcost glideð on geofone (A. 497).

245. sǽmearh plegean recalls the prancing steed.

246. wadan wǽgflotan suggests the swimmer.

247. cwên, *woman*, — *the* woman, queen. Cf. N.E. *quean, queen*.

251. Ms. has sande bewrecene (*sand-whipped*), which is more poetical, and fully as intelligible, as sunde bewrecene.

254. hêo refers to ŷðhofu.

256. To whom does on eorle refer, — Helen ? or is it collective and generic ?

259. **eofurcumbul.** S. 76.

264. I take **sinegim** to be specific, and to refer to the cross which Constantine had had made.

269. **herefeld.** A warrior's conception of fields in general.

273. **Hierusalem.** Cf. **Jerusalem** (1056). The first is the usual form; the second gives the pronunciation, for the word alliterates with *g* and *j*.

IV.

279. **gêmot** recalls the **witena gemot**, or *assembly of counsellors*, whom the king probably appointed, and over whom he presided (Tac. "Germ.," xi.).

294. **wiðwurpon**, regular form; Ms. has **wiðweorpan**.

297. **horu.** According to Sievers (§ 242. 4), instrumental, from **horh.**

300. **spâld.** Cf. **spadl, spatl,** N.E. *spittle.* **Spâld** comes through Northumbrian *spaðl, spalð, spald.*

corðre, from Lat. *cohors.*

309. **webbedan;** for **webbedon** is Mercian or Northumbrian.

320. **codan,** pret. to **gan** (S. § 430).

330. **cynestôle,** from **cyne** [**cyning** or **cyn** (?)] + **stol**, which occurs in "Elene" only in composition.

332. **maðelode,** *spoke, made a speech.* There is something formal in this word.

339. Where did Moses prophecy in these words? Cf. Isaiah ix. 6; Joshua v. 14.

345. Psalms xv. 8.

348. **ic ne wende æfre tô aldre onsîon mîne,** *I never turned my face to life,* i.e. to the things of this life.

353. Where does Essaias make this prophecy?

355. Ms. has **þe** instead of **me.**

356. **nâhton = ne âhton.** From **agan** (S. § 420. 2).

358. **man,** indef. pron. Fr. *on;* N.H.G. *man;* N.E. *one.* **þirsceð**, from **þirscan**, with metathesis **þrescan.** N.E. *thresh.*

359. **nales = ne + ealles, nealles, nales.** Cf. **nalas, nalæs.**

V.

366. **meotod.** This word, which Vilmar ("Alterthümer in Heliand") conceives as *measurer* (cf. Grein, "Sprachschatz," 2. 240), refers, according to him, in the first instance to the measuring god or god who sets boundaries, — i.e. perhaps Thunar, who measured with the hammer, from which were derived those peculiar and prevalent

measures by means of a throw (Grimm, "Deutsche Rechtsalthümer, 54 ff.). The indications are, however, that the god of land-measures, of boundaries, etc., among the Saxons, was Woden. Wanborough (formerly Wodensburh), Wonston (formerly Wodenstan), and numerous others (see Kemble, "S. in E.," i. 344), show his connection with land, while, according to the same author, there are numerous instances in charters of the use of Woden's name in connection with boundary trees, stones, or posts. Hence this meotod, which had, no doubt, lost all of its heathen significance, probably referred originally to Woden, as the god of boundaries.

373. gên. Cf. *again*.

414. Indirect question is usually expressed by optative.

439. þe hit siðð̵an cyð̵de sylfa his eaferan, *which he himself afterwards told his descendant.*

447. mîn swæs sunu. Usual form, mîn sunu se swæs.

452. in woruld weorulda, *in seculum seculi* (Lat. orig.). Cf. *in secula seculorum.*

VI.

461. nergend, from nerian (B. 573). Goth. *nasjan* (cf. *nasjunds*).

466. unasecgendlic, *inenarrabile.*

479. sume hwile, temp. acc., *somewhile.*

483. þrêo niht, pl. fem. with omission of final *e*, or perhaps to be explained as neut. pl.

487. hine is supplied on account of verse.

489. The tangle by which Judas is made the brother of the first martyr, Stephen, the son of Simon and grandson of Sachias, is unintelligible; but the confusion did not originate with Cynewulf. Cf., for instance, "Die Kreuzeslegenden in Leabhar Breac."; Gustav Schirmer, "St. Gallen" (86) ("Leipziger Dissertation," pp. 12-13, 35-36).

501. miltse. Cf. milde (*d* before *s* became *t*).

522. lêoð̵rûne, *secret song, secret instruction, admonitio per carmen.*

533. tô gecyð̵anne, inflected infinitive. S. § 363. 1.

539. nûð̵â, emphatic form of nû.

540. þyslîc (from þŷs), instrumental of sê + lîc (*thusly*), *thus.*

VII.

547. In the Ms. stands weoxon word cwidum (where word must be construed as plural), *the words increased in* (much) *speaking*. This is intelligible; and hence the change to wrixledan is to be rejected.

548. **on healfa gehwæne** (gehwæne, for gehwone, = *each*), acc. sg. masc. Cf. S. § 347.

583. **under womma scêatum** (scêat, according to Grein, *latebra, latibulum*), *in the womb of sins*.

585. **betæhton**, from **betæcan**. **takan** means both *give* and *take*.

600. **tô gîsle**, *zum Geisel* (that is, for torture, in order to evoke from him the desired information).

610. **rex** (Lat.) = *king*, but here equal to *queen*.

618. **beneah**, s. S. 424. 11.

VIII.

622. **eard** has nothing to do with **eorðe**.

629. *Whether he renounced the hope of heaven, as was in his mind, and this kingdom under the heavens, for the present, or revealed the cross.* The two members of this disjunctive sentence are not complete, nor clear, unless we can interpret **rîce under roderum** as parallel with **heofonrîces**, whereas it seems to be in antithesis. It would then mean *whether he should refuse to reveal the cross, and hence renounce heaven, or reveal it and in consequence claim heaven.*

633. Cf. 304.

635. *I cannot report* (supply *more exactly*).

636. **forðgewitenra**, part. from **forðgewitan**, and best translated by relative clause.

640. **cnihtgeong hæleð**, *a young man* (still) *in the period of youth.*

645 ff. See original. This allusion to the Trojan War would hardly have been retained had it not been well known to the poet's public.

647. **þonne**. After an implied comparison. **open ealdgewin þonne**, *a known battle in olden times* (more remote) *than*, etc.

649. **hwæt** = *how many.*

664. Helen seems to have had the power of divination; else how did she know what Judas had told his companions?

668. **wênde him trâge hnâgre**, *he feared the deplorable evil.* **him** is reflexive pronoun.

685. **þurh eorne hyge**, *in her angry soul* (*i.e.* not aloud).

691. See original.

IX.

709. Ten Brink proposes **scrâf** (from **scrifan**); but this is used only of God. See Lat. original.

726. Here begins the prayer. Compare such occurrences in "Crist" and "Juliana."

749. **wlítegaste.** *a,* as connecting vowel, is frequent in Kentish in superlative. **wlítegaste** refers to **wðða.**

750. The hierarchies of angels are several times mentioned in O.E. First are mentioned six angels with six wings each, of whom four are continually doing service before the eternal Judge. These seem to correspond to the four beasts (Rev. iv. 7); they form a heavenly chorus, and are called "cherubim." The other two are "seraphim"; and their duty is to guard paradise, and the tree of life, with fiery swords. The fall of the evil angel and his cohorts is mentioned in the same prayer. The archangels (**hêahengla,** 751) may or may not have represented another class. The passage concerning the seraphim, who guarded the garden of Eden (750), is taken from Gen. iii. 24, where, however, these guardians are called "cherubim." Should the order in which they are named here (and in "Andreas," 719) be intended to indicate relative rank, then it is singular that this order should be just the reverse of that usually assigned them. Cf. Skeat, "Piers the Plowman," p. 100; "Antiq. in A. & E.," 19, 20.

756. **neorxnawang,** *paradise.* The first part of this word is dark; but the constituent **wang** recalls the "fields of the blessed," etc.

766. **in dracan fæðme,** *in the embrace of the dragon.* A part of the Saxon conception of hell was that it was a huge monster, whose mouth was the entrance. Cf. Grein ("Dichtungen der Angelsachsen"), "Die Hölle selbst ward als Drache gedacht"; Plates IV. and XI. of the Cædmon Ms., Ellis's "Archælogia," vol. xxiv.

773. Notice Lat. original.

783. Notice unusual position of **þurh ðâ.**

788. *Bones of Joseph* — where?

790. **þurg þæt beorhte gesceap,** of the image of the cross.

791. **goldhord.** Reference, probably, to cross, without any figurative meaning.

802. *in secula seculorum* = **â bûtan ende.**

X.

818. **fêam** [**feawum, feaum, fêam**]. Cf. A. 615.

825. **wîgges lêan,** *reward of the warrior.* Reference to the reward of Walhalla (S. "Antiq. in A. & E.," 17 f.).

831. **feor** seems to signify *deep.*

832. **niðer,** adv., qualifying **nêolum.**

835. **begrauene.** *u* is an unusual form for O.E.

872. **gefærenne man,** *departed man.* Death, as an entrance upon a

journey, partakes at the same time of Christianity and heathenism: for the former uses such language; the latter held such a doctrine in various forms.

XI.

900. **feond.** The devil — not his son (cf. "Andreas," "Juliana," etc.) — is represented as endowed with the power to fly, and as visiting the earth.

909. Allusion to Christ's death as a malefactor, and his burial.

922. Judas Iscariot.

924. Judas, later Cyriacus the bishop.

928. Julian the Apostate.

XII.

983. **holm.** Grein compares this word denoting the appearance of the sea as rising, and not as a flat surface, with Russian *cholm* and Lat. *culmen*, both denoting elevation. Cf. **ofer hêanne holm**, *over the high sea*.

1001. **Is sylfe** used reflexively?

XIII.

1047. **wyrd.** Among the appellations of the Deity occurs **wyrda wealdend.** It is easy to translate this *Controller of Events*, and to contend, as Köhler ("Germanische Alterthümer in Beowulf," S. 5) does, that the word had lost all its associations with the Norse *Wyrd* or, as the name is in N.E., *Weird.* In this place, **wyrd** is personified. Cynewulf, recalling the checkered and singular career of Judas, — who, from the most ardent of all opponents to surrender to Helen, becomes a most faithful and steadfast defender of Christianity, — exclaims, " Verily, Weird decreed that he should become so faithful," etc.; recording, thus, his belief in fatalism, and attributing this to one of the sisters who presided over the destinies of men. If we recall, now, the expression in 80, it may be added, that, had the poet used this expression deliberately and in its full sense, he would not have been heathenizing God, but rather elevating him above the highest powers of heathen belief, — for even the gods were controlled by the decrees of the Norns, — and giving him a controlling power over the controlling powers of heathen belief.

1059. **Cyriacus** is henceforth the name of *Judas.*

1078. **mec** is old form; in younger poetry, **me** is frequent.

1114. **grunde getenge**, *near the surface, on the ground* (Zupitza).

XIV.

1156. **ðlnga gehwylces**, genitive with **gelimpan**. Cf. "Dan." 114. Generally with dative.

1158. **hwan** is instrumental case. Cf. "Sat." 527; "Crist," 32; "Guðlac," 521.

1185. **on blancan.** Cf. Riddle, 23. 18.

1196. **byreð**, for **biereð**.

1227. **lencten.** The year was divided into seasons, — *spring* (lencten), sumer (1228), *fall* is not mentioned, and **winter** (4). Summer began on the 7th of May; making the seasons, granting their equal duration of three months each, begin on the 7th of May, 7th of August, 7th of November, and 7th of February: which would make midsummer fall about the 21st of June, the time of the summer solstice; midwinter, about the time of the winter solstice, December 21st; while the middle of fall and of spring coincide very nearly with the autumnal and vernal equinoxes (Grein, "A. u. E.," xxiv., and "Nachträge," 171).

1232. **drēam** has the primary meaning of *noisy joviality;* and the derived meaning of *blessedness* is removed by several links in the chain that unites them.

XV.

1237. **frôd**, *prudent, wise, the age of wisdom; i.e. old.* Grimm translates **frôd ond fûs**, *prudens ac promptus.* **fûs** means *ready,* — then *ready* for something, which the context seems to indicate to be death.

hûs, *house, habitation.* Refers, in my opinion, to the body; others think, to the world.

1238. **wæf**, his own work; **læs**, his compilation from other sources.

1239. **reodode** is not found elsewhere.

1240. **nihtes nearwe** (*oppression of night*) seems to suggest sleeplessness, caused by engrossing interest in his work.

1240 ff. That is, that the extended knowledge derived from his reading and aided by his reflection, had given him a clearer insight into the real significance of the cross.

1245. Is **biter** (= *bitter necessity*) neuter or feminine?

1246. **þurh lēohtne hâd,** *in a remarkable manner.* Formerly thought to be indicative of clerical station.

1249. **torht.** Cf. "Gen." 2890; B. 313.

tîdum gerȝmde, *prolonged my days.* Why dative?

1257. Instead of **secg**, read **sæc** (*strife*).

1258. **cên** (*h*), rune for *c*.

1260. **æplede.**   Cf. " Phœnix," 506; " Juliana," 688; Haupt's *Zeit-schrift*, xi. 420.

yr (ᛇ) rune for *y, bow.*   Cf. Wülker's " Grundriss," 158–165.

1261. **nyd** (ᚾ), rune for *n, need.*

1262. **eh** (ᛗ), rune for *e, horse.*

1264. **wên** (ᚹ) rune for *w, hope.*

1266. **ur** (ᚢ) rune for *u, aurochs.*

1269. **lago** (ᛚ) rune for *l, sea, lake.*

1270. **feoh** (ᚠ), rune for *f, cattle.*

The runes, taken together, give ᚻᛖᚾᚹᚢᛚᚠ (*Cynewulf*).   This was discovered by Kemble.   Cf. " Grundriss," p. 148.

1276. *Cave of the winds.*

1277. **þrêam.**   Cf. " Daniel," 294; " Creation," 41.   Here begins a description of purgatory.

1294. **eldes.**   Cf. " Crist," 1060; B. 3125.

GLOSSARY.

———◆———

A.

â, always, aye, 744, 802, 804, 896, 1029, 1082, 1257.

æ, f., law. dryhtnes æ, 198, 971; þurh rihte æ, 281; Moyses æ, 283. ĉowre æ æðelum + cræftige, = versed in the origin of our law, 315; scriptures (written law), revelation, 393, 397; faith, religion, gospel (unrihte æ = false religion), 1042. æ hælendes, 1063.

âbannan, red. vb., to proclaim, to order, 34.

âbêodan, sv. II., to bid, 1004; pret. âbĉad; swa him se âr âbĉad, as the messenger commanded him, 87.

âbrêotan, sv. II., to break to pieces, to destroy, to kill, 510.

æbylgð, n., offence, sin, transgression, 401, 513.

ac, but, (however) 355, (on the contrary) 222, 450, 469, 493, 569, 863(?), 1304.

âcennan, wv. I., to bring forth, bear (child); p.p. âcenned, 5, 178, 339, 639, 776, 816.

âcîgan, wv. I., to call, summon (pret. âcîgde), 603.

æclæca (= ægl-) m., monster; eatol æclæca, dire monster (i.e. devil), 902.

æclêaw, s. æglêaw.

æcræft, knowledge of the law, religion; æcræft eorla (= Jews) 435.

âcweðan, sv. V., to utter, pronounce, express (pret. ûcwæð), 1072.

âcyrran, wv. I., to turn away from, to avert, 1120.

âd, m., fire; âde onæled, burnt with fire, 951; funeral pile, 585; pyre, yfemest in þâm âde, uppermost on this pyre, 1290.

æðelcyning, m., noble king (of Christ), 219; æðelcyninges rôd.

æðele, noble, 275, 300, 476, 545, 591, 647, 662, 733, [1029], 1074, 1107, 1131, 1146, 1174; glorious, 787; costly, valuable, 1025.

æðeling, m., nobleman, prince, (of Constantine) 12, 66, 202, 1003, (of Constantine's followers) 99, (generically) 393, (of Helen's followers) 846, 1198, (of Christ) 886.

æðelu, n. pl., origin, source (dat., ĉowre æ æðelum + crætige, 315, s. æ), race, sect. Israhêla æðelu = the race of the Israelites, 433, [properties, 1029].

âdrêogan, sv. II., endure, bear, suffer; inf., 705, 1291.

âfêdan, wv. I., bring up, rear; p.p. âfêded, 914.

æfen, n., evening, 139.

[æflian, 'comparare,' Gm. 1260.]

æfre, ever, (rendered with negative, hence = never) 349, 361, 524, 572, (rendered without negative, = ever, at any time) 403, 448, 507, (without negative) 961; [always, 451].

æfst, n., hate; æfstum, dat. sg., 207; æfst (acc. sg.) wið âre, hatred with favor, 308; for æfstum, = out of hatred, 496; æfst, acc. sg., 524.

æfter (with dat.), after (temporal or local), 233, 430, 490, 1034, 1155, 1265, 1268; about, 828; throughout, 972; during (æfter woruldstundum = during my sojourn in the world, 363); behind, upon, 135, 675.

âfyrhtan, wv. I., to make afraid, terrify; p.p. âfyrhted, = frightened, 56.

âgalan, sv. VI., to sing, to strike up (a song, etc.); pret. âgôl, fyrdlêoð âgôl wulf, the wolf struck up his song of battle, 27; Dauid ... dryhtlêoð âgôl, David sang a song for the people, 342.

âgan, p.p., to have, possess; 2d p. sg. âhst, 726; 3d p. sg. âh, 1182; 3d p. sg. opt. âge, 1124. (S. § 420. 2.)

âgân, âgangan, red. vb., pass, go; p.p. âgangen, 1; p.p. âgân, 1227.

âgen, own, 179, 422, 599, 1077.

æghwâ, prn., each one, every one; dat. sg., æghwânı, 1270.

æghwylc, prn., each, 1281.

âgifan, sv. V., render, give; andsware âgifan, 167, 545; 3d pret. sg. andsware âgeaf, 455, 462, 619, 662; pret. pl. (not w.s. form), âgêfon, delivered, surrendered, 587.

æglæc, n., terror, distress, oppression, 1188.

æglêaw, wise in the law, 806; æclêaw, 321.

âhangen, s. âhôn.

âhebban, sv. VI., raise, lift up, 10, 17, 29, 112, 724, 844, 862, 868, 879, 885, 976; ic ûp âhôf eaforan ginge, etc., I brought up (reared) a young heir, 353.

âhôn, red. vb., hang, crucify; pret. pl. âhêngon, 210, 475; pp. âhangen, 180, 245, 445, 671, 718, 1076; acc. p.p. âhangnan, 453, 687, 798, 934.

æht, f., council, assembly, deliberation, 473.

æht, f., possession, property, 905, 916; power, 908.

âhyðan, wv. I., plunder, loot, 41.

al, s. eal.

ælærend, instructor in faith, expounder of law, 506.

ælc, prn., every one, each, 1312.

ald, s. eald.

aldor, m., prince (of Constantine), 97, 157.

aldor, n., life, 132, 349, 571, 1218.

aldordôm, authority, dominion, 768.

âlesan, sv. V., select, choose; p.p. âlesen, 286, 380.

ælfylce, n., strange land, foreign land, 36.

all, [1266,] = eall.

ælmihtig, almighty, (of God) 145, 866, 1084, 1091, 1152, (of Christ) 800, 1146.

âlŷsan, wv. I., loose, release (redeem, ransom); âlŷsde lêoda bearn of locan dêofla, released the children of men from the snares of the devil, 181.

âmerian, wv. I., free from dross, purify, refine, 1312.

âmetan, sv. V., measure out, (2d p. sg. pret. ânıæte, thou measurest out, etc.), measure out to, allot, grant; 3d p. sg. pret. âmǽt, the mighty king granted, etc., 1248.

ân, one, 417; acc. sg. m. ǽnne, 585, 599; gen. pl. ânra, in the formula ânra ·gehwylc, every one, every, 1287.

anbîd, n., expectation; on anbîde, in expectation, 885.

ânboren, only-begotten; cyning ânboren, the only-begotten king, 392.

[anbrôce, f., building material, wood? (Gm. 1029)], and

anda, m., vexation, cause of indignation, 970.

andsæc, n.(?), opposition, resistance; andsæc fremede, I offered opposition, resisted, 472.

andswaru, f., answer, 166, 318, 375, 455, 462, 567, 642, 662, 1002.

andswerian, wv. II., answer; 3d p. pret. pl. answeredon, 396.

andweard, present, 630.

andweardlîce, adv., at present, now, 1141.

andwlita, m., countenance, face, 298.

andwyrde, answer, 545, 619.

ǽne, once, a single time, 1253.

ânforlǽtan, red. vb., give up, surrender, desert; 3d p. sg. pret. opt. ânforlête, 630; 2d p. sing. pret. ind. ânforlête, = relinquishedst, 947.

ânhaga, m., solitary (man), recluse, 604.

ânhȳdig, of one mind, fixed in mind, determined, 848; elnes ânhydig, determined in zeal, zealous, 829.

ǽnig, prn., any: (1) subst. w. gen., 159; (2) adj., 166, 538, 567, 660, 916.

ǽnlic, unique, excellent, glorious, 74, 259.

ânmôd, unanimous, with one mind, 396, 1118.

æplede, apple-shaped, 1260.

âr, m., ambassador, messenger, (of the angel) 76, 87, 95, (of Helen's messengers) 981, 906, 1007; âr sêlesta, O best ambassador,— i.e. one who bears the message of one king to another, hence mediator,— (spoken of Cyriacus), 1088.

âr, f., honor, 714; favor, 308.

ǽr, adv., formerly, before, 74, 101, 240, 459, 478, 572, 602, 664, 707, 717, 882, 909, 922, 934, 975, 987, 1044, 1118, 1122, 1144, 1285.

ǽr, prep. with dat. before; ǽr sumeres cyme, before summer's advent, 1228.

ǽr, conj., before, with opt., 447, 676; with ind., before, until, 863, 1241, 1246, 1254; ǽrþan, 1084.

ârǽran, wv. I., raise, build, erect, 129, 887. ârǽred, elated, 804.

ǽrdæg, m., dawn, 105.

areccan, wv. I., expound, report, 635.

ǽrest, first, at first; cf. ǽr, ǽrra, ǽrest, 116.

ârfæst, gracious, merciful, 12, 512.

ǽrgewyrht, n., prior action, former deed, 1301.

ǽriht, n., faith (a system of doctrines), law of the covenant (Gn.), 375; code of law, faith, 590.

ârîsan, sv. I., arise, 803; rise (of resurrection); pret. sg. ârâs, 187, 486; pret. sg. ârâs, 888 (of the young man raised from the dead).

ârlêas, dishonored, wicked, godless, 836, 1301.

ǽrra, adj. comp., former, 305.

ârwyrðe, worthy of honor, venerable, 1129.

ǽrþan, s. ǽr.

âsǽlan, wv. I., to fasten with ropes, illaqueate, ensnare, fetter; synnum âsǽled, fettered by sins, 1244.

æsc, m., ash, a lance made of ash, a lance. [140].

âsceâdan, red. vb., hold aloof; ic symle mec ûscêd þâra scylda, I held myself aloof from their guilt always, 470; separate, to separate from impurities, to purify, 1313.

æscrôf, renowned for skill with the spear, spear-strong, warlike, 202, 275.

æscwîga, m., lancer, 259.

âscyrian, wv. I., separate, free, 1313.

âsècan, âsêcean, wv. I., to seek out, select; imperative pl. sundor ûsêcaþ, 407; inf. sundor âsêcean, 1019.

âseôðan, sv. II., free from dross, refine, purify, 1308.

âsettan, wv. I., place, lay, set, 847, 863, 877; perform, accomplish; sîð ... âseted hæfdon, = had made a voyage, etc., 998.

âspyrigean, wv. I., search out, spy, find out, discover, 467.

âstîgan, sv. I., ascend, 795; 3d p. sg. pret. âstâh, 188, 900; starts up (of the wind), 1273.

âsundrian, wv. II., separate, free, 1309.

æt, prep. w. dat., at, in: (1) locative, 137, 231, 251, 399, 628, 1178, 1182, 1183, 1184, 1186, 1189; (2) specification (æt þâm dægweorce, = upon this day's work, 146; æt þære gesyhðe, = in regards to this view, etc., 965); (3) source (æt þâm, = from him, 191; æt þâm bisceope, 1217); (4) means (æt þâm willspelle, = through this good news, 994).

ætsomne, together, 834.

âtŷdran, wv. I., beget, 1279. –

ætŷwan, wv. I., show, reveal; p.p. ætŷwed, 69.

âþrêotan, sv. II., to be oppressive, burdensome; 3d p. sg. pret. âþrêat, 368.

âwa, always, everlasting, 951.

âweaxan, sv. VI., grow up; 3d p. sg. pret. opt. âwêoxe, 1226.

âweccan, wv. I., awake, arouse (3d p. sg. pret. âwehte, 304, 946; âweahte, 782); incite (ic âwecce wið ðe ôðerne cyning, 927).

âwendan, wv. I., turn; þæt êow þæt lêas sceal awended weorðan to woruldgedâle, that for you this falsehood should be turned to separation from the world (i.e. death), 581.

âweorpan, sv. III., throw, hurl, 703; scorn, reject, contradict, oppose, 771.

âwer = âhwǽr, somewhere, 33.

æwita, m., a man versed in the law, 455.

âwrîtan, sv. I., write upon, inscribe, 91.

âwyrged, accursed, despised; âwyrgede womsceaðan, the accursed sin-besmirched enemies, 1299.

B.

bæð, n., bath; fulwihtes bæð, 490, 1034.

bæðweg, m., bath-way, sea-way, sea, 244.

bǽl, n., fire, funeral pile, pyre, [578].

bǽlfŷr, funeral pile fire, [578].

bald, bold, 412, 593; boldly (adv.), 1073.

baldor, m., prince, (of David) wigona baldor, 344.

bân, n., bone; bân Josephes, 788.

bâncofa, m., bone-chamber, body, 1250.

bannan, red. vb., call, summon, bid, order, 45.

bǽr, f., bier, 873. [beran.]

be, prep. with dat., by, with [(specification) be naman, by name, 78, 505, 756]; by [(over, — nearness, motion alongside), be wolcnum, by the clouds, 1274]; about, concerning, in reference to (be þâm sigebéame (-beacne), 168, 420, 444, 665, 861, 1257; be þâm lifes (wuldres), trêo, 706, 867; be Ꝺǽre róde, 601, 1241; be godes bearne, 562; be þâm (demonstrative), 337, 342, 1068, 1189; be eow (personal), 350).

bêacen, beacon, sign (of the cross), 92, 100, 109, 162, 842; gedó mî, fæder engla, forꝺ bêacen þîn, show forth now, father of angels, thy sign, 784; þæt bêacen (of the nails), 1194.

[bêacenlge, m., sign, K. 842.]

[bêaceninga, ' wäre ominose, fausto omine, feliciter,' Gm. 842.]

beadu, f., battle, war, 34, 45.

beadurôf, renowned in war, distinguished in battle, 152, 1004, 1185.

beaduþrêat, m., battle-throng, troops, army, 31.

bêaggifa, m., ring-giver, king; beorna bêaggifa (of Constantine), 100, 1199.

bealu, n., evil, wrong, injury, 403.

bealudǽd, f., evil deed, sin, 515.

bêam, m., tree, tree of the cross, cross, 91, 217, 424, 851, 865, 887, 1013, 1074, 1225, 1255.

bearhtm (865), breahtm (39), beorhtm (205), m., noise, clang, sound.

bearn, n., child, son (of Christ), bearn, 354, 446, 783; æꝺelust bearna, 476; bearn wealdendes, 391, 851; godes bearn, 179, 525, 562, 814, 837, 964, 1077, 1127; léoda bearn, = children of men, 181.

bebêodan, sv. II., bid, command; 3d p. sg. pret. bebêad, [378], 710, 715, 980, 1018, 1131, 1220; p.p. beboden, 224, 412.

bebod, n., command, 1170.

bebûgan, sv. II., avoid, 609.

bêc, s. bôc.

beclingan, sv. III., surround, enclose, shackle, 696.

becuman, sv. IV., come, reach, 142.

bedǽlan, wv. I., deprive of, rob, [1244].

bedelfan, sv. III., hide by digging, bury; p.p. bedolfen, 1081.

bedyrnan, wv. I., hide, conceal, secrete, 584, 602.

befæstan, make fast; p.p. befæsted, 1300; make safe, entrust to, commit; p.p. befæsted, 1213.

befeolan, sv. IV., grant, bestow upon; p.p. befôlen, 196, 937.

befôn, red. vb., embrace, encompass, seize; 3d p. sg. pret. befeng, 843.

beforan, prep. with dat., before, 108; adv., before, beforehand, 1142, 1154.

begangan, red. vb., execute, fulfil, 1171.

bêgen, prn., both, nom. neut. bû, 614, 889; gen. bêga, 618, 964; bêgra, 1009; dat. bǽm, 805.

begêotan, sv. II., pour into; 3d p. sg. pret. begéat, 1248.

begitan, sv. V., obtain, achieve, procure; 3d p. sg. pret. begeat, 1152, [1248].

begrafan, sv. VI., bury, cover, hide; greote begrauene, buried in the sand, 835; foldan begræfen, hid in the earth, 974.

behealdan, red. vb., hold, keep, inhabit; 3d p. sg. pret. wîc behêold hâlig ... gâst, the Holy Ghost inhabited the dwelling, 1144; behold, gaze on, observe; 3d p. sg. pret. behêold, 111, 243.

behelian, wv. I., hele (Gower), conceal, hide, 429, 831.

behlîdan, sv. I., shut, close; sîe ... behliden helle duru, may the door of hell be closed, 1230.

behŷdan, wv. I., hide, conceal, 793, 988, 1082.

/ **belîðan**, sv. I., rob, deprive of; life belidenes lîc, body robbed of life, 878.

belûcan, sv. II., enclose, lock up, 1027.

bemîðan, to hide, keep secret, 583.

bên, f., prayer, request, 1089.

\ ***benugan**, s. note 618; beneah with gen, to have at one's disposal; þonne hê bega beneah, when he has both at his disposal, 618.

bêodan, sv. II., offer (him wæs hild boŕden), 18; present, declare, (wære bêodan), to declare protection, 80; bid, order, command (swâ him sio cwên bêad), 378; announce, proclaim, 972; 3d p. sg. pret. opt. þe him Cyriacus bude, 1212.

beofian, wv. II., tremble, shake, 759. s. **bifian**.

bêon (often with future significance); bið, 339, 340, 432, 435, [451], 526, 606, 1029, 1187, 1194, 1270, 1294, 1298, 1306, 1310, 1312, 1316; bioð, 1289; beoð, 1295, 1304, 1308.

beorg, m., mountain, mount, hill, 510, 578.

beorgan, sv. III., with dat., save; sume ... feore burgon, some saved life, etc., 134.

beorghlið, n., 788; beorhhlið, mountain slope.

beorht, bright, lucid, shining, glittering, gleaming, brilliant, glorious, sublime, 88, 489, 783, 790, 822, 948, 1089, 1110, 1255.

beorhte, adv., brightly, brilliantly, 92.

beorhtm, s. **bearhtm**.

beorn, m., man (usual in poetry), hero, 100, 114, 186, 253, [614], 710, 805, 873, 1062, 1187, 1199.

berædan, wv. I., rob, deprive, \ 498.

beran, sv. IV., bear, carry, lead; beran ût þræce, to lead out to battle, 45; beran bêacen godes, to bear the standard of God, 109; beraŏ bord ond ord, they bear shield and spear, 1187; sê þæt wicg byrŏ, who guides (directs) this horse, 1196.

berêafian, wv. II., rob; p.p. berêafod, 910.

bescûfan, sv. II., shove, push, hurl, 943.

besencan, wv. I., to sink, [721].

besêon, sv. V., intr., see, look, 83.

besetton, wv. I., set about, adorn (with jewels), bejewel, 1026.

besylcan, wv. I., weaken; sârum besylced, 697.

betæcan, wv. I., to commit, deliver, surrender; 3d p. pl. pret. betæhton, 585.

betera (s. gôd), comp. better, 506; acc. m. beteran, 618; acc. ntr. betere, 1039, 1046, 1062.

Bethlem, Bethlehem, 391.

betwêonum, prep. with dat., between; here with gen., among (sylfra betwêonum, 1207).

beþeccan, wv. I., cover; 3d p. sg. pret. ind. beþeahte, 1236; beþeaht, 76, 884; 3d p. pl. pret. ind. beþeahton, 836; p.p. beþehte, 1298; regularly beþeaht, (s. Sievers, 407, a).

beþringan, sv. III., oppress, burden; sûslum (bisgum) beþrungen, 950, 1245.

beþurfan, pret. pres., impersonal; wisdómes beþearf, there is need of wisdom, 543.

beweorcean, wv. I., work, adorn, ornament, 1024.

beweotigan, wv. II., attend to, perform, 745.

bewindan, sv. III., wrap, envelop, encase; léohte bewundene, wrapped in light, 734; present, deliver, [213].

bewrecan, sv. V., whip, lash; sunde bewrecene, sea-lashed, 251 (s. note 251).

biδ, s. **bêon.**

bîdan, sv. I., with gen., wait for, await (bîdan beorna geþinges, to await the fate of the men, 253); intr. wait, tarry; 3d p. sg. pret. bâd, 329; pres. ptc. bîdende, 484; 3d p. sg. pres. bideδ, 1093.

biddan, sv. V., ask, beg; with acc. of pers. + þæt, pret. bæd, 494, 1069; beg earnestly, pray (with þæt), 3d p. sg. pret., 600, 1101; biddan, 790, 814; imperative bide, 1090.

bifian, s. S. 416, note 5.

bigang, m., course; wyrda bigang, course of events, 1124.

bil, bill, n., sword, 122, 257. Cf. policeman's billy (?).

bioδ, s. **bêon.**

bisceop, m., bishop, 1052, 1057, 1073, 1095, 1127, 1217, [biscop, biscep] [episcopus].

bisgu, f., trouble; dat. pl. bisgum beþrungen, by troubles oppressed, 1245.

bisittan, sv. V., to sit in; with acc. æht bisæton, they sat in council, 473.

bissceophâd, m., bishopric, bishop's dignity, 1212.

biter, adj., bitter, fierce (bitter necessity, 1245).

bitre, adv., bitterly, painfully, [1245]..

blâc, white, bright, brilliant, 91.

blǽd, m., good fortune, 162; prosperity, glory, 354, 489; happiness, 826.

blanca, m.; on blancan, = on the white horse, 1185.

blêo, n., color, appearance, hue, form, 759, 1106.

blîde, blithe, glad, happy, 96, 246; friendly, gracious, 1317.

blind, blind, 1215.

blindnes, f., blindness, 299, 389.

blinn, n. (?), end, ceasing; bûtan blinne, without end, 826.

bliss, f., bliss, joy; dat. pl. blissum hrêmig, = rejoiced with bliss, 1138.

bôc, f., book; (on godes) bôcum, 204, 290, 826; þurh hâlige bêc, 364, 670, 853; bôca gleaw, 1212; on bôcum, 1255.

bôcstæf, m., letter, character; bôcstafum âwriten, 91.

boda, m., messenger, ambassador, 77, 262, 551.

bodian, wv. II., announce, 1141.

bold, u., house, [162].

bord, n., (board), shield ; bord ond ord, 1187 ; borda gebrec, 114 ; wordum ond bordum, 24 ; bordum ond ordum, 235 ; board, hull, 238.

bordhaga, m., protection of the shield ; under bordhagan, 652.

bordhrêð'a, m., cover of the shield (Heyne, " Bêowulf," 2204) ; ornament of the shield (Zupitza), shield, 122.

bôt, f., reparation, reform, remedy, healing, atonement, 299, 389, 1217 ; repentance, 515, 1039, 1126.

brâd, broad, extended, 917.

breahtm, s. bearhtm.

brecan, sv. IV., break, 122, 244 ; 3d p. pl. pret. brǽcon.

bregdan, sv. III., weave, plait ; brogden byrne, plaited corselet, 257.

brêost, n., breast, bosom ; dat. pl. brêostum, 595, 967, 1038, 1095.

brêostloca, m., breast-lock, bosom's recess, soul, 1250.

brêostsefa, mind (heart), in the breast, 805, 842, 1046.

brîdels, m., bridle, reins, 1175, 1185, 1199.

brîdelshring, m., bridle-ring, 1194.

brim, n., surging flood, breakers (of the sea), sea (ocean), 253, 972, 1004.

brimnesen, ' iter marinum ' (Gm.), das glückliche überstehen der seefahrt, (Gn.), [1004].

brimþisa, m., rusher over breakers (brandungsrauscher, Gn.), ship, 238.

brimwudu, sea-wood, ship, 244.

bringan, wv. I., irreg. (cf. S., § 407, a), bring ; 3d p. sg. pret. brôhte 1130 ; 3d p. pl. pret. brôhton, 873,

996, 1016 ; p.p. gebrôht, seldom (cf. S., § 407, a, 7) ; bremgen, 1138.

brôð'or, m., brother, 489, 510, 822.

brogdenmǽl, drawn sword (cf. Sweet) (das geschwungene schwert, Gn.), sword with spiral sign, 759.

brôhte, s. bringan.

bront, steep, high, 238.

brûcan, sv. II., with gen., use, enjoy, [451], 1251, 1315, 1320.

brytta, m., dispenser, distributor, 162, 194 ; originator, author, 958.

bryttian, wv. II., divide, rend asunder, destroy, 579.

bû, s. bêgen.

burg, f., stronghold, fortress, [31] ; gen. sg. byrig, castle (city), 864 ; dat. sg. byrig, castle (city), 822 ; city, 1006, 1054, 1204; gen. pl. burga, cities, 152 ; dat. pl. burgum, cities, 412, 972, 992, 1057, 1062.

burgâgend, possessing castles (citadels), 1175.

bûrgeat, n., tor (nach Ettmüller), 31.

Burgendas, -dan, pl. m., Burgundians, [31].

[burgent (?), f. (?), burg, stadt (??), 31 Zupitza] ; s. burg and ent.

burggeat, n., city gate, [31].

burgsittend, city-dweller, citizen, 276.

burgwîgend, warrior of the city or castle, defender of the city or castle, 34.

bûtan, prep. with dat., without ; (â) bûtan ende, 802, 811, 894, 953 ; bûtan blinne, 826 ; bûtan earfeð'um, 1292 ; save, except, bûtan VI. nihtum, save six nights, 1228 ; with acc. (?), except ; bûtan þec, except thee, 539.

bûtan, conj., unless ; bûtan þû

forlǣte þa lēasunga, unless thou desist from these lies, 689.

byldan, wv. I., incite, impel, encourage, 1039.

bȳme, f., trumpet, 109.

byrgen, f., grave, tomb, 186, 484, 652.

byrig, s. burg.

byrne, f., corselet; brogden byrne, linked corselet, 257.

byrnwî(g)gend, corselet-warrior, mailed-warrior, [34], 224, 235.

C.

câf, quick, vigorous, bold, 56.

Caluarie, Calvary, 676; on Caluarie, 672, 1011, 1098.

campwudu, m., battle-wood, 51.

can(n), s. cunnan.

carcern, n. (Lat. carcer), prison; of carcerne, 715.

câserdôm, m., empire, 8.

câsere, m., emperor, (of Constantine) 42, 70, 175, 212, 262, 330, 416, 551, 669, 999.

cearwelm, m., agitation of grief, wave of trouble; cnyssed cearwelmum, beaten by the waves of trouble, 1258.

cêas, f., strife, battle, 56.

ceaster, f., city, (of Jerusalem); gen. ceastre, 384; acc. ceastre, 274, 846, 1205; gen. pl. ceastra, 973 [castra].

ceasterware, pl., dwellers in the city, citizens, 42.

cempa, m., fighter, warrior, champion, [1258].

cên, m., resin (rosin); name of the rune for c(k), (h), 1258 (s. note 1258).

cennan, wv. I., engender, beget (cende, 354), bring forth, bear, be born (cenned, 346, 392), procreate, give life to (3d p. pl. pret. cendan (cendon), 508), create, give, apply (þâm wæs Jûdas nama cenned, to him was the name Judas given, 587).

cêol, m., keel, ship, 250.

ceruphîn, cherubim, 750.

cild, n., child; in cildes hâd, 336, 776.

cildhâd, m., childhood, 915.

cining, s. cyning.

Ciriacus, s. Cyriacus.

cirice, f., church (Scottish kirk), 1008.

cirran, wv. I., turn; 3d p. sg. pret. cirde; from cyrran, 2d p. sg. pres. cyrrest, thou turnest thyself, betakest thyself, etc., 666.

clǣne, clean, pure; on clǣnra gemang, into the hosts of the pure, 96; clǣnum stefnum, with pure voices, 750.

cleopigan, wv. II., cry, exclaim, 696; 3d p. sg. pret. cleopode, 1100; 3d p. pl. pret. cleopodon, 1319.

clom, m., fetter, 696.

clynnan, wv. I., resound; campwudu clynede, 51.

cnêo, n., knee, 848; cnêow, 1136.

cnêomâgas, pl., compatriot, companions of race, blood relations, 587, 688.

cniht, m., boy, 339.

cnihtgeong, in the period of boyhood (of youth); cnihtgeong hæleð, a young man in the days of youth, 640.

cnyssan, wv. I., strike, beat; cnyssed cearwelmum, 1258.

côlian, wv. II., cool, grow cold, be cold; leomu côlodon, limbs were cold, 883.

collenferhð, of elated mind, proud, courageous, 247, 378, 849.

Constantînus, Constantine, 79, 103, 1008; gen. Constantines, 8; dat. Constantino, 145.

corðor, n., crowd, multitude, following, retinue; dat. sg. on corðre, 70; on wera corðre, 304, 543; acc. sg. corðre, 691; gen. pl. corðra, 374.

cræft, m., craft, power, ability, skill, art, knowledge, 154, 374, 558, 595, 1018, 1059, 1172.

cræftig (crafty), skilled, powerful, 314, [315(?)], 419.

Crêcas, pl., Greeks; on Crêca land, 250, 262, 999.

Crîst, Christ, 460; gen. Crîstes, 103, 212, 499, 973; dat. Crîste, 678, 1011, 1035, 1050, 1120; acc. Crîst, 798.

cristen, Christian (used substantively); cristenra gefêan, joy of the Christians, 980; cristenra cwên, queen of the Christians, 1069: (adjectively), cristenum folce, to the Christian people, 989; cristenum þeawum, to Christian usages, 1211.

cûð, known, familiar, 42, 1192.

cûðe, s. cunnan.

cuman, sv. IV., come, 279, 1205; 3d p. pl. pres. cumað, 1303; 3d p. sg. pret. côm, 150; cwôm, 549, 871, 908, 1110; 3d p. pl. pret. cwômon, 274, 1214; p.p. cymen, 1123.

cunnan, pret. pres. (1) know; 1st p. sg. pres. can, 635, 683; cann, 684; pl. pres. cunnon, 399, 531, 535; pret. sg. cûðe, 1163; pret. pl. cûðon, 328, 393, 398; opt. pl. cunnen, 374. (2) know how (understand), be able, can; 1st p. sg. pres. can, 640, 925; pl. pres. cunnon, 317, 648; pret. pl. cûðon, 167, 281, 284, 1020;

opt. 2d p. sg. cunne, 857; opt. pl. cunnen, 376.

cwacian, wv. II., quake, 758.

cwalu, f., torture, violent death, murder, 499.

cwealm, m., destruction, death, 676.

cweðan, sv. V., say, speak; cweðaþ, 749; cwæð, quoth, 667; cwædon, 169, 871, 1120.

cwên, f., woman, the woman, queen (of the emperor's mother), 247, 275, 324, 378, 384, 411, 416, 533, 551, 558, 605, 662, 715, 849, 980, 1018, 1069, 1152, 1170, 1205; dat. cwêne, 587, 610, 1130; gen. sg. cwêne, 1136.

cwic, quick, living, alive, 691.

cwide, m., speech, address [547].

cwôm, s. cuman.

cwylman, wv. I., afflict, torture-to-death, kill, 688.

cyðan, wv. I., make known, show, tell, 161, 175, 199, 318, 540, 558, 566, 661, 671, 854; pres. (with future significance), cyðe, I will reveal, 702; pret. cyðde, [439]; p.p. cyðed, 827; imperative cyð, 607; wundor cyðan, to work a miracle, 1112.

cyme, m., arrival, 41; advent, 1228; appearance (act of appearing), 1086.

cyman, s. cuman.

cyn, cynn, n., family, race, people, 188, 209, 305, 521, 591, [837], 898, 1204.

cynestôl, m., royal seat, throne, 330.

cyning, king (of earthly kings frequently), e.g. 13, 32, 51, 56, etc., 342; (of God), 79, 145, 291, 494, 1248; (of Christ), 392, 800.

[cyninge, f., queen, (610)].

Cyriacus, proper name, 1059, 1069, 1098, 1211; Ciriacus, 1130. The changed name of the second Judas.

cyrran, s. **cirran**.

D.

dǽd, f., deed, action, 386, 1283.

dǽdhwæt, powerful in deed, 292.

dæg, m., day; gen. sg. dæges, 140; adv. dæges, by day, 198; dat. sg. dæge, 185; acc. dæg, 312, 697, 1223; instrumental, þy þriddan dæg, on the third day, 485; gen. pl. dagena, 193, *and* daga, 358.

dægweorc, n., day's work, 146.

dægweorðung, f., celebration of a day, festival, 1234.

dǽl, m., deal, part, division, 1298, 1306; share, lot, 1232.

dǽlan, wv. I., divide, be divided, 1286.

Danûbie, f., dat. 37, acc. 136, Danube.

dareðlâcende, spear-contenders, lancers; deareðlâcende, 37; dareð-lâcendra, 651.

daroð, m., spear, javelin, lance (140).

daroðæsc (?), m., n. (?), spear of ash, [140].

Dâuid, David; Dâuid cyning, 342.

dêad, dead, 882; deadra, 651, 945.

dêað, m., death, 187, 302, 303, 477, 500, 584, 606, 780.

dêaðcwalu, f., death-throe; drêogað dêaðcwale, they suffer death-throes, 766.

deareð, s. **dareð**.

dêgol, n., concealment, obscurity, 330.

delfan, sv. III., delve, dig, 829.

dêma, m., judge, 746, 1283.

dêman, wv. I., deem, judge, condemn; dêman tô dêaþe, 303, 500; damn, 311.

dêoful, m., devil; gen. sg. dêofles, 1119; gen. pl. dêofla, 181, 302.

dêofulgild, n., sacrifices to the devil, idolatry, idol, 1041.

dêogol, secret, hidden, concealed, 1093; dŷgol, 541.

dêoþ, deep (deep buried), secret, hidden, 584; deep, heavy; dêopra firena, of deep sins, heavy transgressions, 1314.

dêop, adv., deeply, to a great depth, 1190.

dêope, adv., deeply, to a great depth, 1081.

dêophycgende, engaged in deep thought, pensive, 352, 882.

dêoplîce, adv., thoroughly; sup. dêoplîcost, most thoroughly, 280.

dêore, s. **dŷre**.

dêorlîce, dearly, preciously, gloriously; sup. dêorlîcost, in most glorious wise, 280.

dierne, s. **dyrne**.

disig (cf. dysig), foolish, 477.

dôgorgerîm, number of days; dat. adverbially, dôgorrîmum, 705; dogorgerîmum, 780.

dôm, m., doom, judgment, 1280; ordeal (þurh þæs dômes fŷr), through the fire of this ordeal, 1314; choice, will (dôma gewcald), power over wills, 726; glory (dôm unscyndne), blameless glory, 365; dôm, 450; happiness (dômes lêasne), deprived of happiness, 945.

dômgeorn, eager for glory, 1291.

dômweorðung, f., honor through glory, glorious honor, 146.

dôn, irr. vb. (S. 429), do; imperative dô, do, 541; put, place, affix, attach, 1175.

draca, m., dragon, 766 (s. note 766) [draco].

drêam, m., joy, blessedness, [451]; drêam unhwilen, eternal joy, 1261.

drenc, m., drowning; sume drenc fornam, drowning snatched away some, 136.

drêogan, sv. II., endure, suffer, tolerate, bear; wergðu drêogan, 211, 952; drêogað dêaðcwale, 766; pret. nearusorge drêah, 1261.

drifan, sv. I., drive, 358.

[drûsan, sv. II., full, 1258.]

drûsian, wv. II. (?), become turbid, be lazy, burn badly; cen drûsende, rosin burning badly, 1258.

drŷge, dry; in drŷgne sêað, into the dry well, 693.

dryhten, Lord (of God), 81, 193, 198, 280, 292, 352, 365, 371, 726, 760, 948, 971, 1010, 1140, 1160, 1168, 1206, 1280; (of Christ) 187, 346, 491, 500, 717, 897.

dryhtlêoð, n., song for the people (national song), 342.

dryhtscipe, m., valor, heroism, 451.

dûfan, sv. II., plunge, thrust; pret. bil in dufan, they thrust in the swords, 122.

dugan, avail, be worth, [451].

dugoð, uð, f., worth, excellence, joy; duguða lêas, deprived of joys, 683; throng, multitude, 1291; heavenly hosts, duguða dryhten, 81; mankind, men, 450, 1093, 1160.

dûn, f., dune, hill, 717.

duru, f., door; helle duru, 1230.

dŷgol, s. dêogol.

dynnan, wv. I., make a noise (cf. v. a. din), 50.

dŷre, dear, beloved, 292; precious, glorious; sup. dêorestan, 1234.

dyrnan, wv. I., hide, secrete, keep secret, 971; pret. pl. dyrndun, 626.

dyrne, secret, hidden, concealed, 723, 1093; dierne, 1081.

dysig, n., folly; mid dysige þurhdrifen, pervaded with folly, 707.

dyslic, foolish; acc. dyslice dæd, foolish deed, 386.

E.

êac, adv., also, 742, 1007; swylce êac, also, likewise, 3; with ond (frequent elsewhere), 1278.

êaðe, adv., easily, 1292.

êadhrêðig, rejoicing in prosperity, triumphant, blessed; sêo êadhrêðige Elene, 266.

êadig, rich, happy, blessed, 806; sêo êadige, 619; êadigra gedryht, 1290.

êaðmêdu, f., reverence; pl. eallum êaðmêdum, 1088, 1101.

êadwela, m., riches, prosperity, 1316.

eafera, m., child, descendant, heir, 439; eafora, 353.

êage, n., eye; gen. pl. êagena, 298.

eal, eall, (1) all (without substantive); gen. sg. ealles, 512, 1236; nom. pl. ealle, 1118; gen. pl. ealra, 187; eallra, 370, 475; dat. pl. eallum, 1220; acc. pl. ealle, 385: (with substantive), nom. sg. eal, 26 (?), 753; gen. sg. neut. ealles, 486; gen.

sg. f. eallre, 446; dat. sg. ealre, [293]; acc. sg. m. ealne, 731; neut. eall, 1197; gen. pl. eallra, 422, 483, 519, 894, 1285; ealra, 769; alra, 645; allra, 816; dat. pl. eallum, 1088, 1101. (2) entire, whole; calle gesceaft, whole creation, 729; þeos world eall, this whole world, 1277. (3) every; ealre synne, 772; adv. entirely, wholly; eal, 856; eall, 1131, 1155, 1293, 1311; eallra, in all, 649.

eald, old, 207, 455, 905; ald, 252, 1266; comp. yldra, elder, older, 159; min yldra, my father, 462; yldra fæder, grandfather, 436.

ealdfeond, m., old foe, hereditary foe, embittered adversary, 493.

ealdgewin, n., battle in olden days (of the Trojan war), 647.

earc, f., ark, ark of the covenant; æt godes earce, 399.

eard, m., country, home, dwelling-place, 599, 622.

earfeðe, n., hardsnip, distress, torture, 700, 1292.

earhfaru, f., the circuit of the arrow (s. note 44 and 116); (pfeilflug, kampf, Zupitza) (Umlauf des Heerpfeils, 44; Anprall der Geschosse, 116 (Grim.)). Impetus sagittarum (Dietrich).

earhgeblond, n., sea, 239.

earm, m., arm, 1236.

earn, m., eagle, 29, 111.

eart (2d pers. sg. ind. of bêon), art, 809, 815.

eastweg, m., eastern road, path from the east, 255, 996.

eatol, dreadful, dire, terrible; eatol ecleca, dire monster, 902.

eaxlgestealla, m., shoulder-companion, trusted friend, 64 (s. note 64).

Ebrêas, pl., Hebrews, 287, 448. ebrêisc, Hebrew; ebrêisce æ, 397; weras ebresce = Ebrêas, 559; on ebrisc, in Hebrew, 725.

êce, eternal, everlasting; êce lif, 526; êcra gestealda, everlasting mansions, 802; êces êadwelan, 1316; êces dêman, 746; êce cining, 800; êce rex, 1042.

êce, adv., eternally, continually, forever, 1218, 1231.

êðe, easy, agreeable, pleasant; superl. êðost, 1294.

êðel, country, native land, home, 1220, [1294].

êðgesŷne, readily seen, visible, 256.

êðigean, wv. II., breathe, ascend, 1107.

ednîowunga, anew (cf. geednîwian, to renew), 300.

êdre, adv., immediately, forthwith, at once, 649; syððan ... êdre, as soon as; syððan andsware êdre gehŷrdon, 1002.

efnan, wv. I., do, perform, execute, 713.

eft, adv., again, 143, 148, 382, 514, 516, 903, (921), 924, 1000, 1155, 1220, 1275; afterwards, later, 255, 350, 500.

egesa, m., fear, terror (consternation, dismay); egsan geâclad, with fear disquieted, 57, 1129; egesan hwôpan, to threaten with terror, 82; egesan geþrêade, by fear oppressed, 321.

êgstrêam, m., sea-stream, current, river (of the Danube); êgstrêame nêah,66; sea, (onêgstrêame, 241).

eh, m., n. (?), horse, name of the rune for e, (M), 1262.

êhtan, wv. I., with gen. pursue;

pret. ehton elþeoda, 139; persecute
(se ehteð þin, who will persecute
thee, 928).

elde, pl., 476; ilde, 521; ylde,
[451], 792; men.

eled, m., fire, (1294).

Elene, Helen, 219, 266, 332, 404,
573, 604, 620, 642, 685, 953, 1051,
1198, 1218; gen. Elenan, 848; dat.
Elenan, 1003, 1063.

ellen, n., courage, strength, zeal;
elnes oncýðig, unacquainted with
strength, powerless, 725; elnes
ânhýdig, determined in zeal, 829.

elþêod, f., strange nation, hostile
nation, enemy, 139.

elþêodig, strange, hostile (without substantive); elþeodig, 908;
elþeodige, 57, 82.

ende, m., end, 590, 802, 811, 894,
953; limit, boundary, lifes æt ende,
at the limit of life, 137; on Rów-
wara rices ende, on the boundary
of the empire of the Romans, 59.

endelîf, n., end of life, 585.

enge, narrow; fram þâm engan
hofe, out of this narrow (contracted) court, 712; in þâm engan
hâm, in that contracted home (i.e.
hell); enge rûne, close secret, 1262.

engel, m., angel; gen. pl. 79,
476, 487, 773, 777, 784, 858, 1101,
1231, 1281, 1307, 1316; dat. pl. englum, 622, 1320.

engelcyn, n., race of angels,
733.

ent, m., giant (31).

êode: pret. to gân (s. S. § 430),
went, went away; eode, 1096; eodon,
411, 557; 846; eodan, 320, 377.

eoforcumbul, n., sign of the bear
(an image on the helmet), helmet,
259; eofur-, 76.

eofot, n., sin, guilt, crime; un-

scyldigne eofota gehwylces, innocent of every sin, 423.

eofulsæc, n., blasphemy, 524.

êom; 1st p. sg. pres. ind. of
bêon, am; ic (the devil) . . . eom,
etc., 923.

eorcnanstân, m., precious
stone (cf. eorclanstân, B. 1209);
mid þâm æðelestum eorcnanstânum, with the most costly precious
stones, 1025.

eorðcyning, m., earthly king;
þâm æðelestan eorðcyninga, to the
noblest of the kings of earth, 1174.

eorðe, f., earth, 753; dat. for
eorðan, 591; on eorðan, 622, 878,
1109; of eorðan, 1226; acc. eorðan,
728, 829; instr. eorðan, 836.

eorðweg, m., path of earth, earth;
of eorðwegum, from the paths of earth,
736; on eorðwege, on earth, 1015.

êoredcest, f., crowd (?); feðan
trymedon eoredcestum, the infantry
was strengthened by crowds, 36
(s. note 36).

eorl, m., earl, warriors, (of Constantine's retinue) 12, 66; (of
Helen's retinue) 225, 256, 275, 620,
848, 1198; (of the Jews) 321, 332,
404, 417, 435; (of Moses) 787;
(Judas is) eorla hlêo, 1047. Selec-
tion on account of excellence is the
dominant factor in this word.

eorlmægen, n., multitude of noble men, 981.

eorre, s. yrre.

êow, pers. prn., you; dat. pl.
from ðû, thou, 298, 309, 339, and
frequently.

êow, pers. prn. you; acc. pl.
from ðu, thou, 295, 318, 368, and
frequently.

êower, poss. prn., your, 305, 315,
375, etc.

erm$\eth$u, f., misery; yrm$\eth$u, 953; pl. in erm$\eth$um, 768.

Essñias, Essûias, 350.

êst, favor, love grace; þurh meotodes êst, 986.

Eusebius, Eusebius; acc. Eusebium, 1051.

êwigcan, wv. I., to show one's self, [1107].

F.

fæc, n., period of time, interval, while; ymb lytel fæc, after a little while, 272, 383; on swâ lytlum fæce, in such a little while, 960.

fæcne, deceitful, delusive, 577; uncertain, unreliable, 1237.

fæder, m., father, (of God) 784, 891, 1084, 1106, 1151; (of earthly relationship) 343, 463, 517, 528; mîn yldra fæder, my grandfather, 436; dat. fæder, 438, 454; pl. fæderas, forefathers, ancestors, fathers, 388, 398, 425, 458.

fæderlic, paternal, ancestral; þà fæderlican lâre, ancestral teaching, 431.

fæ$\eth$m, m., fathom, expanse; sæs sidne fæ$\eth$m, the wide expanse of waters, 729; outstretched arms, encircling arms (on fæ$\eth$me, 881); embrace (in dracan fæ$\eth$me, in the embrace of the dragon, 766).

fæ$\eth$man, wv. I., embrace, encircle, surround, 972.

fæge, doomed to death (nothing to do with N.H.G. feige, cowardly), 117; dead ofer þæt fæge hûs, over that dead frame, 881.

fæger, fair, beautiful, joyful, 98, 242, 891, 911, 949.

fægere, adv., beautifully, admirably, 743, 1213.

fâh, colored, stained, variegated, spotted; weorcum fâh, spotted by works, 1243.

fâh, hostile, guilty, abhorred (of the devil), 769, 925, (1243?).

fæle, faithful, good, lovely; fæle fri$\eth$owebba, lovely weaver of peace, 88.

fâmig, foamy, foaming, 237.

fær, n., journey, warlike journey, war, [93].

fær, m., danger, 93, 646.

faran, sv. VI., go, travel, march, march thither, advance; pret. sg. fôr, 27, 35, 51; pret. pl. fôron, 21, 261; þe geond lyft fara$\eth$, who fly through the air, 734; fære$\eth$ (of the wind), 1274.

fæst, fast, firm, secure, 252, 723, 771, 883, 909; fæste on fyr$\eth$e, 570; fæst on ferh$\eth$e, 1037, steadfast in heart.

fæste, adv., fast, firmly, steadfastly, [213], 933, 937, 1208.

fæsten, n., fastness, 134.

fæstlîce, adv., firmly, securely, 427, 797.

fæt, vessel, casket, 1026.

fêa, few; þêah hira fêa wêron, although there were few of them, 174; fêam sî$\eth$um, few times, seldom, 818.

feala, with gen., many; obj. acc. feala wun$\eth$ra, 362, 778; feala hearma, 912; dêadra feala, 945; adv. acc. feala mæla, 987; feala tîda, 1044; nom. feale, is nû feale si$\eth$þan for$\eth$gewitenra, etc., 636 (s. S. 275). [Ger. viel.]

feallan, red. vb., fall; pret. pl. fêollon, 127, 1134.

fearo$\eth$hengest, m., seahorse, ship, 226.

fê$\eth$a, m., infantry-man, foot-soldier, infantry, army; fê$\eth$an, 35.

feðegest, m., guest coming on foot, newcomer, stranger; pl. fê-ðegestas, 845.

feng, m., grip, embrace; in fýres feng, in the fire's embrace, 1287.

fêogan, fêon, wv. III., hate, 360; pret. pl. fêodon, 356.

feoh, n. (Ger. vieh), cattle, possessions, money. Name of the rune for f. (ᚠ), 1270.

feohgestrêon, n., possessions, riches; gen. pl. feohgestrêona, 911.

fêond, enemy; gen. pl. fêonda, 68, 108, 1179; acc. pl. fêond, 93 (S. 286). (Of the devil), 207, 900, 954; gen. sg. fêondes (721?).

fêondscipe, m., enmity, hatred; þurh fêondscipe, 356, 498.

feor, far, distant (from the surface), deep; on .xx. fôtmǽlum feor, twenty feet deep, 831; distant (from present), remote past, far back in the past, 1142.

feorh, m. n., life; gen. sg. feores, 680; dat. sg. feore (?), 498; acc. pl. feore, 134; period of time, time; tô widan feore, for extended time, for eternity, forever, 211, 1321; on widan feore, throughout (in) extended time, 1288 (S. 273).

feorhlegu, f., life's end, death, murder; tô feorhlege, 458.

feorhneru, f., preservation of life, rescue, deliverance, salvation, 898.

feorran, adv., from afar, 993, 1213.

fêower, four, (744).

fêran, wv. I., go, march, journey, 215.

ferhð, m. n., soul, mind, heart; ferhð, 174, 991; dat. sg. on ferhðe, 1037, 1164; on fyrðe, 463, 570, 641; in fyrhðe, 196; acc. sg. ferhð, 797;

acc. pl. ferhð, 427: (adverbially) life time (widan fyrhð, 761; widan ferhð, 801), throughout eternity, eternally.

ferhðglêaw, wise in heart, wise; 327; fyrhð-, 881.

ferhðsefa, life-spirit, mind, heart; on ferhðsefan, 316, 850, 895; on firhðsefan, 213); on fyrhðsefan, 98, 1079; acc. fryhðsefan, 534.

ferian, wv. I., carry, bear, 108. Cf. N.E. ferry.

fêt, s. fôt.

fiðru, n. pl., feathers, wings; mid syxum fiðrum, with six wings, 743.

fîfelwǣg, m., sea-monster's waves, sea, 237.

fîfhund, five hundred, .d., (379).

findan, sv. III., (1) find, 924; 2d p. sg. pres. findest, 84; 3d p. pl. pres. findaþ, 373, 1032; pret. sg. fand, 202, 1255; also funde, 831 (s. 386, n. 2); pret. pl. fundon, 327, 379, 1217; pret. opt. funde, 1080; p.p. funden, 974, 987. (2) find out, discover, 632, 641.

finger, m., finger; þurh fingra geweald, 120.

firas, m. pl., men; nerigend fira, 1078, 1173; fira cynne, 898.

firen, f., transgression, sin; on firenum, 909; dêopra firena, 1314.

firhð-, s. ferhð-.

flân, m. f., arrow; flâna scûras, showers of arrows, 117.

flêogan, sv. II., fly; pret. pl. daroðas flugon, spears flew, 140.

flêon, sv. II., flee; pret. pl. flugon, 127, 134.

fliht, m., flight; on flihte, a flight, on the wing, in motion, 744.

flôd, m., flood, flow of the tide,

current; flôdas gefýsde, currents set in motion, 1270.

flôdweg, m., current's road, water-way, sea, [215].

flot, n. [from flêotan, to float], [water deep enough to float a ship (B.)]; sea (Grein), swimming, sea-voyage (Z.); tô flote fysan, to prepare for the sea-voyage, 226.

fôdder, n., fodder (Ger. futter), 360.

folc, n., folk, people, nation, 872, 1287; gen. sg. 157, [213], 499, 1095; dat. sg. folce, 415, 895, 989, 1050; acc. sg. folc, 117; instr. sg. folce, 891 : pl. men, people, 302; gen. folca, 27, 215, 502; dat. folcum, 1143.

folcscearu, f., folkshare, part of a people, nation, people; on þyre folcscere, 402; in þǣre folcsceare, 968.

foldbûende, pl., earth-dweller, inhabitant of earth, 1014.

folde, f., earth; foldan getyned, 702; foldan begrǣfen, 974; in foldan, 987, 1080.

foldgrǣf, n., earth-grave; of foldgrǣfe, out of its earth-grave, 845.

foldweg, m., earth-way, road over the earth; feran foldwege, 215.

folgaꝺ, m., following, retainers, retainers' service, 904.

folgian, wv. II., follow, obey, be subject to; mânþêawum minum folgaþ, he is subject to my sinful usages, 930.

folm, f., hand; his folme, 1066; hâꝺenum folmum, 1076.

for, prep., for. I. with dat. (1) local, before, in the sight of, in the presence of, 4, 110, 124, 170, 175, 180, 332, 351, 362, 404, 406,

417, 587, 591, 596, 620, 688, 782, 979, 1198, 1273; (2) causal (objective), because of, on account of, 63, 491, 521, 677, 703; (subjective), out of, from, for, on account of, 496, 564, 687, 1134; (3) in regard to (for þâm nǣglum, in regard to the nails, 1065). II. with acc., for, in the place of, instead of, 318, 546.

fôr, f., journey, [1262].

foran, adv., before, in front, 1184.

forꝺ, adv., forth. I. (with verbs of motion giving direction); forꝺ onsendan, send forth, 120; gedo-forꝺ, show forth, disclose, 784; forꝺ gewitan, go forth, depart, die, 636, 1268; forꝺ ... up eꝺigean, ascend, 1105. II. (temporal), (1) forth, from now on, from this time on, 318, 1062; fram orde oꝺ ende forꝺ, from the beginning (even) until the end, 590; oꝺ þæt æfen forꝺ fram dæges orde, from the beginning of day (even) until evening, 139 (in these two phrases it gives direction in time); (2) continually, 192, 213.

forꝺgewitan, sv. I., go, vanish; forꝺgewitenra, 636.

forꝺsnoter, forꝺsnotter, very wise; acc. m. forꝺsnoterne, 1053; forꝺsnotterne, 1161; gen. pl. forꝺ-snotterra, 379.

fore, prep., before, with dat. or acc. (1) (local), mê fore, before me, 577; fore onsýne, before the sight, 746; fore Elenan cnêo, before Helen's knee, 848; (2) (temporal), ûs fore, before us, 637.

fore, adv., before, beforehand, aforetimes, once upon a time, once, 345, 1262.

foresnotter, very wise, [379].

foreþanc, m., forethought; pl. núhton foreþancas, they had no forethought, 356.

forgifan, sv. V., give, grant, bestow; pret. sg. forgeaf, 144, 164, 354, 1218.

forlǽran, wv. I., mis-teach, lead astray by false teaching, seduce, 208.

forlǽtan, red. vb., (1) let (with inf.); pret. sg. forlet . . . sêcan, 598; imperative, forlǽt . . . ástigan, 793. (2) with adverb of direction; pres. opt. mê of . . . ûp forlǽten, let me up out of, 700; pret. opt. hine of . . . ûp forléte, 712. (3) let go, relinquish, abandon, renounce; pres. opt. þa fæderlîcan lâre forlêten, 432; bûtan þû forlǽte þa lêasunga, unless thou desist from this lying, 689; pres. ind. (with future significance); hê forlæteþ lâre þîne, he will renounce thy teaching, 929.

forniman, sv. IV., take away, snatch away, 578; pret. sg. fornam sume wîg fornam, 131; sume drenc fornam, 136.

forsêcan, wv. I., to follow closely, to punish, persecute; sârum forsôht, 933.

forsêon, sv. V., scorn, abhor; pret. pl. forsâwon, 1318; forsegon, 389 (S. 391. 5).

fortyhtan, wv. I., mislead, lead astray; pret. sg. fortyhte, 208.

forþan, forðan, for that, therefore, on that account, 309, 517, 522, 1319.

forþryccan, wv. I., crush, oppress; þrêam forþrycced, 1277.

forþylman, wv. I., surround, envelop; þeostrum forþylmed, enveloped in darkness, 767.

forwyrd, f., destruction; in wîta

forwyrd, in the destruction of hell, 765.

fôt, m., foot; pl. fêt, 1066.

fôtmǽl, n., foot-measure, foot, 831.

fram, prep. with dat. (instr.). (1) from (motion away); fram rûne, 411. (2) from (measure of distance — in time), 140; (from), 590. (3) from (with idea of separation), 296, 299, 301, 1120, 1309. (4) from, by (agent with passive), 190, 701, 1142. (5) from, out of (source), 712.

Francan, pl., Franks, 21.

frætwan, wv. irr. (S. 408. 6), adorn, 1199.

frætwe, f. pl., ornament; frætwum beorht, bright with ornaments, 88; landes frætwe, the ornaments of the land, 1271.

frêa, m., lord, king (of God), 680, 1307; (of Christ), 488, 1067.

frêcne, terrible; on þâm frêcnan fǽre, in the terrible danger, 93.

fremman, wv. I., do, accomplish, 646; exercise, offer (andsæc fremede, I offered opposition, 472; wiðersæc fremedon, they offered contradiction, 569); commit, (þæt þû hospcwide, æfst nê eofulsæc ǽfre ne fremme, that thou mayest never commit scornful speech, hate or blasphemy, 524).

frêobearn, n., noble child; cyninges frêobearn, the King's noble child, 672.

freoðian, wv. II., have a care for, protect, guard; freoðode, 1147.

frêond, m., friend, 954; pl. frŷnd, 360 (S. 286).

frêondlêas, friendless, 925.

frêondrǽdden, f., friendship; frêondrǽddenne, 1208.

fricca, m., herald; hreopan

(hreopon) friccan, the heralds made proclamation, 54, 550.

fricggan, sv. V., inquire, ask, 157, 560; fricgendra, 991.

fri', m. n., peace, protection, safety, 1184. [Ger. friede].

fri'eléas, peaceless, deserted of peace, 127.

fri'ian, s. **freo'ian**.

fri'owebba, m., weaver of peace; fæle fri'owebba (of the angel), 88.

frignan, sv. III., ask; frignan ongan, 443, 570, 850, 1008, 1104; 2d p. sg. frignest, 589; 3d p. sg. frigne', 534; p.p. frugnen, 542.

frigu, f., love; þurh weres frige, 341.

frôd, prudent, wise, 343, 431, 438, 463, 531, 542; frôdne, 1164; frôdra, 637; experienced, old, frôd, 1237. Adverb, wisely; frode, 443.

frôfor, f., consolation, joy; gen. sg. frôfre gast, 1037, 1106; dat. sg. tô frôfre, 502, 1143; gen. pl. frôfra mæst, 196, 993.

from, s. **fram**.

from, active, bold, brave; fyrdrincas frome, warriors bold, 261.

fromlîce, adv., boldly, quickly, 454.

fruma, m., beginning, origin (fram fruman worulde, from the beginning of the world, 1142); originator, author, 772, 793, 839; the first, the chief, prince (herga fruman, 210, [213, 518]).

frym', m. f., beginning, 345, 502.

frŷnd, s. **frêond**.

ful, full, 752, 939. Adv., fully, full; ful geare, 167; ful gere, 860.

fûl, n., foulness, uncleanliness, impurity, 769.

fultum, m., help; on fultum, in help, 1053.

fulwiht, f. n. m. (?), baptism; þurh fulwihte, 172; fulwihte onfêng, receive baptism, 192; onfêng . . . fulwihtes bæ', 490, 1034.

fur'um, even, just; sy''an fur'um, just as soon as, 914.

fur'ur, further, more, 388.

fûs, ready, ready for (with gen.); sî'es fûs, ready for the journey, 1219; ready to die, 1237.

fylgan, wv. I., follow; gedwolan fylgdon, followed error, 371.

fyllan, wv. I., fell, cause to fall, discard; gedwolan fylde, he discarded error, 1041.

fyr, comp. to feor, [646].

fŷr, n., fire; 'urh fŷres blêo, through the form of fire, 1106; in fŷres feng, in the embrace of fire, 1287; þurh ofnes fŷr, 1311; þurh þæs dômes fŷr, through the fire of this ordeal (purgatorial), 1314.

fŷrbæ', n., fire-bath, hell-fire; on fyrbæ'e, 949.

fyrd, m., army; fyrda mæst, 35.

fyrdhwæt, brave in war, warlike, 21, 1179.

fyrdlêo', n., war-song; fyrdlêo' âgôl wulf, the wolf sang his battle-song, 27.

fyrdrinc, m., warrior; fyrdrincas frome, 261.

fŷrhât, hot as fire, ardent; fŷrhât lufu, 937.

fyrh', s. **ferh'**.

fyrh'wêrig, sad at heart, sorrowful; fyrh'wêrige, 560.

fyrmest, adv., first, at first, 68; first of all, especially, 316.

fyrn, adv., formerly, in olden days, of yore, long ago, 632,641,974.

fyrndagas, m. pl., days of yore; (on) fyrndagum, 398, 425, 528, [722].

fyrngeflit, n., old strife; þurh fyrngeflit, 904.

fyrngemynd, n., recollection of former deeds, history, 327.

fyrngewrit, n., old writing, ancient scripture; þurh fymgewrito, 155; fyrngewritu, 373, 431, 560.

fyrngid, n., ancient word, ancient prophecy; fyrngidda fród, 542.

fyrnweota, m., wise old man, prophet; fród fyrnweota (of David), 343; fród fyrnwiota (of Sachius), 438; þurh fyrnwitan, 1154.

fyrst, m., space of time, time (Ger. frist); nihtlangne fyrst, 67; æfter fyrste, 490; vii. nihta fyrst, 694.

fyrstmearc, f., definite time, appointed time; æfter fyrstmearce, 1034, 1268.

fyrwet, n., curiosity, desire of knowledge; mec . . . fyrwet myn-gaþ, desire of knowledge reminds me, etc., 1079.

fýsan, wv. I., hasten, make haste, prepare one's self; tô flote fýsan, to get ready for the sea-voyage, 226; fýsan . . . tô râde, get ready for the journey, 981.

G.

gâd, n., lack, 992.

galan, sv. VI., sing, scream; hrefen ûppe gôl, the raven screamed on high, 52; þâ wæs . . . sigeleoð galen, 124.

gǽlan, wv. I., hesitate, delay; scealcas ne gǽldon, the servants did not delay, 692, 1001.

galdor, m., sound, tone, song, speech; galdrum cýðan, 161.

galga, m., gallows, cross; on galgan, 179, 489, 719.

gamel, old, aged; me . . . game-lum tô gêoce, to me an old man for my assistance, 1247.

gang, m. [Ger. gang], course; dat. pl. wintra gangum, 633; geâra gongum, 648; wyrda gangum, 1256.

gangan, red. vb., go; imperative gangaþ nû (snûde), go now (quickly), 313, 372, 406.

gâr, m., spear; gâras lixtan, the spears glittered, 23, 125; gâras . . . forð onsendan, send forth . . . spears, 118.

gârþracu, f., storm of spears, battle; æt gârþræce, 1186.

gârþrîst, bold with the spear, 204.

gâst, m. (1) ghost, spirit (as principle of life); his gâst onsende, gave up the ghost, 480; gâste ge-gearwod, supplied with spirit, 889. (2) spirit, soul; gâste mînum, 471. (3) pl. spirits (demons) (of Christ); se gâsta helm, 176; (of God), gâsta gêocend, 682, 1077, — scyppend, 791, — weard, 1022; fram unclǽnum . . . gâstum, from unclean spirits (i.e. demons), 302; geômre gâstas, 182. (4) the spirit, spirit of God, Holy Ghost; hâlig gâst, 936, 1145; frôfre gâst, 1037, 1106; þurh gâstes gife, 199, 1058, 1157; gâstes mih-tum, 1070, 1100; þurh dryhtnes gâst, 352.

gâstgerýne, n., spirit's secret, spiritual mystery; gâstgerýnum, 189, 1148.

gâsthâlig, holy in spirit, endowed with the Holy Ghost, 562.

gâstlêas, without spirit, soulless, dead; gingne gâstlêasne, 875.

gâstsunu, m., spiritual son; godes gâstsunu, God's spiritual son (Christ), 673.

gê ... gê, both ... and, 965, 966; whether ... or, 629, 631.

gê, prn.; 2d pers. pl. ye, you, 290, 293, 294, and often.

geâclian, wv. II., frighten, excite, disquiet; egsan geûclad, by fear disquieted, 57; egesan geâclod, 1129.

gêacnian = ge-êacnian, become pregnant, fructify; wæstniuin gêacnod, 341.

geador, adv., together, 26, 889.

geagncwide, m., contradiction, answer; grimne geagncwide, angry contradiction, 525; gêncwidas glêawe, wise answers, 594.

geagninga, adv., directly, completely, perfectly, 673.

geâr, n., year, 7; geâra hwyrftum, 1; geâra gongum, 648; æfter gêârum, 1265.

geâra, adv., formerly, of yore, 1266.

geârdagas, m. pl., days of the year, days of life, 1267; days of yore (gcârdagum, 290, 835).

geare, (gere, gearu, gearwe,) adv., readily, clearly, well, accurately, exactly, fully, completely, 167, 399, 419, 531, 648, 719; gere, 860; gearwe, 1240; (gearu, 1045?); comp. geawor, 946; superl. gearwast, 328.

gearolîce, adv., readily, fully, thoroughly, 288.

gearu, ready, 85, 222, 605, 1029, 1045 (?); pl. gearwe, 23, 227, 555.

gearusnotter, very wise, skilled; with gen. gidda gearosnotor, 418; with dat. giddum gearusnottorne, 586.

gearwe, s. geare.

gearwian, wv. II., make ready, prepare one's self, 1000.

geâsne, with gen., poor in, destitute of; gôda geâsne, 924.

geatolîc, adorned, splendid, stately; geatolîc gûðscrûd, splendid battle dress, 258; geatolîc gûðcwên, stately queen of battle, 331.

gebann, n., commission, order, behest; þurh heard gebann, by strict behest, 557.

gebæro, n. pl., conduct, demeanor (beornes gebæro, 710); actions, deeds (þêoda gebæru, 659).

gebêodan, sv. II., bid, command, direct, 276, 1007.

gebîdan, sv. I., wait, 865.

gebindan, sv. III., bind; p.p. sûsle gebunden, 772; bitrum gebunden, 1245.

geblissian, wv. II., rejoice, make glad, delight; p.p. geblissod, 840, 876, 990, 1126.

gebrec, n., breaking, crash, noise; borda gebrec, crash of shields, 114.

gebringan (s. bringan), gebrôht, [614].

gebyrde, by birth, innate, natural; him gebyrde is, it is innate in him, 593.

gecêosan, sv. II., choose, select; pret. sg. gecêas, 1039, 1166; p.p. gecorenne, 1059; tô gecêosanne (gerund), 607.

geclænsian, wv. II., cleanse, 678; p.p. geclænsod, 1035, 1311.

gecnâwan, red. vb., know, recognize; pret. sg. gecnêow, 1140; pret. sg. opt. gecnêowe, 708; p.p. gecnâwen, 808.

gecost, tried, proved; bill gecost, tried sword, 257; hêape gecoste, with a tried band, 269; guman gecoste, 1186.

gecweðan, sv. V., speak; pret. sg. gecwæð (formula) þæt word gecwæð, this word he spake, 338, 344, 440, 939, 1191.

gecwême, pleasing, dear, 1050.

gecŷðan, wv. I., announce, to make known, 409, 588, 861; opt. pres. gecŷðe, 690; imperative, þonne þû snûde gecŷð, then speak out quickly, 446; gerund, tô gecŷðanne, 533; show, reveal, 595; opt. pres. gecyðe, 1091; p.p. gecŷðed, 816, 1050; gecŷðde . . . wundor, showed a miracle (i.e. worked a miracle), 866.

gecynd, f., nature; manna gecynd, nature of men, human nature, 735.

gecyrran, wv. I., turn [Ger. kehren], change; nama wæs gecyrred, the name was changed, 1061; geogoð is gecyrred, youth is passed, 1265.

gedafenlic, becoming, suitable, proper, 1168.

gedôn, (S. 429), do, apply; tô hwan hio þa næglas . . . gedôn mealhte, to what purpose she might apply these nails, 1158; show; gedô nû . . . forð bêaccu þin, show forth now thy sign, 784.

gedryht, f., multitude, host, 27, 737, 1290.

gedwola, m., error, heresy, 311, 371, 1041, 1119.

gedŷrsian, wv. II., honor, glorify; gedŷrsod, [451].

geearnian, wv. II., earn, deserve, 526.

geefnan, wv. I., accomplish, execute; hio geefnde swâ, she executed it thus, 1015.

gefær, n., journey, warlike expedition, army, 68.

gefaran, sv. VI., go, depart, depart hence, die; gefærenne man, 872.

gefæstnian, wv. II., fasten, make fast; p.p. gefæstnod, 1068.

gefêa, m., joy, 195; gefêan, 870, 949, 980.

gefeallan, red. vb., fall; p.p. gefeallen, 651.

gefeoht, n., fight, combat, battle; þurh gefeoht, 646; æt gefeohte, in battle, 1184.

gefêon, sv. V. (1), rejoice, be delighted; contracted participle, (S. 373); ferhð gefêonde, the soul rejoicing, 174, 991; pret. pl. leode gefægon, the people were delighted, 1116. (2) rejoice at, glory in (with gen. of object of joy); weorces gefeat, rejoiced at the work, 110, 849; cwên siðes gefeah, the queen gloried in the voyage, 247.

gefêran, wv. I., fare, come, go; ûp gefêran, ascend, 736; feorran gefêrede, those come from afar, 993.

gefetian, wv. II., fetch, bring, 1053; gefetigean, 1161.

gefic, n., fraud, deceit; mid fæcne gefice, with delusive deceit, 577.

geflit, n., contention, strife; geflitu ræran, raise strife, 443; geflitu rærdon, joined strife, 954.

gefrætwian, wv. II., fret, adorn; p.p. gefrætwad, 743.

gefrêge, known, 968.

gefremman, wv. I., do, perform, commit; gif wê . . . bôte gefremmaþ, if we do repentance, 575; feala . . . wundra gefremede, 363 (cf. 779, 912); oft gê dyslîce dæd gefremedon, 386; þe wê gefremedon, which we committed, 402 (cf. 415, 818); effect (fram blindnesse bôte gefremede, 298); grant (miltse gefremede, 501).

gefricgan, sv. V., learn by inquiry, learn; p.p. gefrigen, 155; gefrǣgon, [1116].

gefrignan, sv. III., find out by asking, learn; pret. pl. gefrugnon, 172; gefrugnen, 1014.

gefullǣstan, wv. I., help, 1151.

gefulwian, wv. II., baptize; p.p. gefulwad, 1044.

gefylgan, wv. I., follow, persist in (with dat.); gif gê þissum lease leng gefylgað, if you persist in this lie longer, 576.

gefyllan, wv. I., fill (opt. sg. gefylle, 680; p.p. gefylled, 452, 1143); finish, fulfil (opt. sg. gefylle, 1084; pret. sg. gefylde, 1071; p.p. gefylled, 1131, 1135).

gefȳsan, wv. I., hasten, incite, set in motion; flodas gefȳsde, 1270; with gen. be ready for; sîðes gefȳsde, [22], 260.

gegearwian, wv. II., make ready, equip (p.p. gegearwod, 47); equip, supply (gâste gegearwod, provided with spirit, 889).

geglengan, wv. I., adorn, decorate; golde geglenged, 90.

gehæftan, wv. I., chain, hold captive, torture; hungre gehæfted, tortured by hunger, 613.

geheaðrian, wv. II., confine; in nêdcleofan nearwe geheaðrod, confined in its narrow prison, 1276.

gehealdan, red. vb., hold, observe; ond þæt forð gehêold, and observed it (i.e. Christianity) from that time forth, 192.

gehðu, f., care, grief, sorrow; acc. gehðu, 609; on gehðu, 667; dat. pl. gehðum, 322, [531].

gehigd, f., thought; heortan gehigdum, with the heart's thoughts, 1224.

gehladan, sv. VI., load; pret. pl. gehlôdon, 234.

gehlêða, m., companion, comrade; holtes gehlêða, the wood's companion, 113.

gehwâ, prn., each, every (with following gen.); gen. worda gehwæs, 569; dat. sg. daga, niða, beorna, manna gehwâm, 358, 465, 1187, 1229; acc. on healfa gehwæne, (548); dat. sg. fem. in ceastra gehwære, 973 (s. note 548).

gehwæðer, prn., each of two, either, both; gehwæðres wâ, woe in either event, 628; bega gehwæðres, in both respects, 964.

gehwǣr, adv., everywhere, [548], 1183.

gehweorfan, sv. III., turn; sê ðe tô bôte gehwearf, who turned to repentance, 1126.

gehwylc, prn. (with gen.), each; tâcna gehwylces, 319 (cf. 423, 910, 1030, 1156, 1310)); gumena gehwylcum, 278; scylda gehwylcre, 1313; fêonda gehwylcne, 1179; þinga gehwylc, 409 (cf. 645, 1317); ânra gehwylc = each, 1287 (S. 347): (without following substantive), gehwylcne, 598: (as adj.), dǣdra gehwylcra, of all deeds, 1283.

gehȳdan, wv. I., hide, conceal; p.p. gehȳdde, 832; gehȳded, 1092.

gehȳnan, wv. I., bring low, humiliate, afflict, weaken, 923; hungre gehȳned, weakened by hunger, 720.

gehȳran, wv. I., hear, perceive, learn (by hearsay), 333, 364, 442, 511, 660, 709, 957, 1002, 1282; hear = hearken unto; swâ ðû gehȳrdest þone hâlgan wer, as Thou heardest that holy man, 785.

gehyrstan, wv. I., adorn, decorate; golde gehyrsted, 331.

gehyrwan, wv. I., neglect; word gehyrwan, 221.

gefewan, geŷwan, wv. I., show; pret. geŷwdest, 787; geŷwde, 488; p.p. geŷwed, 74, 183; geîewed, 102. [gelǽcan, 43; translated by Kemble, move.]

gelǽdan, wv. I., lead, conduct; hine . . . ûp gelǽddon of carcerne, they led him up out of prison, 714.

gelǽstan, wv. I., accomplish, carry out, perform, do (Ger. leisten); tô gelǽstenne, 1166; gelǽste, 1197; exercise, practice, 1208.

gelêafa, m., belief, faith, 491, 966, 1036, 1137.

gelêafful, faithful, 960; gelêaffull, 1048.

gelêodan, red. vb., grow, increase; geloden under lêafum, grown under leaves, 1227.

gelettan, wv. I., hinder; geletest lâð werod, thou shalt hinder the hated crowd, 94.

gelic, like; englum gelice, like the angels, 1320; superl. adv. winde geliccost, very like the wind, 1272.

gelîðan, sv. I., go, reach (syþþan tô hŷðe . . . geliden hæfdon, after they had attained to the harbor (reached the harbor), 249); go, pass away, vanish (lifwynne geliden, vanished with the joy of living, 1269).

gelimpan, sv. III., happen (swâ hit gelamp, 271, 1155); befall, happen to, 441; succeed, be successful, 963.

gelŷfan, wv. I., believe, 518, 796.

gemang, n., troop, crowd; on gemang, among, etc.; on clǽnra gemang, into the hosts of the pure (i.e. among the pure), 96; on fêonda

gemang, in the midst of the enemies, 108 (cf. 118).

gemengan, wv. I., mix, mingle, contaminate; mâne gemengde, 1296.

gemêtan, wv. I., meet, find; p.p. gemeted, 871, 1013, 1225.

gemetgian, wv. II., moderate, temper; him gemetgaþ eall êldes lêoma, He tempers for them entirely the fire's glare, 1293.

gemôt, n., meeting, assembly; on gemôt, 279.

gemyltan, wv. I., melt; gemylted, 1312.

gemynd, n. f., memory, mind; on gemynd, in memory, 644; in gemynd comaþ, they come into mind, 1303; þe on gemynd nime, who taketh in mind (i.e. remembers), 1233; on gemynd begêat, He poured it into my mind, 1248.

gemynde, mindful; gemynde ymb, mindful of, 1064.

gemyndig, mindful, heedful (with ymb), 213; (with gen), 266, 819, 902, 940.

gên, adv., again, once again, 373, 925; moreover, furthermore, 1218; still, now, 1063, 1078, 1080, 1092.

gêncwide, s. geagn-.

geneahhe, adv. enough, sufficiently, in the highest degree, very, 1065, 1158.

genêgan, wv. I., address; wordum genêgan, 385.

genemman, wv. I., name; þûra . . . sint . . . syx genemned, of these six are named, 741.

generian, wv. I., save; pret. generede, 163; generedon, 132; free, deliver (ond fram unclǽnum eft generede dêafla gâstum, and he often delivered from the unclean spirits of devils, 301).

geníðla, m., enemy, enmity, hostility; oncyrran geníðlan, avert the enmity, 610; fram hungres geníðlan, by the hostile attacks of hunger, 701.

geniman, sv. IV., take; pret. sg. genam, 599.

gêoc, f., help, assistance, consolation; tô gêoce, 1139, 1247.

gêocend, helper (of God); gâsta gêocend, 682; (also of Christ), 1077.

geofen, n., sea; ymb geofenes stæð, about the sea-coast, 227; ofer geofenes strêam, over the sea's current, 1201. .

geogoð, f., youth; on geogoðe, in youth, 638; geogoð is gecyrred, youth is past, 1265.

geogoðhâd, m., period of youth, youth; geogoðhâdes glæm, the joy of youth, 1267.

geolorand, m., yellow border, shield, 118.

gêomor, sad, saddened, 627; gêomrum, 922; pl. gêomre, 182, 322.

gêomormôd, sad at heart, sorrowful in mind; gêomormôde, 413, 555.

geond, prep. (with acc.), through, throughout, beyond; geond middangeard, 16, 1177 (cf. 278, 734, 969).

geopenigean, wv. II., open, reveal, disclose, 1102; pres. opt. geopenie, reveal, 792; p.p. geopenad, opened, 1231.

georn, zealous; georn on môde, zealous in spirit, 268.

georne, adv., zealously, eagerly, earnestly, 199, 216, 322, 413, 471, 600, 1157, 1171; exactly, accurately, 1163.

geornian, wv. II., desire, [1260].

geornlîce, adv., zealously, 1097, 1148.

gêotan, sv. II., pour; p.p. goten, 1133.

gerǽde, n., hæleða gerædum, for mediation with the men, (Grein, Pompe), 1054; hæleða gerædum, by the interposition of men (durch der Helden Anstiften, Grein), 1108 (veranstaltung, vermittlung?, Zupitza).

gereccan, wv. I., report, narrate, 649.

gerestan, wv. I., rest; ond geresteð nô, and resteth nevermore, 1083.

gerûm, n., room; on gerûm, away, apart, 320.

gerȳman, wv. I., make room, prolong, extend; tîdum gerȳmde, extended with time (?), 1249.

gerȳne, n., secret; dryhtnes gerȳno, the secret of the Lord, 280; þæt gerȳne rihte, that true secret, 566; wryda geryno, secret of events, 589, 813.

gesǽlig, blessed, saved (Ger. selig), 956.

gesamnian, wv. II., assemble; p.p. gesamnod, 26, 282.

gesceâdan, red. vb., separate, decide; hild wæs gesceâden, the battle was decided, 149. (Cf. N. E. shed in watershed.)

gesceaft, f., creation (samod ealle gesceaft, likewise all creation, 729; (of heaven), 1089; creature, 729 (?); eallra gesceafta, of all creatures, 894); what is created, object (of the cross), þurh þû . . . gesceaft, 183, 1032.

gesceap, n., creature, object (of the cross); þurg þæt beorhte gesceap, 790.

gescrîfan, sv. I., prescribe, determine, decree; wyrd gescrâf, the Fate decreed, 1047.

gescyrdan, wv. I., injure, destroy; hêap wæs gescyrded, the multitude was destroyed, 141.

gescyrtan, wv. I., shorten, lessen, 141 (?).

gesêcan, wv. I., seek; dôm gesêceð, He seeketh judgment (i.e. comes to pass judgment), 1280; pret. gesôhte, 230, 255, 270.

gesecgan, gesecggan, wv. I., say, speak, proclaim; gesecggan, speak, 108; gesecgan, proclaim, announce, 985.

gesêðan, wv. I., verify, prove, 582.

gesêft, softened, mild, pleasant; superl. gesêftost, most pleasant, 1205.

gesêon, sv. V., see, 1308; gesîon, 243; pres. pl. gesêoð, 1121; pret. sg. geseah, 88, 100; geseh, 842; pret. pl. gesægon, 68; gesâwon, 1111; pret. sq. opt. gesêge, 75; p.p. gesegen, shown (?), 71 (S. 391. 2).

gesettan, wv. I., set, place, put, destine, determine, [614]; tô þegnunge þinre gesettest, Thou predestinedst (them) to Thy service, 739; þæt hê gesette on sacerhad ... Jûdas, that he should establish Judas in the priesthood, 1055.

gesihð, s. gesyhð.

gesîon, s. gesêon.

gesittan, sv. V., sit, sit down; gesæton, they sat down, 868.

gespon, n., plaiting, etc., web, twist; wîra gespon, twist of wires (nails), 1135.

gesprecan, sv. V., speak; pret. sg. opt. gesprǣce, 667; p.p. gesprecenra, 1285.

gesteald, n., dwelling, mansion; êcra gestealda, the eternal mansions, 802.

gesund [Ger. gesund], sound, healthy, happy, prosperous; gesundne sîð, a prosperous voyage, 997.

gesweorcan, sv. III., darken, grow dark; rodor eal geswearc, the whole heavens grew dark, 856.

geswerigan, sv. VI., swear; ic þæt geswerige þurh sunu meotodes, this I swear by the Son of the Creator, 686.

geswîcan, sv. I., omit, forsake, cease from (with gen.); þæs unrihtes eft geswicaþ, we cease again from this unrighteousness, 516.

geswiðrian, wv. II., lessen, diminish, weaken; p.p. geswiðrod, 698, 918; geswiðrad, 1264.

gesyhð, f., sight, view, appearance, a vision; þurh þâ fægeran gesyhð, on account of this joyful vision, 98; æt þǣre gesyhðe, at this sight, 965; on gesyhðe, in a vision, 184; in sight, visible, 346; in sight, 847; on gesihðe, before his eyes, in sight, 614.

gesyllan, wv. I., give, 1284.

gesŷne, visible, evident, clear; þâ wæs gesŷne, 144, 264.

getǣcan, wv. I., show, reveal (2d p. sg. pret. getǣhtesð, 1075), impart; pret. opt. getǣhte, 601.

getellan, wv. I., tell, count; geteled rîmes, 2; geteled rîme, 634.

getengan, wv. I., devote, dedicate; hine ... sylfne getengde ... in godes þeowdôm, and devoted himself to the service of God, 200.

getenge, resting on, near, adjacent; sunde getenge, resting on the sea, 228; grunde getenge (lying on the ground), near the surface, 1114.

getimbrian, wv. I. and II., build, erect; getimbrede, 1010.

getrŷwe, true, faithful; Criste getrŷwe, 1035.

getŷd, taught, skilled, practised; cræftum getŷde, skilled in arts, 1018.

getŷnan, wv. I., shut in, enclose, bury, getŷnde, 921; getŷned, 722.

geþanc, m., thought; on geþance, 267, 807; geþanc, 1239; geþonca, 1286; geþancum, 312.

geþeaht, f., reflection, consideration, counsel; þurh snyttro geþeaht, through the counsel of wisdom, 1060; næfre ic þâ geþeahte . . . sêcan wolde, I was never willing to visit the conferences, etc., 468; knowledge; rûmran geþeaht, more extended knowledge, 1241.

geþencan, wv. I., think, consider, think of; snyttro geþencaþ weras wîsfæste, in prudence think of your wisest men, 313.

geþinge, n., fate; bîdan beorna geþinges, await the fate of the men, 253.

geþôht, m., thought; þæt wæs þrêalîc geþôht, that was a horrible thought, 426.

geþolian, wv. II., endure, suffer, 1292.

geþonc, s. geþanc.

geþrêan, wv. III. (S. 416, n. 4), torture, torment, oppress; egesan geþrêade, with fear oppressed, 321.

geþrêatian, wv. II. persecute; hungre geþrêatod, persecuted with hunger, 695.

geþrec, n., rush; beorna geþrec, 114.

geþringan, sv. III., overcome, devastate, 40.

geþrôwian, wv. II., endure, bear, suffer; pret. sg. geþrôwade, 519, 563; geþrôwode, 859; pret. pl. geþrôwedon, 855.

gewadan, sv. VI., go, advance, press in; sefa dêop gewôd, the mind pressed in to great depth, 1190.

gewælan, wv. I., torture, pain; sorgum gewæled, pained by sorrows, 1244.

geweald, n., might, power [Ger. gewalt]; þurh fingra geweald, through the fingers' power, 120; dôma geweald, power over the wills, 726; on þære cwêne gewealdum, in the power of this queen, 610.

gewendan, wv. I., wend, turn; gewended tô wuldre, turned toward heaven, 1047; gewende tô wædle, turns to poverty, 617.

geweorðan, sv. III., be, become, happen, occur, 456, 611; pres. cûþ þæt gewyrðeð, this will become known, 1192; swîge gewyrðeð, it becomes still, 1275; on gesihðe . . . geweorðað, they become visible, are before his eyes, 614; pret. sg. gewearð, happened, occurred, 632, 641; became, was, 923; pret. pl. gewurdon, were, 1288; p.p. hu is þæt geworden, how has that happened? 643; wæs him frôfra mæst geworden in worlde, to them the greatest of consolations was come in the world, 994.

geweorðian, wv. II., distinguish, honor; wîgge geweorðod, distinguished in battle, 150 (cf. 823, 1193 [1196]); in þrýnesse þrymme geweorðad, honored in the glory of the Trinity, 177.

gewerian, wv. I., cover over,

clothe; hilderincas hyrstum gewerede, the knights in armor clad,
263.

gewîtan, sv. I., go; pret. gewât
. . . hâm, he went home, 148; go
away, vanish, 1272, 1277; gewât,
94.

gewitt, n., wits, understanding,
mind; wîsdômes gewitt, understanding of wisdom, 357, 1190 (cf. 459,
938).

gewlencan, wv. I., adorn, decorate, bedeck; wîrum gewlenced,
bedecked with metal wires, 1264.

gewrit, n., writ, scripture, book;
gewritu herwdon, you neglected the
Scriptures, 387; on gewritu setton,
put in writing (*i.e.* record), 654,
658; nom. pl. gewritu, 674; prt.
pl. on gewritum, in writing, 827,
1256.

gewunian, wv. II., dwell in,
inhabit; siððan frôfre gâst wîc gewunode, after the Spirit of consolation inhabited the dwelling, 1038.

gewyrcan, wv. I., work, con-
struct, 104; create (þû geworhtest,
Thou createdst, 727, 738); commit
(þêah wê æbylgð . . . gewyrcen,
though we commit transgression,
513).

gewyrd, f., event, occurrence,
647.

geŷwan, s. geîcwan.

gidd, n., song, speech; gidda
gearosnotor, skilled in speech, 418
(cf. [531?], 586) (s. gearusnotter).

gif, if (with ind.), 435, 459, 514,
533, 576, 1004; (with opt.), 441, 542,
621, 773, 777, 782, 789, 857.

gifan, sv. V., give (gifad, 360);
grant (geaf, 365).

gifu, f., gift, present, benefit,
grace, favor, 265; acc. godspelles

gife, 176 (cf. 596, 1144); gife, 182,
967, 1033, 1201, 1247; þurh gâstes
gife, 199, 1058, 1157.

gildan, sv. III., yield, return,
repay; ne geald hê yfel yfele, he
did not return evil for evil, 493.

gim, m., gem; gimmas lixtan,
the gems glistened, 90.

gîman, wv. I., care for, be careful of, pay attention to, observe
(with gen.); hlâfes ne gîme, and
take no notice of the loaf, 616.

gimcyn, n., kind of gems, precious stones; gimcynnum, 1024.

gîna, yet, still, 1070.

ging, young, 353, 404, 875; (comp.
gingra, 159).

gîo, once, 436.

girwan, wv. I., prepare, erect;
girwan godes tempel, to build a
temple of God, 1022.

gîsel, m., hostage; tô gîsle, as a
hostage, 600.

glæd, bright, gleaming, glad;
þê glædra, the gladder, 956.

glædmôd, glad at heart, 1096.

glæm, m., gleam, splendor, joy;
ûr wæs gêara geogoðhâdes glæm, in
the days of yore the buffalo was
the joy of youth, 1265.

glêaw, skilled, sagacious, wise,
594, 638, 807, 1163, 1212; superl.
þâ glêawestan, the wisest, 536.

glêawhŷdig, wise-in-mind, 935.

glêawlîce, adv., prudently, wisely, 189.

glêawnes, f., wisdom, prudence;
glêawnesse þurhgoten, impregnated
with wisdom, 962.

glêd, f., heat, fire, flames (Ger.
glut); in glêda gripe, in the grip
of the flames, 1302.

gnornian, wv. II., be sorrowful,
moan, bemoan; ŷr gnornode nŷd-

gefera, the bow bemoaned its companion in need, 1260.

gnornsorg, f., sadness, sorrow; gnornsorge wæg, he bore his sorrow, 655; gnornsorga mæst, the greatest of sorrows, 977.

gnyrn, f., sadness, 1139; wrong, blemish; eallra gnyrna lêas, free from all blemishes, 422.

gnyrnwrǽc, f., revenge for wrong; nales gnyrnwræcum, in nowise with revenge for wrong, 359.

god, m., God, 4, etc.; gen. godes, 109, etc.; dat. gode, 965, 1135; acc. god, 209, etc.

gôd, good; gen. pl. gôdra, 637; substantive good; gôda geâsne, poor in goods, 924.

godbearn, n., God's Son, Christ, 719.

godcund, godlike, divine; godcunde gife, 1033.

gôddênd, pl., benefactors, 359.

godgimmas, m., pl., heavenly jewels (gottes gemmen, sterne des himmels, Gm.), (jewels, Kemble), [1114].

godspel, n., gospel; godspelles gife, 179.

gold, n., gold; swâ smǽte gold, as purified gold, 1309; æplede gold, appled gold, 1260 (s. note, 1260); instr. golde, 90, 331, 1024.

goldgim, m., goldgem; goldgimmas, 1114.

goldhoma, m., garment ornamented with gold; unter goldhoman, among the gold-bespangled (garments), 992.

goldhord, n., gold hoard, treasure of gold, treasure, 791.

goldwine, gold distributing friend, ruler, king (of Constantine), 201.

gomen, n., game, rejoicing, joy, pleasure, 1265.

gong, s. gang.

gram, hostile; on gramra gemang, in the midst of the hostile, 118; gramum gûðgelǽcan, against the hostile warriors, 42.

grâp, f., grasp, clutch; grâpum gryrefæst, terribly firm in grasp, 760.

grêot, m., grit, sand, earth; grêote begrauene, covered with sand, 835.

grim, grim, fierce, angry; grimme geagncwide, angry contradiction, 525.

grîma, m., helmet; gylden grîma, 125.

grîmhelm, mark-helm, helmet, (with visor), 258.

gring, f. n. (?) slaughter, downfall; herga gring, fall of the masses, 114.

gringan, sv. III., fall, perish; hǽðene grungon, the heathens fell, 126. (For gring and grinnan, compare cring and cringan.)

gripe, m., gripe, grip, grasp; in glêda gripe, in the flames' grip, 1302.

grund, m., ground, bottom; grunde getenge, near the surface (or on the ground?), 1114; in wylmes grunde, on the bottom of the waves of fire, 1299; earth (ofer sîdne grund, throughout the wide earth, 1289); bottom, abyss (in sûsla grund, into the abyss of tortures, 944).

gryrefæst, terribly firm, 760.

gûð, f., battle, combat, 23, [43].

gûðcwên, queen of battle (of Helen), 254, 331.

gûðgelǽca, warrior; gramum

gûðgelæcan, against the hostile warriors, 43.

gûðheard, brave in battle (of Constantine), 204.

gûðrôf, renowned in battle, renowned, 273.

gûðscrûd, n., battle-dress; geatolîc gûðscrûd, 258.

gûðweard, ward of battle, leader, prince; gûðweard gumena, 14.

guma, m., man (human being), 464, 531; pl. guman, 561, 1186; gen. pl. gumena, 14, 201, 254, 278, 638, 1096, 1203.

gumrîce, n., kingdom of men, kingdom; on þâm gumrîce, 1221.

gylden, golden, 125.

gylt, m., guilt, sin; mînra gylta, of my guilty actions, sins, 817.

H.

habban, wv. III., anv. (1) have, hold, possess, 621; 3d p. sg. ind. hafað, 825; pres. opt. sg. hæbbe, 594; opt. pl. hæbben, 316, 408; pret. ind. sg. hæfde, 63, 1253; pret. pl. hæfdon, 49, 381. (2) auxiliary vb., have; 1st p. sg. ind. hafu, 808 (S. 416 1); 3d p. sg. hafað, 910; opt. pres. sg. hæbbe, 288; pret. sg. ind. hæfde, 224, 412, 1130, 1254; pret. pl. hæfdon, 155, 249, 369, 415, 870, 998.

hâd, m., rank, class; þara on hâde sint . . . syx genemned, of those in this class six are named, 749; shape, form (on weres hâde, in the form of a man, 72; in cildes had, in the form of a child, 72, 336, 776; þurh lêohtne hâd, in a glorious manner, 1246 [s. note, 1246]) (N. E. suffix hood).

hæder, bright, clear (Ger. heiter); hædrum stefnum, with clear voices, 748.

hæðen, heathen, 126, 1076.

hæft, m., bondage, imprisonment, 703.

hæftnêd, f., necessity of captivity, bondage, thraldom; of hæftnêde, 297.

hæl, f., hail, health; Elenan hæl âbêodan, to bid Helen hail, 1003.

hæleð, m., man, hero, warrior, 511, 640, 936; acc. sg. hæleð, 538; nom. acc. pl. hæleð (S. 281 2), 273, 1006, 1297; gen. pl. hæleða, 73, 156, 188, 852, 1054, 1108, 1204; dat. pl. hæleðum, 661, 671, 679, 709, 1012, 1273.

hæland, m., healer, Saviour (Ger. heiland), (of God), 726; (of Christ), 809, 862, 912, 920, 1063.

hâlig, holy (attributive), 218, 625, 679, 740, 751, 843, 885, 936, 976, 1087, 1145, 1195; f. hâlige rîme, 333, 1169 (cf. 720, 1012, 1224); n. þæt hâlige trêo, 107, 128, 429, 442, 701, 841; m. se hâlga god, 751; dat. tô þêre hâlgan byrig, 1006, 1054, 1204; acc. m. þone hâlgan wer, 785; acc. f. þurh þâ hâlgan gesceaft, 1032; acc. n. hâlig, 758; acc. pl. þurh hâlige bêc, 364, 670, 853; (substantive), se hâlga, 1094; þæs hâlgan, 86; on þone hâlgan, 457; hâligra, 821; hâlgum, 988.

hælo, f., health, healing, cure, 1216.

hâm, m., home; in þâm engan hâm, in that narrow home (i.e. hell), 921; acc. hâm, home, 143, 148.

hand, f., hand; mid bæm handum, with both hands, 805 (cf. 843); handa sendan, lay hands (on), 457.

handgeswing, n., swing of the

hands, combat; heard handgeswing, 115.

hǣs, f., behest; þurh þæs hâlgan hæs, at the behest of this holy one, 86.

hât, hot, 628, 1133; in hâtne wylm, 1297; superl. hâttost, 579.

hâtan, red. vb. (1) call, name (hê wæs . . . be naman hâten, he was called by name, 505; be naman hâteð, 756). (2) bid, order, enjoin, command; pret. sg. heht, 42, 79, 99, 105, 129, 153, 276, 691, 863, 877, 999, 1003, 1007, 1023, 1051, 1161, 1198, 1202; hêt, 214; pret. sg. opt. hehte, 509; imperative, hât, 1173.

hê, he, 9, 13, etc.; she, hêo, 570, 1136; hio, 268, 325, 420, 568, 569, 571, 598, 710; it, hit, 170, 271, etc.; gen., his, his, 147, 162; her, hiere, 222; hire, 1200; dat., him, him, 18, 72, etc.; her, hire, 223, 567, etc.; acc., him, hine, 14, 200, etc.; it, hit, 350, 702; pl. nom. and acc., they and them, hie, 48, 175, etc.; hêo, 116, 254, etc.; hio, 166, 324, etc.; gen. pl., their, hiera, 360; hira, 174, 359; dat. pl., them, him, 173, 182, etc.

heaðofremmende, giving battle, fighting, 130.

heaðowelm, m. (war-wave), fierce flame; hottost heaðowelma, 579; of þâm heaðuwylme, 1305.

hêafodwylm, m., tears; hât hêafodwylm, 1133.

hêah, high, on hêanne bêam, 424; ofer hêanne holm, beyond the high sea, 983; superl. hîhst (197?).

hêahengel, m., archangel, 751.

hêahmægen, m., high strength, mighty power; godes hêahmægen, 464 (cf. 753).

healdan, red. vb., hold; rîce healdan, to hold dominion, 449;

hold, keep, preserve, observe; opt. sg. pres. þæt dû dryhtnes word healde, 1169; pret. sg. hê wære wið þec . . . hêold, he kept his faith in (toward) thee, 824; pret. pl. hêoldon . . . hælcða rǣdas, 156; hold, defend, keep (lîfes trêo . . . hâlig healdan, to keep the tree of life undefiled, 758).

healf, f., side; on healfa gehwǣne, 548 (s. note, 548); on twâ halfa, 955; on twâ healfe, 1180.

healfcwîc, half-quick, half-alive, half-dead, 133.

healsian, wv. II., adjure; ic êow healsie þurh heofona god, 699.

healt, halt, 1215.

hêan, abject, poor, miserable, 1216; depressed, 701.

hêanne, s. hêah, hêan.

hêannes, f., height; on hêannesse, on high, 1125.

hêap, m., heap, troop, multitude, army, 141, 269, 549, 1206.

heard, hard; on heardum hige, in my hard heart, 809; comp. stane heardran, harder than stones, 565; hard, cruel, terrible (heardre hilde, with cruel battle, 83); heard hundgeswing, hard combat, 115; strict, imperative (þurh heard gebann, by imperative order, 557); hard (to bear), severe, intolerable (wîtum heardum, with intolerable tortures, 180; cf. 704).

hearde, adv., fiercely, very; hearde . . . eorre, very angry, 400.

heardecg, hard of edge, sharp-edged, 758.

hearding, m., bold man, hero; heardingas, 25, 130.

hearm, m., harm, injury; feala mê hearma gefremede, he did me . . . many injuries, 912.

hearmloca, m., place of afflic₊ tion, prison; under hearmlocan, 695.

hebban, sv. VI., raise, lift, 107; pret. pl. hôfon, 25; p.p. hafen, 123, 890.

heht, s. hâtan.

hel, f., hell; helle duru, 1230.

helan, sv. IV., cover, hide, conceal; leng helan, 703, 706.

helledêofol, m., devil of hell, 901.

hellegrund, m., abyss of hell, 1305.

hellesceada, m., hellish enemy, devil; þone hellesceaþan, 957.

helm, m., helmet, protector (of Constantine), 148, 223; (of Christ), 176, 475.

help, f., help; tô helpe, 679, 1012; acc. helpe, 1032.

hêo, n., hue, form; þurh mennisc hêo, in human form, 6.

heofen, heofon, 728, heofun, 753, m. (1) heaven, 728, 753; heofones, 1230; heofona, 699; heofonum, 188, 527; heofenum, 801. (2) heavens (heofenum, 83, 976; heofonum, 101).

heofoncyning (cining), m., King of Heaven, 170, 367, 748.

heofonlic, heavenly, 740, 1145.

heofonrîce, n., kingdom of heaven; heofonrîces weard, 197, 445, 718; heofonrîces god, 1125; heofonrîces hyht, 629; in heofonrîce, 621.

heofonsteorra, m., star of heaven; swylce heofonsteorran, 1113.

heolstor, n., darkness, concealment, 1082, 1113.

heolstorhof, n., dark dwelling; under heolstorhofu (of hell), 764.

heorte, f., heart; gen. sg. heortan, 1224; dat. sg. æt heortan, 628.

heorucumbul, n., standard of war, ensign, 107.

heorudrêorig, sword-gory, - bloody, 1215.

heorugrim, savagely, fierce; hetend heorugrimme, dire enemies, 119.

hêr, adv., here; bûtan hêr nûða, except here now, 661.

here, m., army, multitude, troops, 65; gen. sg. herges, 143; heriges, 205; dat. sg. herge, 52; acc. sg. here, 58; gen. pl. heria, 101; herga, 115, 210; heriga, 148; dat. pl. hergum, 32, 41, 110, 180; herigum, 406.

herebyrne, f., war corselet, [22].

herecumbol, n., battle-standard, ensign, 25 (?).

herefeld, m., battle-field, field; on herefelda, 126; ofer herefeldas, 269.

heremægen, n., warlike force, multitude; for þâm heremægene, 170.

heremeðel, n., assembly of the people, assembly; tô þâm heremeðle, 550.

hererǽswa, m., warrior, leader of the army; him hererǽswan, to him the leader of the army (of Constantine), 995.

heresîð, m., warlike expedition, 133.

heretêma, m., army-leader; âhæfen ... tô heretêman, raised to leader of the forces, 10.

hereweorc, n., army-work, battle; þæs hereweorces, 656.

hereþrêat, m., army's troop, cohort; on þâm hereþrêate, 265.

herg, s. here.

hergan, herian, wv. I., praise, adore; (with reference to God), god hergendra, 1097; god hergendum, 1221; (with reference to Christ), ᘐe þone ähangnan cyning heriad, 453; sunu wealdendes ... heredon, 893.

heria, s. here.

herigean, wv. III.(?), despise; ic þā rôde ne þearf hleatre herigean, I dare not despise this cross with the laughter of scorn, 920.

herwan, wv. I., neglect, scorn, despise; ac hîe hyrwdon mê, but they despised me, 355; ond gewritu herwdon, and the scriptures neglected, 387.

hete, m., hate; þurh hete, 24.

hetend, pl., haters, enemies; wiᘐ hetendum, against the enemies, 18; hetend heorugrimme, dire enemies, 119. (Cf. hettend.)

Hierusalem, 273, Jerusalem, 1056; Jerusalem (s. note, 273).

hige, s. hyge.

higefrôfor, f., consolation for the heart, heart-consolation, 355.

higegléaw, of wise mind, prudent; gehŷraᘐ, higegléawe, hâlige rûne, hear, O ye of wise minds, the holy secret, 333.

higeþanc, m., thought of the mind; higeþancum, 156.

hild, f., battle, fight, combat, 18, [22]; dat. tô hilde, 32, 49, 52, 65; instr. hilde, 83.

hildedêor, daring in battle, brave in battle, 936.

hildegesa, m., terror of battle; hildegesa stôd, terror of battle spread, 113.

hildemecg, m., warrior, [22].

hildenædre, battle-adder, war-snake, missile; hildenædran, arrows (?), 119; spears, 141.

hilderinc, m., warrior, hero; hilderincas hyrstum gewerede, battle-knights in armor clad, 263.

hildeserce f., battle-sark, coat of mail, 234.

hildfruma, m., battle-prince (of Constantine), 10, 101.

hîwbeorht, bright of hue, beautiful, brilliant, 73.

hlâf, m., loaf, bread, 613; hlâfes, 616.

hlæfdige, f., lady, 400; hlæfdige mîn, 656 (of Helen).

hlâford, m., lord (of Constantine), 265, 475, 983.

hleahtor, m., laughter of scorn; hleatre, 920.

hlêapan, red. vb., leap, run, 54 (s. note, 54).

hlêo, m., protection; under swegles hlêo, under the protection of heaven, 507; wiᘐ hundres hlêo, as a protection against hunger, 616; protector, shield; (of Constantine), æᘐelinga hlêo, 99; wigena, 150; (of Judas), eorla, 1074.

hlêoᘐrian, wv. II., (utter sounds), speak, 901.

hlêor, n., cheek, 1099, 1133.

hlihan (hlihhan), sv. VI., laugh, laugh for joy, rejoice; hlihende hyge, the heart rejoicing, 995.

[hlôwan, red. vb., low, roar, blow loudly; hlêowon hornboran, the trumpeters blew loudly, 54.] (See hleapan.)

hlûd, loud, 1273.

hlûde, adv., loudly, 110, 406.

hlŷt, m., lot, portion, throng; mid hâligra hlŷte, with the throng of the holy, 821.

hnâg, debased, deplorable; wênde him trâge hnâgre, feared the deplorable evil, 668.

hnesce, soft, 615.

hof, n., court-yard, house, dwelling (Ger. hof); tô hofe, to court, 557; fram þâm engan hofe, out of this narrow dwelling (Judas'prison), 712; in þâm rêonian hofe, in this sad spot (of the burial place of the crosses), 834.

holm, m., rounded height (cf. N. 983) [230]; ofer hêanne holm, over the high sea, 983.

holmþracu, f., tossing of the sea, restless sea, 728.

holt, n., forest, wood; holtes gchlêða, 113. (N.E. holt.)

hôn, red. vb., hang, crucify; pret. pl. hengon, 424; p.p. hangen, 852.

hord, n., hoard, treasure; hord under hrûsan, 1092.

horh, filth, defilement; instr. horu, 297 (S. 242. 2).

hornbora, m., hornbearer, trumpeter; hornboran, 54.

horu, s. horh.

hospcwide, m., contemptuous words, insulting, scornful speech, 522.

hrû, n., body, 579; body without life, corpse, 885.

hraðe, adv., quickly, straightway, promptly, 76, 406, 669, 710.

hrædlîce, adv., quickly, 1087.

Hrêðas, same as Hrêðgotan.

hrêðer, m. (?), the inside, soul, 1145.

hreðerloca, m., inclosure of the interior, breast; hreðerlocan onspêon, opened his bosom, 86.

Hrêðgotan, the renowned Goths, 20.

hrefen, m., raven, 52; hrefn, 110.

hrêmig, rejoicing, exulting (with instr.); hûðe hrêmig, exulting in booty, 149; blissum hrêmig, exulting with joy, 1138.

[hreodlan, 1239 (zittern, Leo).]

hrêof, rough, leprous; hrêofe, 1215.

hrêosan, sv. II., fall, 764.

hring, m., ring, sound; wôpes hring, sound of weeping, 1132.

hringedstefna, m., ringed-prow (vessels with prows provided with rings for making them fast to the land); hringstefnan, 248.

hrôðer, m., joy, consolation, delight; tô hrôðer, 16, 1160.

hrôf, m., roof; ofer wolcna hrôf, upon the roof of the clouds, 89.

hrôpan, red. vb., call, proclaim, make proclamation; hrêopan friccan, 54, 550.

hrôr, strong, brave; hrôrra tô hilde, of the brave in battle, 65.

hrûse, f., earth; under hrûsan, 218, 625, 843, 1092.

hû, adv., how (in dir. interr.), 456, 611, 632, 643; (in indir. interr.), 176, 179, 185, 335, 367, 474, 512, 561, 954, 960, 997.

hûð, f., plunder, booty; hûðe hrêmig, 149.

Hûgas, pl., proper name, (21 ?).

Hûnas, pl., Huns, [21]; gen. pl. Hûna, 20, 32, 41, 49, 58, 128, 143.

hund, n., hundred; tû hund, 2; d, = fîf hund, 379; cc, = tû hund, 634.

hungor, m., hunger; hungres, 616, 701; dat. hungre, 703; instr. hungre, 613, 687, 695, 720.

hûru, adv., verily, certainly, 1045, 1150.

hûs, n., house, frame; þæt fæge hûs, that doomed frame, 881; þurh þæt fæcne hûs, on account of this uncertain human body (*i.e.* frame), 1237.

hwæð̄re, adv., however, yet; hwæð̄re . . . nyste, yet he did not know, 719.

hwan (from hwâ); tô hwan, to what (purpose), 1158.

hwậr, interr. adv., where (in indir. interr.), 205, 217, 429, 563, 624, 675, 720, 1103.

hwæt (from hwâ), n., what (in indir. interr.); hwæt se god wậre, 161; hwæt sio syn wære, 414; þurh hwæt, etc., 400; (in indir. interr., with gen.), hwæt . . . þậs, 532, 608, 1165; hwæt þæs wậre dryhtnes willa, 1160; hwæt þậr eallra wæs ou manrîme morð̄orslehtes, dareð̄-lâcendra dêadra gefeallen, 649; (in dir. interr.), hwæt is þis, 903; (interjection), forsooth! indeed! how! etc., 293, 334, [357], 364, 397, 670, 853, 920.

hwæt (sharp), bold, brave; hwate wêras, 22.

hwætêadig, rich in courage, very brave; sê hwætêadig, the brave man, 1195.

hwætmôd, bold in mind, courageous; hæleð̄ hwætmôde, 1006.

hwîl, f., while, time; sume hwile, somewhile (?), 479; acc. hwile nû, now for a while, 582, 625; dat. pl. hwilum, sometimes, once [1252].

hwît, white, 73.

hwonne, adv., when, until; bî-dan . . . hwonne, to wait . . . until, 254.

hwôpan, red. vb. (whoop), threaten with; acc. pers. and dat. of thing, þê elþêodige egesan hwô-pan, the enemies threaten thee with terror, 82.

hwurfe [629], excederet (Grimm).

hwylc, prn., which, what; on hwylcum þâra bêama, 851; on hwylcne, 862.

hwyrft, m., course; dat. pl. geâra hwyrftum, in the course of years, 1.

hycgan, wv. III., think, hope, [629].

hŷdan, wv. I., hide, conceal; p.p. hŷded, 218; hŷdde, 1108.

hŷð̄, f., harbor, haven; tô hŷð̄e, 258.

hyder, adv., hither; sume hyder, sume þyder, 548.

hyge, m., mind, heart, soul; hige onhyrded, the soul strengthened, 841; hlihende hyge, the rejoicing heart, 995; mîn hige, 1082; dat. sg. on heardum hige, in my hard heart, 809; on hyge, in thy heart, 1169; acc. sg. hyge, 685, 1094.

hygegômor, of sad heart, mournful, 1216; higegeômre, 1297.

hygerûn, f., heart's secret; hy-gerûne ne mâð̄, he did not keep back the secret of his heart, 1099.

hyht, m., hope, joy; acc. sg. heofonrices hyht (629?); hyht un-twêonde, an unwavering hope, 798; gen. pl. hyhta hîhst, the highest (of) joy(s), 197.

hyhtful, full of joy; ic þurh Iûdas ậr hyhtful gewearð̄, 923.

hyhtgifa, giver of joy (of Christ); hæleð̄a hyhtgifa, the mens' Giver of joy, 852.

hŷnð̄, or hŷnð̄o, oppression, affliction, misery; in hŷnð̄um, 210.

hŷran, wv. I. (1) hear, learn [1st p. pret. sg. hyrde, 240; pret. pl. hyrdon, 538, 672, 670, 853]. (2) hear, hearken, obey (with dat.) [heofoncyninge hŷran sceoldon, should hearken to the King of Heaven, 307; pret. sg. 2d p. þâm ðû hŷrdest ǽr, whom thou formerly obeyedst, 934; pret. pl. lârum ne hŷrdon, they did not obey the teachings, 839 (cf. 1210)].

hyrde, m. (-herd), keeper, guardian (Ger. hirt); þrymmes hyrde, 348, 859.

hyrst, f., armor; hyrstum gewerede, 263.

hyrwan, s. herwan.

hyse, m., youth, young man, son; hyse lêofesta, dearest son, 523.

I.

Ic, prn., I, 240, 288, 319, and often.

îcan, wv. I., eke, increase; îceð ealdne nîð, increases the old hate, 905.

ides, f., woman, wife, queen (of Helen), 405; dat. idese, 229; acc. sg. idese, 241.

Ierusalem, s. Hierusalem.

ilca, prn. (with def. art.), the same; þurh þâ ilcan gesceaft, 183; þæt ilce, 436.

ilde, s. elde.

In, prep. (1) with dat. *in* (in rîce, 9; in þrŷnesse þrymme, 177; in fŷrðe, 196; in hynðum, 210 [cf. 391, 412, 425, 484, and often]); *upon* (þone mæran dæg . . . in ðâm, that glorious day . . . upon which, 1224); *on, upon* (in cynestôle, on the throne, 330; in beorge, upon the mountain, 578). (2) (with acc.) *in, into* (in middangeard, 6, 775; in godes þêowdôm, 201, etc., 274, 305, 693, 765, 775, 931, 943, 944, 1026, 1089, 1205, 1287, 1297, 1290, 1302, 1303, 1305; in cildes hâd (â)cenned, 336, 776; in lêoht cymen,

to come to light: [temporal] in woruld weorulda, in the world of worlds [*i.e.* in eternity], 452; in hira lifes tîd, during their lifetime (s. note, 1209), 1209).

In, adv., *in* (bil in dufan, plunged the sword in, 122); *in, into* (êodon . . . in on þâ ceastre, they went [within] into the city, 846).

inbryrdan, s. onbryrdan.

ingemynd, f., n., inward thought, ardent thought, 1253.

ingemynde, impressed; on ferðsefan ingemynde, impressed upon the minds, 896.

ingeþanc, m., inner thought, earnest thought; feores ingeþanc, 680.

innoð, inner parts, breast; æðelne innoð, the noble breast, 1146.

innan, adv., within (on innan); prep. with dat. within, in (burgum on innan, within the cities, 1057).

instæpes, adv., on the spot, immediately, 127.

inwit, n., iniquity; þurh inwit, through wickedness, 207.

inwitþanc, m., wicked thought; inwitþancum wrôht webbedan, wove crime with wicked thoughts, 308.

inwrêon, s. onwreon.

Ioseph, Joseph; bân Iosephes, Joseph's bones, 788.

is, 3d p. sg. pres. *is*, 426, 465, 512, 553, 591, 593, 633, 636, 643, 703, 750–752, 771, 822, 903, 906, 917, 918, 1123, 1168, 1264, 1265.

Israhêlas, pl. Israelites; gen. pl. Israhêla, 338, 361, 433, 800.

Iûdas, (1) Judas Iscariot, 922; (2) Judas (afterwards Cyriacus), 418, 586, 600, 609, 627, 655, 667, 682, 807, 860, 875, 924, 935, 1033, 1056 (undeclined).

Iûdêas, pl. Jews; gen. pl. Iûdêa, 206, 268, 837; dat. pl. Iûdêum, 216, 328, 977, 1203; acc. Iudeas, 278.

îwan, wv. I., show [842].

K.

kalendas, pl., calends, first day of the Roman month; on maias kalendas, on the calends of May, 1229 (s. note, 1229).

L.

lâ, interj., lo! behold! forsooth! 903.

lâc, n., gift, present; acc. lîc, 1137; dat. tô lâce, as a present, 1200.

lâcan, red. vb., spring, jump; (of flames) flicker, flare (lâcende lîg, flaring flame, 580, 1111); fly (lâcende fêond, flying enemy [of devil], 900).

lâð, loathsome, loathed, hated; geletest lâð werod, thou shalt hinder the hated crowd, 92; gen. pl. lâðra lindwered, the shield-bearing band of the loathed, 142; dat. pl. lâðum on lâste, behind the loathed ones, 32; superl. wyrda lâðost, the most detested of occurrences, 978.

lædan, wv. I., lead, 241, 691; lead, hold (sê ðe foran lædeð brîdels on blancan, who holds in front the bridle on the white horse, 1184); spread (wîde læded, spread far, 969).

laðian, wv. II., invite, summon; 3d p. sg. pres. laðað, 551; p.p. laðode, 383; laðod, 556.

lâðlic, loathsome, hateful; lâðlic wîte, hated punishment, 520.

lago, m., lake, sea, ocean, name of the rune for l (ᚱ), 1260.

lagofæsten, n., water-fastness, sea; ofer lagofæsten, 249; ofer lagufæsten, 1017.

lagostrêam, m., water-stream, (of Danube) river; on lagostrêame, 137.

lama, m., a lame person; pl. laman, the lame, 1214.

laud, n., land; acc. land, 270 (on Creca land, 256, 262, 999); land (earth) (landes frætwe, ornament of the land, 1271).

læne, lent, transitory, 1271.

lang, long, 432.

lange, adv., long, 602, 723, 793, 1119; comp. leng, 576, 702, 706, 907.

lâr, f. (lore), teaching, instruction, doctrine (acc. lâre, 335, 368, 388, 432, 929; dat. pl. lârum, 839, 1210); instruction, advice, information (lâre, 1166, 1246; dat. sg. tô lâre, 286); advice, instigation (dat. pl. Sawles larum, at the instigation of Saul, 497).

læran, wv. I., teach (Ger. lehren), instruct (pret. sg. lærde, 529:) p.p. lærde, 173, 191; exhort, urge (1st p. sg. pres. lære, 522; læran, 1206).

lârsmið, m., teacher; þurh lârsmiðas, 203.

læs, adv., less; (conj.) þŷ læs, lest; (with opt.) þŷ læs tôworpen sîen, lest there be destroyed, etc., 430.

læssa, comp., less; werod læsse, less men, 48.

lâst, m., trace, track (cf. shoe-last); on lâste, = behind; lâðum on lâste, 30.

læstan, wv. I., perform, carry out, follow; lâre læstan, to follow the teaching, 368.

lǽtan, red. vb., let, allow, cause; imper. lǽt mec ... wunigan, let me dwell, etc., 819; pret. sg. leort ðâ tâcen forð ... ûp êðigean, He caused the sign to ascend, 1105; pret. pl. lêton ... scrîðan, they let ... stride, 235; cêolas lêton æt sǽfearoðe ... bîdan, they let the ship await at the seashore, etc., 250.

late, adv., late, 708.

lâttêow, m., leader; lîfes lâttîow, 520, 899; gen. sg. lâttêowes, 1210.

lêaf, n., leaf, foliage; under lêafum, 1227.

leahtor, m., reproach, sin; leahtra fruman lârum, to the teachings of the source of sins, 839.

leahtorlêas, sinless, 1209.

lêan, n., reward, gift; wîgges lêan, a warrior's reward, 825.

lêas, loose, free (with gen.), 422, 497, 778; free, deprived, robbed (with gen.) (duguða lêas, bereft of joy, 693; dômes lêasne, robbed of happiness, 945), loose, false (lêase lêodhatan, the false haters of men, 1300).

lêas, n., falsehood, lying, 580; dat. sg. lêase, 576.

lêasing, f., lie; lêasunga, 689; mid lêasingum, 1123.

lêasspell, n., false news, [580].

lef, weak, feeble, 1214.

lêgen, flaming, fiery; lêgene sweorde, with fiery sword, 757.

leger, n. (cf. lair), lying-place, bed, couch; in legere, in its bed, 602; legere fǽst, 723; lîc legere fǽst, the body fast on its couch (i.e. dead), 883.

lencten, m., spring (lent), 1227 (s. note, 1227).

leng, s. **lange**.

lêod, f. pl., men, people; leode, 20, 128, 163, 208, 1111; leoda, 181, 285; leodum, 666, 723.

lêodfruma, m., prince of the people (of Constantine), 191.

lêodgebyrga, people's protector (of Constantine), (11), 203; lêodgebyrgean (of representative), Jews, 536.

lêodhata, m., hater of the people; lêase lêodhatan, the false haters of men, 1300.

lêodhwæt, very valiant, [11].

lêodmæg, relation of the same people, one of the people, people's companion; lêodmǽga, 380.

lêoðrûn, f., song-secret, secret instruction; þurh lêoðrûne, 522.

lêoðucræft, m., art of poetry; lêoðcræft onlêac, opened up the art of poetry, 1251.

lêof, dear, valued, 1036, 1048; wk. nom. m. lêofa, 511; neut. lêofre, = pleasant, 606; gen. pl. lêofra, 1206; superl. leofesta, 523.

leofað, s. **lifgan**.

lêoflic, lovely; lêoflic wîf, 286.

lêofspell, n., dear news; lêofspell manig, many a message of love, 1017.

lêoht, bright, light, illuminating, beautiful, 163; lêohtne gelêafan, 491; þurh lêohtne hâd, 1246; mid þâ lêohtan gedryht, 737; lêohte gelêafan, 1137.

leoht, light; him wæs leoht sefa, his heart was light, 173.

lêoht, n., light, 7, 94, 1045 (?); (of Christ) ealles lêohtes lêoht, 486; acc. lêoht, 298, 307, 1123; instr. lêohte, 734; gen. pl. lêohta, 948.

lêohte, adv., brightly, clearly, 92, 966, 1116.

lêoma, m., ray of light, light,

glare; êldes lôoma, fire's glare, 1294.

leomu, s. **lim.**

lcornian, wv. II., learn; pret. pl. leornedon, 397.

leornungcræft, m., learning, 380.

lcort, s. lætan, 1105.

lesan, sv. V., collect; wundrum læs, I collected (it) wonderfully, 1238.

libban, wv. I., live; lifdon, 311.

lîc, n., body; life belidenes lîc, body robbed of life (corpse), 877; lîc legere fæst, body fast on the couch (corpse), 883.

lîcgan, sv. V., lie, [921].

lîchoma, m., body (home of the soul); in lichoman, in the fleshly tabernacle, 737.

lîf, n., life, 526, 606; gen. sg. lifes, 137, [518], 520, 664, 706, 757, 793, 899, 1027, 1209; dat. sg. life, 575, 878; acc. sg. lîf, 305, 622, 1046.

lîfdæg, m., day of life; gif þê þæt gelimpe on lifdagum, if this happen to thee in the days of thy life, 441.

lîffruma, m., author of life (of Christ), 335.

lîfgan, wv. II., live; leofað, 450; lifgende, alive, 486.

lîfwcard, m., lifewarden, guardian of life (of Christ), 1036.

lîfwyn, f., joy of life; lifwynne, with the joy of living, 1269.

lîg, m., fire, flame; lâcende lîg, 580, 1111; lige befæsled, 1300.

lîgewalu, f., fiery torment; fram lîgewale, from the torture of fire, 296.

lîge, m., lie, 575; acc. lige, 307; dat. on lige, 666.

lîgesearu, n., lying cunning;

lígesearwum, with lying deceptions, 208.

lígesynnig, sinning by lies, lying; ligesynnig . . . fêond, 899.

lim, n., limb; pl. leomu; leomu côlodon, the limbs were cold, 883.

limsêoc, limb-sick, lame, 1214.

lindgeborga, m., protector armed with a shield, [11].

lindhwæt, valiant with the shield; se lindhwata lêodgebyrga, the protector of the people, valiant with the shield, (11).

lindwered, n., troops armed with shields; shield-bearing band, 142.

lindwîgend, m., shield-warrior; hêape gecoste lindwîgendra, with a chosen band of shield-bearing warriors, 270.

lîxan, wv. I., shine, glitter, glisten; pret. pl. gâras lixtan, 23, 125; gimmas lîxtan, 90; næglas . . . lixton, 1116.

loc, n., lock; locum belûcan, to lock up with locks, 1027.

loca, m., imprisonment, snare; of locan dêofla, from the devil's snares, 181.

lôcian, wv. II., look; pret. lôcade, 87.

lof, m., praise (with obj. gen.); Cristes lof, praise of Christ, 212; heofonciningos lof, 748; lof, 890.

lofian, wv. II., praise; lofiað, 453.

lûcan, sv. II., lock, enclose, set in gold; sincgim locen, 264.

lufe, f., love; lufan dryhtnes, 948, 1206; for lufan, for the love of, for the sake of; for dryhtnes lufan, for the Lord's sake, 491; for sawla lufan, for the love of souls, 564.

lufian, wv. II., love; swâ þin môd lufaþ, as thy heart desireth, 597.

lufu, f., love; fŷrhât lufu, ardent love, 937.

lungre, adv., soon; forthwith, 30, 368.

lust, m., pleasure, joy (Ger. lust) (cf. lust); on luste, = rejoiced,138; with joy, 261; lustrum, willingly, 702; with pleasure, 1251.

lyft, m., f., air (Ger. luft); under lyfte, 1271; geond lyft, 734; on lyft, 900.

lyftlâcende, floating in the air, 796.

lŷsan, wv., loose, release; lŷsan . . . of hæftnêde, to release from bondage, 296.

lŷt, little, few; (with gen.) hæfde wigena tô lŷt, he had too few warriors, 63.

lŷtel, little; on swâ lŷttum fæce, in such a little while, 960; ymb lŷtel fæc, 272, 383; adv. nû lŷtle âr, now a little before, 664.

lŷthwôn, little, but few; lŷthwôn becwom Hûna herges hâm,but few of the army of the Huns reached home, 142.

M.

mâ (s. mûra, comp. from micel), more, 634; more, hereafter, 817; more, longer, 434.

maðelian, wv. II., speak, harangue; pret. sg. maþelode, 332, 604, 685, 807; maþelade, 404, 573, 627, 642, 655.

mâðum, m., treasure, object of value; þeah he . . . maðmas þege, though he received the treasures, 1259.

mæg, f., kinsman, relation; câseres mæg, 330, 669.

magan, pret. pres. can, be able;

ic mæg, 632, 635, 702, 705; ðû meaht, 511; hê mæg, 448, 466, 588, 611, 735, 770; pl. magon, 582, 583, 1291; opt. mæge, 677, 1178; pret. sg. meahte, 33, 160, 243, 609, 860, 1159; pret. pl. meahton, 166, 324, 477, 979.

mægen, n., strength, power, might, 698; instr. mægene, 1223; acc. mægn, 408; gen. pl. mægena, 347, 810; troop, multitude, army, 55, 61, 138, 233, 283, 1293; acc., 242.

mægencyning, m., mighty king, 1248.

mægenþrym, m., mighty strength, great glory; mycle mægenþrymme, with very great glory, 735.

maias, May; on maias kalendas, 1229.

mæl, n., time; âr fœla mæla, a long time before, 987 (s. note, 987).

mælan, wv. I., speak; wordum mælde, 351; wordum mældon, 537.

man, n., man, person, 467; mannes, 660; man, 872; gen. pl. manna, 326, 735, 923, 1229, 1312; dat. pl. mannum, 16, 626; indef. prn., one, 358, 711, 755.

mân, n., wickedness, crime; mâne gemengde, 1296; þurh morðres mân, 626; gen. pl. mâna gehwylc, 1317.

mânfrêa, m., criminal lord; morðres mânfrêa, the wicked prince of murder (i.e. devil), 942.

mânfremmende, sin-committing; sâwla . . . mânfremmende, sin-committing souls, 907.

maneg, many (attrib.), 231, 258, 1017; monige, 499; manegum, 15; (subst.) manegum, 501; manigum, 970, 1176.

manrîm, n., number of men; on manrîme, 650.

mânweorc, sinful; mê . . . swâ manweorcum, to me . . . so sinful, 812.

mânþêaw, m., sinful custom; ond manþêawum mînum folgaþ, and follows my sinful usages, 930.

manþêaw, m., man's habit, custom, 930 (?).

mǣrð, f., glory; mǣrðum ond mihtum, with glory and power, 15; mǣrðum, with glory, gloriously, 871.

mǣre, bright, glorious, 970 (gen. sg. þǣre mǣran byrig, 864; acc. sg. ymb þæt mǣre trêo, 214; þurh þâ mǣran word, 990; þurh þâ mǣran miht, 1242; ymb þâ mǣran wyrd, 1064; superl. mǣrost bêama, 1013, 1225); known, well known, 1177; well known, renowned (mihtum mǣre, renowned in power, 340; þone mǣran dæg, 1223).

Mâria, Mary; mid Mârian, 1233; þurh Mârian, 775.

mǣst (superl. from micel), most, greatest (with gen.), 31, 35, 196, 977, 984, 993; pl. mǣste, 274; (attrib.), mǣste-snyttro, 381, 408.

mê, me, to me (dat.), 163, 164, 317, 375, 409, 462, 679, 812, 912, 1074; me (acc.), 361, 700, 920; mec, 469, 528, 819, 910, 1078.

meaht, mealte, s. magan.

mear, s. mearh.

mearcpæð, n., mark-path, path running through the marks, 233 (see note, 233).

mearh, m., horse (cf. mare), 55, 1193; dat. meare, 1176.

mec, s. mê.

mêðe, weary, tired (mêðc ond metelêas, 612, 698), miserable (mê swâ mêðum, to me so miserable, 812).

meðel, n., council, assembly (on meðle, 546, 593), speech (to God), prayer (on meðle, in prayer, 786).

meðelhêgende, holding conclave, deliberating, 279.

meðelstede, m., place of assembly, council-chamber; on meðelstede, 554.

medoheal, f., mead-hall; in medohealle, 1259.

melda, m., informer, betrayer; þæs morðes meldan, betrayers of the murder, 428.

mengan, wv. I., mingle; mengan ongunnon, mingled, confounded, 306.

mengo, f., many, multitude; dat. mengo, 377, 596; mengu, 225; menigo, 871.

mennisc, human; þurh mennisc, hêo, in human form, 6.

meotod, m., Creator, 366; meotud, 1040; metud, 819; gen. sg. meotodes, 686, 986; meotudes, 461, 474, 564; metudes, 1313.

merestrǣt, f., sea-street, seaway, 242.

metan, sv. V., mete, measure, traverse; þær him eh fore mîlpaðas mǣt, where the horse once traversed with him the mile-paths, 1263.

mêtan, wv. I., meet, find; pret. sg. mêtte, 833; pret. pl. mêtton, 116; p.p. mêted, 986.

metelêas, without food; mêðe ond metelêas, 612, 698.

metud, s. meotod.

micel, great; mycel, 426, 646; þurh þâ myclan miht, 597; instr. mycle mægenþrymme, 755; dat. pl. ôfstum myclum, with great haste, 44, 102, 1000; myclum, adv., greatly, 876.

mid, prep. (1) with dat. or instr.,

with, 105, 377, 577, 622, 707, 714, 742, 805, 821, 843, 844, 854, 865, 1025, 1067, 1123; *among*, 328, 407, [451], 1203; mid Marian, 1233. (2) with instr. mid þŷs bêacne, 92; mid þŷ, 1178; *among* (mid þŷ folce, 891). (3) with acc., *with* (mid þâ æðelan cwên, 275; mid horu, 297; mid sigecwên, 998; mid þâ lêohtan gedryht, into the presence of the brilliant hosts, 737).

miðan, sv. I., conceal, keep secret; pret. sg. wælrûne ne mâð, he did not conceal the battle secret, 28; hygerûne ne mâð, he did not keep back the secret of his heart, 1099.

middangeard, m. (middle world), world, earth; gen. sg. middangeardes, 810; acc. in middangeard, 6, 775; geond ——, 16, 1177, ofer ——, 434, 918.

middel, m., middle; in þâm midle þrêad, punished in the middle (of the purgatorial fire), 1296; on þone middel, 864.

midl, n., bit of a bridle, 1176, 1193.

miht, f., might, power; dat. sg. mihte, 584, 1163; acc. sg. miht, 295, 310, 558, 597, 727, 1242; gen. pl. mihta, 337, 366, 786, 819, 1043; dat. pl. mihtum, 15, 340, 1070, 1100.

mihtig, mighty, 680, 1068; se mihtiga cyning, 942.

milde, mild, gracious, 1043, 1317.

mîlpæð, mile-path; mîlpaðas mæt, 1263.

milts, f., mercy, 501.

mîn, prn. (gen. of ic), of me; mîn on þâ swîðran, on the right of me, 347.

mîn, poss. prn., my, mine, 163, 349, 436, etc.

môd, n., mood, spirit, soul, heart, 597, 990, 1064; gen. sg. môdes snyttro, 554; on môdes þeaht, 1242; dat. môde, 268, 629 (?), 1223.

môdblind, blind in heart, 306.

môdcræft, m., mood-craft, power of mind, 408.

môdcewânlg, sad at heart, sorrowful, 377.

môdeg, s. **môdig**.

môdgemynd, f., n., memory; þurh môdgemynd, 380; heart, 840.

môdgeþanc, m., thought of the heart, inmost thought; môdgeþanc mînne cunnon, you know my inmost thought, 535.

môdig, spirited, proud, brave, 1263; môdigra mægen, 138, 1293; mearh under môdegum, midlum geweorðod, among the courageous, the horse adorned with the bit, 1193.

modor, f., mother, 214, 340.

môdsefa, m., mind, heart; on môdsefan, 876.

môdsorg, f., heart-sorrow; môdsorge wæg ... cyning, grief of heart experienced the king, 61.

molde, earth, mould; mearh moldan træd, the horse trod the earth, 55.

moldweg, m., way upon the earth, earth; on moldwege, 467.

monig, s. **maneg**.

monigfeald, manifold; swâ monigfeald, such manifold things, 644.

morðor, n., murder, violent death, deadly sin; morðres, 428, 626, 942.

morðorhof, n., place of punishment (murder-court); of þâm mordorhofe (of hell), 1303.

morðorsleht, m., slaughter; morðorslehtes, 650.

morgenspel, n., morning news; mære morgenspel, the happy news of morning, 970.

môrland, n., moorland, 612.

môtan, pret. pres., may, be allowed, etc.; 3d p. sg. môt, 916; pl. môton, 906, 1307, 1315; opt. môten, 433; pret. pl. môston, 175, 1005.

Moyses, Moses, 283, 337; dat. Moyse, 366; acc. Moyses, 786.

mûð, m., month; þurh æniges mannes mûð, 660; þurh þæs dêman mûð, 1283.

mund, f., hand; mundum þînum, with Thy hands, 730.

mycel, s. micel.

myndgian, wv., II. remember; wê þæs hereweorces ... myndgiaþ, we remember this work of the army, 657.

mynglan, wv. II., remind; mec þæra nægla ... fyrwet myngaþ, desire of knowledge reminds me of these nails, 1079.

myrgan, wv. I., be merry, "rejoice," (Kemble), [244].

N.

næfre, adv., never, 388, 468, 538, 659, 778.

nâgan, pret. pres, not have; pret. pl. nâhton foreþancas, they had not forethought, 356.

nægel, m., nail; pl. n. and a. næglas, 1109, 1115, 1158, 1173; gen. pl. nægla, 108, 1078; dat. pl. næglum, 1065, 1103, 1128.

nales, adv., not at all, by no means, 359, 470, 1253; nalles, 818, 1134.

nama, m., name, 418, 437, 530, 586, 750, 1061; naman, 465, 503; be naman, by name, 74, 505, 756.

nænig, m., no one, none, 505.

nære = ne wære, was not; þæs twêo nære, of this there was no doubt, 171; gif hê þin nære sunu, if he were not Thy son, 777.

næs = ne wæs, was not; næs; næs . . . gâd, 991.

næs, m., ness (naze), headland, promontory; under nêolum niðer næsse, under the steep descending cliff, 832.

nât = ne wât, not know; þæt ic nât, which I do not know, 640.

nâthwylc, indef. prn. (I know not which), some, some one or other, 73.

Nazareð, Nazareth, 913; in Nazareð, 913.

ne (adv.), not (non), 28, 62, 81, 166, 219, etc.

nê (conj.), and not, nor (nec), 167, 221, 240, 399, 524, 567, 684, 860; nê . . . nê, neither . . . nor, 572.

neah, adv., enough, sufficiently, continually; neah myndgaþ, we remember continually, 657.

nêah, near; superl. nihst, nearest, last, [197].

nêah, adv., near; êgstrêame neah, 66.

nêan, from near, near by, nearly, [657].

nearo, f., narrowness, restraint, oppression, embarrassment (nîwan on nearwe, in this new embarrassment, 1103; nihtes nearwe, in the oppression at night, 1240?), narrow room, prison (of nearwe, 711), hiding-place, concealment (of nearwe, 1115).

nearolic, narrow, oppressive; nîða nearolicra, oppressive enmity, 913.

nearusearu, f., secret cunning, intrigue; þurh nearusearu, 1109.

nearusorg, f., crushing sorrow; nearusorg drûah, suffered the crushing sorrow, 1261.

nearwe, adv., narrowly, exactly, 1158, 1276.

nêat, n., neat-cattle, ox, etc.; þa wêregan nêat, 357.

nêawest, f., vicinity, neighborhood; on nêaweste, 67, 874.

nêd, s. nŷd.

nêgan, wv. I., approach, address; wordum nêgan, 287, 559.

nemnan, wv. I., name; pret. nemde, 78, 1060; p.p. nemned, 1195.

neoðan, adv., beneath, 1115.

nêol, steep, deep; under nêolum niðer næsse, under the steep-descending naze, 832.

nêolnes, depth, abyss; in nêolnesse nyðer bescûfeð, hurleth down into the depth, 943.

neorxnawang, m., paradise, 756 (s. note, 756).

nêosan, wv. I. (with gen.), visit, go to; burga nêosan, 152.

nêowe, s. nîwe.

nergend, nerigend (saving), saviour, deliverer (of God), 503, 1086 (nerigend), 1173; (of Christ), 461, 465, 799, 1065 (nerigend), 1078.

nesan, sv. V., endure, survive, 1004 (s. note, 1004).

nêsan = nêosan, wv. I., visit, [1004].

nið, m., man, person; pl. gen. niða, 465, 503, 1086.

nið, strife, violence, enmity, hostile acts; acc. hîe wið godes beam nið âhôfun, they stirred up strife against the Son of God, 838; ealdne nið, old feud, 905; gen. pl. niða

nearolîcra, oppressive acts of hostility, 913.

niðer, adv., nether, downward, down, 832; nyðer, 943.

niðheard, brave in strife, 195.

nigoða, ninth; wæs þû nigoðe tîd, it was the ninth hour, 874; oð þâ nigoðan tîd, until, etc., 870.

nîhst, s. neah.

niht, f., night; pl. þrêo niht, 483; .vii. nihta fyrst, 694; bûtan .vi. nihtum, 1228; adv. gen. nihtes, by night (cf. Ger. nachts), 198, 1240.

nihthelm, m., helmet of night, darkness; nihthelm tôglâd, the helmet of night fell apart, 78 (s. note, 78).

nihtlang, lasting the night; nihtlangne fyrst, for the space of the night, 67.

niman, sv. IV., take; þæt hê þone stân nime, that he should take the stone, 615; þe on gemynd nime, who takes in mind, remembers, 1233; take away, snatch away; tîonlêg nimeð, the destructive flame snatcheth away, etc., 1279; ær þec swylt nime, ere death snatch thee away, 447 (cf. 676).

nîod, f., eagerness, zeal, purpose, [629].

nis = ne is, is not, 911.

nîwe, new, 195; niwan stefne, 1061, 1128; nîwan on nearwe, 1103; nêowne gefean, 870.

nîwigan, wv. II., renew, 941.

nô, adv., never, not at all, by no means, 780, 838, 1083, 1302.

noldon = ne woldon, did not wish, 566.

nû, adv., now, 313, 372, 388, 406, 426, etc.; (strengthened), nûþâ, bûtan þec (hêr) nûþâ, 539, 661; (conj.), inasmuch as, since, now that, 534, 635, 702, 815, 908, 1171.

nûþâ, s. nû.

nŷdcleofa, m., prison, dungeon; of nŷdcleofan, 711; in nêdcleofan, 1276.

nŷðer, s. nîðer.

nŷdgeféra, m., companion in (time of) need; ŷr gnornode nŷd-geféra, the bow bemoaned its companion in need, 1261.

nŷdþearf, f., need, necessity; for nŷdþearfe, out of necessity, 657.

nysse = ne wisse, nyste = ne wiste (S. 420), did not know, 1240, 719.

nyton = ne witon, do not know, 401.

O.

ôð, prep. with acc. (temporal), until, 139, 312, 590, 870; ôð þæt, until then, 1257; conj., until, 866, 886.

oððe, or, 74, 159, 508, 634, 975, 1114.

ôðer, prn., other, 506; æfter ôðrum, 233; ôðerne, 540, 928.

ôðfæsten, wv. I., inflict upon; him . . . déað ôðfæsten, to inflict death upon him, 477.

œðil = êðel, (1260 ?).

ôðŷwan, wv. I., show, appear; pret. ôðŷwde, appeared, 163.

of, prep. with dat. (instr.), of, out of, from (separation), 75, 181, 186, 187, 282, 295, 297, 303, 440, 482, 700, 711, 715, 736, 762, 780, 794, 803, 845, 1226, 1303, 1305, (source), 915, 1023, 1087, 1113, 1115.

ofen, m., oven, furnace; þurh ofnes fŷr, through the fire of the furnace, 1311.

ofer, prep. with dat., over; ofer þâm æðelestan engelcynne, 733; with acc., over, 31, 118, 158, 233, 237, 244, 249, 255, 269, 385, 881, 918, 981, 983, 996, 997, 1017, 1133, 1135, 1201; over, upon, 89, 230, 434, 1289; ofer riht godes, against the truth of God, 372; ofer þæt, after that, 432, 448.

ofermægen, n., over-might, superiority, greater number, 64.

oferswîðan, wv. I., overcome, 1178; oferswîðeð, 93; oferswî-ðedne, 958.

oferwealdend, m., highest lord, sovereign (of Christ); se rîcesða ealles ofer wealdend, the mightiest Sovereign of all, 1236.

oferþearf, f., great need; for oferþearfe ilda cynnes, on account of the great need of mankind, 521.

ofost, f., haste; ofstum myclum, with great haste, 44, 102, 1000.

ofstlîce, adv., hastily, with haste, 225, 713, 1197.

oft, adv., often, 238, 301, 386, 471, 513, 1141, 1213, 1253.

on, prep. with dat. (instr.), on, 37, 59, 101, 232, etc.; in (on rîme, in number, 284 [cf. 650]); on, upon, 126, 133, 241, 242, 253, etc.; in (circumstantial), 28, 36, 53, 67, 69, 70, etc.; among, 754, 820 (on gesyhðe [s. gesyhð]; on .xx. fôtmælum feor, at a distance of twenty feet, 830); in (temporal), 105, 398, 441, 528, 571, 638, 639, 960, 1288; with acc., on, 179, 206, 250, etc.; upon, 84, 117, 717, etc.; to, in, into, 96, 134, 262, 291, etc. (on willsîð, for the journey, 223; on healfa gehwæne, on every side, 548 [cf. 955, 1180]; on unriht, wrongly, 582; [temporal], in his dagana tîd, during the period of his days, 193; on þone seofeðan dæg, on the seventh day, 697; on þâ æðelan tîd, in that glorious day, 787; on þâ slîðan tîd, at that dreadful hour, 857; on maias kalendas, on the calends of May, 1229, [cf. innan and gemang]).

onǽlan, wv. I., set fire to, inflame, burn; âde onǽled, burnt by the fire, 951.

onbindan, sv. III., unbind, loose; bâncofan onband, unbound my body, 1250 (s. note, 1250).

onbregdan, sv. III., start up; hê of slǽpe onbrægd, he started up out of his sleep, 75.

onbryrdan, wv. I., excite, inspire; p.p. onbryrded, 1095; inbryrded, 842, 1046.

oncnâwan, red. vb., know, perceive, recognize, acknowledge, [229], 302, 395; pret. oncnêow, 966.

oncnâwe, "cognitus," (Gm.), oncnǽwe, "declared" (K.), [229]. Does this word occur anywhere?

oncor, m., anchor; oncrum fæste, made fast with anchors, 252.

oncweðan, sv. V., answer, 324; pret. oncwæð, 573, 669, 682, 935, 1167.

oncýðig, [sorrowful, 725] (cf. uncýðig).

oncyrran, wv. I., turn, change (naman oncyrde, changed his name, 503); turn away, avert (oncyrran rex geniðlau, avert the enmity of the ruler, 610.

ond (so written, 931, 977, 984, 1210,—otherwise abbreviated), and (never written and, Zupitza).

ondrǽdan, red. v., fear; ne ondrǽd þû ðê, do not fear, 81.

onfôn, red. vb., receive, take, with acc., gen., dat. (instr.); pret.

sg. fulwihte onfêng, 192; swengas, 238; fulwihtes bæð, 490, 1033; þâm nǽglum, 1128; pret. pl. lâre on fêngon, 335.

ongeân (ongên), prep. with dat., against (ongean gramum, 43; hire ongên þingode, spoke to her, 609, 667 [post positive]).

onginnan, sv. III., begin, with inf. (often best translated by the historical aorist of the inf.); pret. sg. ongan, 157, 198, 225, 283, 384, 558, 570, 696, 828, 850, 901, 1068, 1094, 1148, 1156, 1164, 1205; pret. pl. ongunnon, 303, 306, 311; with acc., begin, institute, 468.

ongitan, sv. V., understand, perceive, recognize (ongitaþ, 359); impera. ongit, 464; p.p. ongiten, 288.

onhyldan, wv. I., bow; hleor onhylde, he bowed his face (lit., cheek), 1099.

onhyrdan, wv. I., strengthened, encouraged; hige onhyrded þurh þæt hâlige trêo, 841.

onhyrtan, wv. I., "animare, recreare" (Gm.), [841].

onlêon, sv. I., lend, grant; dat. pers. and gen. rei, ǽr mê lâre onlag, before he granted me instruction, 1246.

onlîce, adv., like, 99.

onlûcan, sv. II., unlock, open; lêoðucræft onlêac, opened up the art of poetry, 1251.

onmêdla, m., haughtiness, pride, glory; ald onmêdla, 1266.

onscunian, wv. II., shun, fear, detest, despise; onscunedon þine scîran scrippend eallra, 370.

onsendan, wv. I., send (forð onsendan, 120; þine bêne onsend, send up thy prayer, 1089); send away, give up (on galgan his gâst onsende, He gave up His ghost on the cross, 480).

onsîon, s. onsŷn.

onspannan, red. v., unspan, unloose, open; hrêðerlocan onspêon, he opened his bosom, 86.

onsŷn, f., sight, face, countenance; fore onsŷne êces dêman, before the face of the Eternal Judge, 746; ic ne wende æfre tô aldre onsion mîne, I never turned my face to life (i.e. earthly things), 349.

ontŷnan, wv. I., open; pret. ontŷnde, 1249; p.p. ontŷned, 1230.

onwindan, sv. III., unwind, loosen, open; brêostlocan onwand, opened the bosom's enclosure, 1250.

onwrêon, sv. I. and II., uncover, discover, disclose, reveal, 589, 674; pret. sg. onwrâh, 1243; pret. opt. onwrige, 1072; p.p. onwrigen, 1124, 1254; with, 1072 (cf. inwrige, 813).

open, open, known; open ealdgewin, a known battle in olden times, 647.

ôr, [1266] (Leo, "geld").

orcnæwe, evident, well known, 229.

ord, m., point, point of a spear, spear (bord ond ord, 1187; bordum ond ordum, 235); beginning (fram [dæges] orde, 140, 590; æfter orde, 1155); first, chief, prince (of Christ) (æðelinga ord, 393).

ôwiht, aught, something; ôwiht swylces, anything at all of this sort, 571.

P.

Paulus, Paul; sanctus Paulus, 504.

plegean, pres. sv. V. (S. 391. 1),

pret. wv. II., move rapidly, play, prance (sæmearh plegean, the seahorse prance, 245); to move (the hands) rapidly, clap, applaud (hê mid bæm handum . . . ûpweard plegade, he clapped with both hands toward heaven, 806).

R.

râd, f., ride, expedition, journey; tô râde, for a journey, 982.

ræd, m., counsel, advice (rede) (hæleða rædas, the counsels of men, 156); foresight (rædes þearf, need of foresight, 553); power, might (mîn is geswiðrod ræd under roderum, my dominion under heaven is diminished, 919); advantage, weal (begra rædum, for the weal of both, 1009).

rædan, red. vb., advise, counsel; swâ hire gâsta weard reord of roderum, as the Guardian of spirits counselled her from heaven, 1023.

raðe = hraðe.

rædgeþeaht, f., counsel, consultation, deliberation, 1052, 1162.

rador, s. rodor.

rædþeahtende, taking counsel, sagacious, wise, 449, 869.

rand, m., border (of shield); þonne rand dynede, then the shield made a noise, 50.

ræran, wv. I. (rear), promote, stir up, enkindle; geflitu ræran, 443; sæce ræran, 941; geflitu rærdon, 954.

rêc, m., smoke, 795, 804.

reccan, wv. I., explain, expound, narrate, 281, 284; opt. pres. reccen, 553.

rêniend, m., arranger, [880].

reodian, wv. II., pass through a sieve, sift; geþanc reodode, sifted the thought, 1239.

rêonig, rêoni, sad, 1083; in þam rêonian hofe, in that sad court, 834.

rêonigmôd, sad-hearted, down-hearted, 320.

reordberend, endowed with speech, man; reordberenda, 1282.

reordian, wv. II., speak, say; reordode, 405, 417, 463, 1073 [speisen, Gm., 1239].

rêotan, sv. II., weep, mourn; rêonig rêoteð, mourneth in sadness, 1083.

rex (Lat.), king, ruler (of God), 1042; (of Helen), 610 (!).

rîce, n., might, power, dominion, 13, 449, 917; supremacy, victory, 147 (rices ne wênde, he did not hope for victory, 62); kingdom, empire, 1231 (rices, 59, 820; in rîce, 9; acc. rîce, 40, 631).

rîce, powerful, mighty; sîo rice cwên, 411; superl. se rîcesða ealles oferwealdend, the most powerful Sovereign of everything, 1235.

ricene, adv., instantly, at once, 607, 623, 982, 1162.

rîcsian, wv. II., be mighty, rule, 434; þæt rîcsie sê, that He rule, 774.

rîdan, sv. I., ride; pret. pl. ridon, they rode, 50.

riht, right, true, 13; þurh rihte æ, 281.

riht, n., right (ofer riht godes, against the right of God, 372); that which is right, true judgment, truth (rihtes wêmend, the discloser of truth, 880; rihte, 390, 663; ryhte, 369; riht, 601, 1241; sceall . . . riht gehŷran dæda gehwylcra, shall hear judgment for all deeds, 1282); right, possession (rihta gehwylces,

of every right, 910; ænige rihte, with any possession, 917).

rihte, adv., rightly, exactly, truthfully, 553, 566; ryhte, 1075.

rîm, n., number (geteled rîmes, 2; geteled rîme, 634); the number told (on rîme, 284; rîm, 635).

rîmtalu, f., number; on rîmtale rîces þînes, in the number of Thy kingdom, 820.

rinc, m., man, warrior, hero; pl. rincas, 46.

rôd, f., rood, cross, 219, 624, 720, 887, (973), 1012, 1224; gen. rôde, 147, 856, 1235; dat. rôde, 103, 206, 482, 601, 774, 1067, (1241); acc. rôde, 631, 919, 1023, 1075; gen. pl. rôda, 834, 869, 880.

roder, s. rodor.

rodor, m., heaven (rodora [radora] waldend, 206, 482, 1067; cyning on roderum, 460, 1075; fæder on roderum, 1151; of roderum, 762, 1023); heavens (rodor eal geswearc, 856; under radores ryne, 795; under radorum, 13, 46, 147, 631, 804, 919, 1235.

rodorcyning, m., King of heaven (of Christ); rodorcyninges bêam, 887; rôd . . . radorcyninges, 624.

rôf, strong, valiant, renowned, 50.

Rôm, f., Rome; Rôme bisceop, bishop of Rome, 1052.

Rômware, pl., Romans, 46; gen. Rômwara, 9, 40, 59, 62, 129; Rômwarena, 982.

rûm, roomy, wide, extensive; rûmran geþeaht, more extended knowledge, 1241.

rûn, f., mystery, secret (rune) (hâlige rûne, 333, 1169; enge rûne, 1262); (secret) council (êodon þâ fram rûne, 411; tô rûne, 1162).

ryht, ryhte, s. riht, rihte.

ryne, m., expanse; under radores ryne, under the expanse of the heavens, 795.

S.

sǽ, m., f., sea, ocean, 240; sǽs sidne fæðm, the sea's wide expanse, 720.

sæc, f., contest; æt sæcce, 1178, 1183, [1257].

sacan, sv. VI., contend, [1181].

sacerdhâd, m., priesthood; on sacerdhâd, 1055.

Sachîus, Sachias, 437.

sacu, f., contest, strife, war; þis is singal sacu, this is constant strife, 906; sæce, 1031; sæce rǽran, to stir up strife, 941.

sǽfearoð, m., sea-coast; æt sǽfearoðe sande bewrecene, in the sand-whipped sea-coast, 251.

sægde, s. secgan.

*__saglan,__ wv. II., say, tell; saga, 623, 857.

sǽl, m., f., happiness: on sǽlum = happy, 194.

sǽlan, wv. I., tie, bind, make fast with ropes (Ger. seilen); sǽlde, 228.

sǽlð, f., good fortune, prosperity, [1244].

Salomôn, Solomon; gen. Salomônes, 343.

salor, n. (?), hall, room, royal hall; tô salore, 382, 552.

same, adv., similarly; swâ some, = similarly, in like manner, 653, 1066, 1278; swâ same, 1207, 1284.

sǽmearh, m., sea-horse, ship, 245; pl. sǽmearas, 228.

samnian, wv. II., collect, assemble, gather; mægen samnode, 55;

werod samnode, 60; werod samnodan, 19.

samod, adv., together, simultaneously, (614), [620], 729, 889; somed, 95.

sâmwîslîce, adv., semi-wisely, half-wittedly, foolishly, [293].

sanctus (Lat.), saint; sanctus Paulus, 504.

sand, n., sand (shore), 251.

sǽne (with gen.), slow, slack, negligent; þæs sîðfates sǽne, neglectful of this journey, 220.

sang, m., song; earu sang âhôf, the eagle raised his song (= screech), 29; wulf sang âhôf, the wolf raised his song (= howl), 112; sang âhôfon, they raised a song, 868.

sâr, n., (sore), pain, sorrow; acc. sâr, 941; dat. pl. sârum, 479, 697, 933.

sâwl, f., soul, 890; gen. pl. sâwla, 461, 564, 799, 906, 1172.

sâwllêas, soulless, lifeless; sâwllêasne, 877.

Sawlus, Saul; Sawles lârum, at the instigation of Saul, 497.

sceacan, sv. IV., shake, move rapidly, escape, vanish; p.p. sceacen, 633.

sceâdan, red. vb., divide, separate, decide, rule; pret. scêad, 709.

sceaða, m., scather, injurious enemy; (of devils), scyldwyrcende sceaðan, the sin-committing foes, 762.

sceal, s. sculan.

scealc, m., slave, servant, subject; scealcas ne gældon, the subjects did not delay, 692.

sceamu, f., shame; sceame, 470.

sceat, m., corner, lap, bosom; under womma sceatum, in the bosom of sins, 583; (Grein), latebra, latibulum.

scêawian, wv. II., (show), see, behold; pret. sg. scêawode, 345; scêawedon, 58.

sceðð̄an, sv. VI. and wv. I., scathe, injure, oppress; êow sêo wergðu forðan sceðþeð scyldful-lum, for that reason this punishment oppresses you laden with guilt, 310, [709?].

[scênan? wv. I., "in die höhe heben (zeigen, scheinen machen), aber auch rütteln, schütteln" (Grimm), (151)].

sceolde, s. sculan.

sceolu, f., school, troop, (shoal), multitude, 763; ârlêasra sceolu, the throng of the godless, 836, 1301.

scînan, sv. I., shine, gleam; scînaþ, 743, 1319; scinende, 1115.

scippend, m., creator, 370; scyp-pend, 791.

scirian, wv. I., arrange in parts, determine; hira dǽl scired, 1232.

scîr, sheer, bright, clear, pure, 310, 370.

scrîðan, sv. I., stride, move; ofer fifelwǽg . . . scrîðan . . . brim-þisan, (they let) the rusher over the sea (= ships) stride (= move) over the sea, 237.

scrîfan, sv. I., determine, rule, [709].

scûfan, sv. II., push, throw; scûfan scyldigne . . . indrŷgne sêað, to throw the guilty one in the dry well, 692.

sculan, pret. pres., should, ought; 2d p. sg. scealt, 673; 3d p. sg. sceal, 545; pl. sceolon, 756; pret. sg. sceolde, 764, 1049; pret. pl. sceol-don, 367, 982; (with omission of infinitive), sceol, 1192; opt. pres. scyle, 896; sceoldon, 838; (para-

phrase of future), scealt cwylmed weorðan, thou shalt be tortured to death, 687; scealt . . . drêogan, 951; sceol . . . âwended weorðan, 580; sceal . . . þrowian, 768; sceall . . . weorðan, 1176; sceall . . . gehŷran, 1281; pl. sculon . . . drêogan, 210.

scûr, m., shower; flâna scûras, showers of arrows, 117.

scyld, f., debt, obligation, crime, sin (Ger. schuld); gen. pl. scylda, 470, 1313.

scyldful, f., full of guilt, laden with guilt; êow . . . scyldfallum, 310.

scyldig, guilty; scyldigne, 692.

scyldwyrcende, sin-committing, 762.

scyndan, wv. I., hurry, hasten; lungre scynde, hastened hurriedly, 30.

scyppend, s. scippend.

sê, prn. demonstrative, m., 465, 928, 1195; (f. sîo, sêo); n. þæt, 426, 456, 1050, etc.; gen. m. n. þæs, 39, 60, 86, etc.; (adverbial), so (inten-sive), 704; (conj.), for that reason, therefore, 210, 768; that, because, 812, 823, 963; gen. f. þǽre, 293, 610, etc.; dat. m. n. þâm, 70, 133, 146; dat. f. þǽre, 324, 545; acc. m. þane, 294; þone, 243, 302, etc.; acc. f. þâ, 98, 183, 274, etc.; acc. n. þæt, 107, 117, 128; instr. m. n. þŷ, 185, 485, 891, 1178; (before comparatives), the — þŷ blîþra, 96; þŷ fæstlîcor, 797; þê sorglêasra, 97; þê sêl, 796; þê gearwor, 946; (conj.), þŷ lǽs, in order that . . . not, that . . . not, lest, 430; pl. nom. acc. þâ, 153, 169, etc.; gen. þǽra, 285; þâra, 450, 470, 740, etc.; dat. þâm, 277, 754, etc. Prn. rel., m., sê, 243, 545, 1196; sê þe, 303, 774, 913, etc.; f. sîo, 709; n. þæt, 101; gen. m. n. þæs, 1251; (conj.), þæs þe, since, after (temporal), 4, 68; since, because, 957, 1140, 1317; dat. m. n. þâm, 421, 444, etc.; acc. m. þone, 423; acc. f. þâ, 398, 1235; pl. nom. acc. þâ, 172, 317, etc.; þû þe, 154, 280, etc.; gen. þæra, þâra þe, 508, 818, etc. (with sing. predicate), 975, 1226; dat. þâm. 354, 1067. *Art. def.*, m., se, 11, 42, 76, 87, etc.; (with vocative), hæled mîn se lêofa, 511; f. sio, 254, 378, 384, etc.; sêo, 266, 309, 558, etc.; n. þæt, 94, 272, etc.

sêaðˇ, m., well, cistern; in drŷgne sêaðˇ, into the dry cistern, 693.

searo, s. searu.

searu, n., plot, deceit; þurh feondes searu, 721.

searucræft, searo, m., artistic skill, art; searocræftum, 1026; [artifice, treachery, 721].

s e a r u þ a n c, m., ingenious thought, shrewdness, sagacity; searoþancum, in wise thoughts, 414; snottor searuþancum, wise in sage thoughts, 1190.

sêcan (sêcean), wv. I., seek, look for, inquire, 216, 420, (sêcean), 1149, 1157; sêcaþ, 1180; pret. pl. sôhton, 322, 414, 474; person, from whom something is sought, with dat. and tô (post positive); þe ic him tô sêce, 319, 410; him tô sôhte, 325, 568; seek, visit, 469, 598, (sêcean) 983.

secg, m., man, warrior, (1257); pl. secgas, 47, (secggas) 260, 552, 998, 1001; secga, 97, 271.

secgan, wv. I., say, inform, tell, (secggan) 160, 317, 376, 567, 574; secgaþ, 674; pret. sægdest, 665; sægde, 366, 437; sægdon, 190, 588, 1117.

sefa, m., mind, heart, 173, 627, 956, 1190; on sefan, 382, 474, 532, 1149, 1165; þurh sîdne sefan, through expanded mind, 376.

segn, m., token, field-ensign, banner (of cross), 124; (Lat. signum).

sêl, good (only in superl.); sêlest, 532, 1170; sêlost, 1165; âr sêlesta, 1088; sêlestan, 1019; (with following gen.), sêlust, 527; sêlest, 975, 1028; sêleste, 1202.

sêl, adv., comp. better; þê sêl, the better, 796; superl. sêlest, 374; sêlost, 1158.

self, s. sylf.

sellan, wv. I., give, grant; pret. sg. sealde, 182, 1171; p.p. seald, 527.

semninga, adv., immediately, forthwith, 1110, 1275.

sendan, wv. I., send; sendeðˇ, 931; pret. sende, 1200; þæt on þone hâlgan handa sendan . . . fæderas ûsse, that our fathers lay hands on this holy one, 457.

seoðˇðˇan, s. sîðˇðˇan.

seofeðˇa, seventh; on þone seofeðˇan dæg, on the seventh day, 697; seofon, seven; vii., (694).

scolf, s. sylf.

seolfren, (silvern), made of silver; in seolfren fæt, in a silver casket, 1026.

sêon, sv. V., see; pret. pl. sægon. seonoðˇdôm, m., synodal resolution, assembly's conclusions; seonoðˇdômas, 552.

seppan, or sêpan? wv. I., teach, instruct; septe sôðˇcwidum, taught with true speeches, 530.

seraphin, seraphim; þe man seraphin be naman hâteðˇ, 755.

settan, wv. I., set, put (on gewritu setton, put in writing, 654,

658); set, put, place (héo híe on cnéow sette, she put them on her knee, 1136; gesundne síð settan, make a prosperous voyage, 1005); count, reckon (þæt hê him þâ wéa-ðæd tô wræce ne sette, that he might not reckon this evil deed for vengeance against them, 495; sârum settan, persecute with pains, 479).

sib, s. syb.

sîd, wide, extended, large; ofer sîd weorod, among the large crowd, 158; ofer sîdne grund, over the wide earth, 1289; sæs sîdne fæðm, the ocean's wide expanse, 729; þurh sîdne sefan, through expanded mind, 376.

sîde, far; sîde ond wîde, far and wide, 277.

sîdweg, m., wide way, great distance; of sîdwegum, 282.

sîð, m., journey, voyage, expedition; sîðes, 247, 260, 1219; sîðe, 1001; sîð, 111, 243, 997, 1005.

sîð, adv., comp., later, afterwards; ær oððe sîð, 74 (cf. 975); sîð nê ær, 240 (cf. 572).

sîðdagas, pl. m., later days, later time; on sîðdagum, 639.

sîððan, syððan (sioððan, 1147), adv. dem., after that, afterwards, later, 271, [439], 481, 483, 504, 507, 518, 636, 639, 677, 926, 1028, 1060, 1147, 1302, 1315; rel. conj., since, when, as soon as, after, 17, 57, 116, 230, 248, 502, 842, 914, 1002, 1016, 1037, 1051.

sîðfæt, m., journey, voyage, 229; þæs sîðfates sæne, negligent of this expedition, 220.

sîðian, wv. II., journey, go; [sîðigean, 1107]; sîðode, 95.

*sîðmægen, n., [Grein, 26].

sîðwerod, n., [Körner, 26].

sîe, pres. opt. of subst. verb (S. 427), 542, 675, 773, 789, 799, 810, 817, 893, 1229; pl. sien, 430.

sige, m., victory, 144, (1181).

sigebêacen, n., beacon of victory, victory's sign (of the cross), 888; be þâm sigebêacne, 168, 1257; sêlest sigebêacna, 975.

sigebêam, m., tree of victory, cross; þæs sigebêames, 965; be þâm sigebêame, 420, 444, 665, 861; gen. pl. sêlest sigebêama, 1028; acc. pl. sigebêamas, 847.

sigebearn, n., child of victory, victorious son; (of Christ) sigebearn godes, 481, 863, 1147.

sigecwên, f., victorious queen (of Helen), 260, 998.

sigelêan, n., reward of victory; sêlust sigelêana, the best of the rewards of victory, 527.

sigelêoð, n., lay of victory, song of victory, 124.

sigerôf, famous for victory, strong in victory; sigerôf cyning, 158 (cf. 437); secgas sigerôfe, 41; sigerôfe, the renowned in victory, 868; sigerôfum, 71, 190.

sigespêd, f., victory, fortune in arms, 1172.

sigor, m., victory; gen. sg., sigores tâcen, 85, 104, 1121; acc. sigor æt sæcce, 1183; gen. pl. sigora dryhten, 346 (cf. 488, 732, 1140, 1308.

sigorbêacen, n., sign of victory (of cross), 985.

sigorcynn, n., victorious race; victorious beings (of angels), 755.

sigorlêan, n., reward of victory; sigorlêan in swegle, reward of victory in heaven, 623.

Siluester, Silvester; fram Siluestre, by Silvester, 190.

sîn, his, [438].

sinc, n., treasure, riches, gold; sinces brytta, dispenser of treasure, 194.

sincgim, m., valuable gem, jewel, 264.

sincweorðung, gift of treasure, gift; him Elene forgeaf sincweorðunga, Helen granted him gifts, 1219.

sindon, 1081; sint, 740, 744, 826; syndon, 754; synt, 605, 742, 1267; pl. pres. indic. of subst. verb.

sindrêam, m., everlasting joy; in sindrêame, 741.

singal, continual; þis is singal sacu, 906.

singallîce, adv., continuously, 747.

singan, sv. III., sing, (sound); singaþ, 747; sang, 337, 1189; sungon, 561; p.p. sungen, 1154; bŷman sungon, the trumpeters sounded, 109.

sint, s. sindon.

siomian, wv. II., tarry, linger; siomode in sorgum .vii. nihta fyrst, lingered in sorrow for the space of seven nights, 694.

sionoð, m., synod, assembly; tô sionoðe, 154.

sittan, sv. V., sit; þû sylf sitest, Thou Thyself sittest, 732.

six, s. syx.

slǣp, m., sleep; on slǣpe = asleep, 69; of slǣpe, out of sleep, 75.

slîðe, cruel, dire, dreadful; on þâ slîðan tîd, at that dire hour, 857.

smǣte, pure (of gold); swâ smǣte gold, as pure gold, 1309.

smêagan, wv. II., search into, reflect; georne smêadon, reflected earnestly, 413.

snoter, prudent, wise; snottor searuþancum, skilled in wise thoughts, 1190; super. þâm snoterestum, 277.

snûde, adv., quickly, swiftly, 154, 313, 446.

snyrgan, wv. I., hurry, hasten, 244.

snyttro, f., shrewdness, sagacity, wisdom, 154, 293, 313, 374, 382, 407, 544, 554, 938, 959, 1060, 1172.

sôð, sooth, true, 444, 461, 488, 564, 888, 1122; þone sôðan sunu wealdendes, 802; sôðra ... wundra, 778.

sôð, n., sooth, truth; dat. sôðe, 390, 603; wið sôðe, 307; acc. sôð, 395, 588, 690, 708, 1140; tô sôðe, in truth, truthfully, 160, 574; þurh sôð, in truth, verily, 808.

sôðcwide, m., true speech; septe sôðcwidum, taught in true speeches, 530.

sôðcyning, m., true king, 444.

sôðfæst, fast in truth, true; sôðfæste, 1289; sôðfæstra lêoht, 7.

sôðfæstnes, f., state of being grounded in truth, truthfulness, piety, justice; sôðfæstnesse sêcean, to seek piety, 1149.

sôðlîce, adv., truthfully, 317, 665; in truth, indeed, 799; indeed, verily, 200, 577.

sôðwundor, n., true miracle; sôðwundor godes, 1122.

some, s. same.

somed, s. samod.

sôna, adv., soon, forthwith, 47, 85, 222, 514, 713, 888, 1031.

sorg, f., sorrow, grief; dat. sg. sorge, 922, 1031; dat. pl. sorgum, 694, 1244.

sorgian, wv. II., sorrow; sorgað, 1082.

sorglêas, without sorrow, free from care; þê sorglêasra, the freer from care, 97.

spâld = spâdl,•spâtl, n., spittle, 300.

spêd, f., speed (Godspeed), success, good fortune; hê âh æt wigge spêd, he had success in battle; mihta spêd, fulness of powers, 366.

spêowan, wv. I., spew, spit; spêowdon, 297.

spild, m., destruction, annihilation; þurh dêofles spild, through the devil's destruction, 1119.

spôwan, red. vb., with instr., have success, be successful; ne môt ǣnige nû rihte spowan, I cannot now be successful with any right, 917.

sprecan, sv. V., speak; pret. sg. sprǣc, 332, 404, 725.

stæð, n., beach, shore (Ger. gestade), bank (of river), of Danube, 38, 60; ymb geofones stǣð, 227, (cf. 230).

staðelian, wv. II., found, fix, establish, make steadfast; opt. pres. staðelien, 427; ind. pres. staðelige, 797; staðolian, 1094.

stân, m., stone, 613; acc. 615; stâne, pl., 565; instr. pl. stânum, 492, 509.

stânclif, n., crag, cliff; æfter stânclifum, behind the cliffs, 135.

standan, sv. VI., stand; standaþ, 577; pret. pl. stôdon, 227, 232; stand forth, spread (hildegesa stôd, fear of battle spread, 113).

stângefôg, n., stone-fitting, stone-laying; stângefôgum, 1021.

stângripe, m., handful of stones, (Grim); dat. pl. stângreopum, 824.

stânhlið, n., rocky slope, cliff; under stânhleoðum, 653.

stærcedfyrhð, strong-minded, brave, 38.

stêam, m., steam, vapor, smoke; stêam ûp ârûs, the smoke arose, 803.

stearc, stark, stiff, stiff-necked, hard-headed; stearce, 565; streac ond hnesce, hard and soft, 615.

stede, m., stead, place, locality, region; stede ... ymb Danûbie, the region round the Danube, 135.

stedewang, m., field; æfter stedewange, on the field, 675, (cf. 1021).

stefn, f., voice; hǣdrum stefnum, 748; clǣnum stefnum, 750.

stefn, m., time (in multiplication); nîwan stefne, anew, again, 1061, 1128.

stênan, wv. I., decorate with stones (gems), 151.

Stephanus, Stephen, 492, 509, 824.

steppan, sv. VI., step, advance, storm; stôpon stîðhidige, the courageous stormed, 121; stôpon ... stîðhycgende, the steadfast in mind advanced, 716.

stîðhîdig, of determined mind, stout-hearted, courageous, 121.

stîðhycgende, stout-minded, steadfast in mind, 683, 716.

stôw, f., stow, place, spot, 675; dat. stôwe, 716, 803; acc. stôwe, 653, 683.

strang, strong, severe; tô ðan strang, so severe, 703.

streac, s. stearc.

strêam, m., stream, current; ofer geofenes strêam, over the sea's current, 1201.

strûdan, sv. II., spoil, rob, plunders; ǣhta strûdeð, despoils my possessions, 905.

stund, f., period, time (Ger.

stunde); dat. sg. stunde, at that time, 724; dat. pl. stundum, awhile (?), 121; stundum, from time to time, time and again, 232.

sum, indef. prn., some one, some; sume hwile, some while, 479 ; sume ... sume, some ... others, 131, 132, 133, 136, 548.

sumer, m., summer; ær sumeres cyme, before the advent of summer, 1228.

sund, m., swimming, sound, sea; sunde getenge, made fast on the sea, 228 ; sunde bewrecene, sea-whipped, (251).

sundor, adv., apart, aside, asunder, 407, 603, 1019.

sundorwîs, especially wise; sægdon hine sundorwisne, they called him especially wise, 588.

sunne, f., sun ; sunnan beorhtra, brighter than the sun, 1110.

sunu, m., son (of Christ) ; sunu meotudes, 461, 474, 564, 686, (cf. 592, 778, 892, 1318) ; voc. sunu, 447 ; gen. suna, 222 ; dat. suna, 1200.

sûsl, n., misery, torture, torment; sûsle gebunden, bound in torment, 772; sûslum beþrungen, oppressed by miseries, 950; in sûsla grund, into the abyss of tortures, 944.

swâ, adv., so (intensive), so (in this manner), 153, 306, 325, 350, etc.; swâ þéah, and yet, nevertheless, 500 ; as, 87, 100, 190, 207, etc. — (swâ brimo fæðmaþ, as far as the sea (extends) embraces, 972; swâ = as soon as, 128; swâ ... ne, without, although . . . not, 340.

swâmian, wv. II., become obscure, vanish, [629].

swǽs, beloved, own; mîn swǽs sunu, 447; mîn swǽs fæder, 517.

sweart, black, dark, superl. in þâ sweartestan ... witebrôgan, into the blackest . . . of the torturing terrors, 931.

swefan, sv. V., sleep ; pret. sg. swæf, 70.

swefen, m., sleep, dream, vision; swefnes woma, noise of a dream, 71 (s. note, 71).

swegl, n., heaven; under swegles hléo, 507; under swegle, 75; in swegle, 623; on swegle, 755.

swelling, m. or f. (?), swelling, swelling sail; under swellingum, under swelling sails, 245.

sweng, m., stroke, blow ; ýða swengas, blows of the waves, 239.

s w e o r d, n., sword ; lêgene sweorde, with fiery sword, 757.

sweordgenîðla, m., sworded foe, foe armed with a sword, 1181.

sweot, n., band, multitude, troop, [26]; for sweotum, before the troops, 124.

sweotole, adv., visibly, clearly, plainly, 26, 168, 861.

sweotollîce, adv., clearly, 690.

swîcan, sv. I., fail, fall short, become untrue, [293].

swîð, strong ; comp. swîðra ; séo swîðre, = the strong (hand), the right (hand) ; mîn on þâ swîðran, on my right hand, 347.

swîðe, adv., very, strongly, severely, fiercely ; tô swîðe, too fiercely, 663 ; swâ swîðe, so strongly, 940; super. swîðost, = most, very much ; twéon swîðost, very much in doubt, 668 (cf. 1103).

swîge, still, silent, 1275.

swilt, s. swylt.

swinsian, wv. II., sound, resound; sǽ swinsade, the sea resounded, 240.

swonrâd, f., swan-road, sea; ofer swonrâde, over the sea, 997.

swylc, such, of this sort (owiht swylces, anything of this kind, 571); such as, whoever (swylce ... Hûna cyning ... meahte âbannan, such as the king of the Huns might order, etc., 32).

swylce, adv., likewise, in the same manner, 3, 1033; like, resembling, as (swylce rêc, as smoke, 804; swylce heofensteorran, like the stars of heaven, 1113).

swylt, m., death, 447; swilt, 677.

syb, sib, f., peace; gen. sybbe, 446, 1315; dat. sybbe, 598; acc. sybbe, 1183; relationship, love, 1207; (Ger. sippe), [26].

syððan, s. sîððan.

sylf, prn., self; sylf, 303, 466, 732, 855, 1280; sylfa, [439]; gen. f. hiere sylfre, 222; dat. m. n. sylfum, 69, 184, 1295; acc. m. sylfne, 200, 209; gen. pl. sylfra, 1207; acc. pl. sylfe, 1001; — seolf, 708, 808; seolfum, 985; seolfne, 488, 603; pl. seolfe, 1121; gen. f. hire selfre, 1200.

symle, adv., always, continually, 469, 915, 1216.

Sŷmon, Simon, 530.

syn, f., sin, 414; gen. sg. synne, 772; gen. pl. synna, 497, 514, 778, 940, 958, 1318; dat. pl. synnum, 677, 1244, 1309.

syndon, s. sindon.

synful, sinful; synfulle, those laden with sin, 1295.

synnig, sinful, 956.

synt, s. sindon.

synwyrcende, sin-committing, 395, 944.

syx, six, 741; mid syxum ...

fiðrum, with six wings, 742; butan .vi. nihtum, 1228.

syxta, sixth; syxte geâr, sixth year, 7.

T.

tâcan, wv. I., show, point out; tâhte, 631.

tâcen, n., token, mark, sign, 171 (sigores tâcen, 85, 184, 1121; tâcen, 104, 1105; tâcna torhtost, the brightest of signs, 164); sign, wonder, miracle (tâcna gehwylces, of every wonder, 319; tâcnum cŷðan, declare in signs, 854; alra tâcna gehwylc, each of the old heroic deeds, 645). —

têar, m., tear; têaras fêollon, the tears fell, 1134.

tellan, wv. I., count, reckon, consider, believe; þonc ic ... fæstne talde, whom I believed made fast, etc., 909.

tempel, n., temple; tempel dryhtnes, 1010; godes tempel, 1022; tô godes temple, 1058.

têona, m., injury, insult, vexation; tô têonan, as a vexation, 988.

tîd, f., tide, time, period (on his dagana tîd, throughout the period of his days, 193; on þâ æðelan tîd, in that glorious day, 787; in hira lifes tîd, in her lifetime, 1209; feala tîda, many times [lit., much of times], 1044; tîdum gerŷmde, prolonged [my time] with time [?], 1249); hour (on þâ slîðan tîd, at this dreadful hour, 857; oð þâ nigoðan tîd, until the ninth hour, 870; nigoðe tîd, ninth hour, 874).

til, good; swâ tiles, swâ trâges, whether good or evil, 325.

tîonlêg, m., destructive flame, 1279.

tîr, m., glory, 164 (s. note, 164); tîre getâcnod (decore insignitum, Gm.), stamped with Thy glory, 754.

tîrêadig, glorious, rich in glory, renowned; tîrêadig cyning, 104; tîrêadig cwên, 605; tîrêadig, 955.

tô, prep. (1) with dat. (to whom?), to, 604, 1073, 1100, 1318; (wherefore? to what?) to, etc., 10, etc.; (often best translated by ["as" and] apposition), tô hrôðer, a joy, 16; tô wræce, a vengeance, 17 (cf. 23, 34, 45, 48, etc.) (whither?), 32, 52, 83, 216, etc.; (after sêcan), of, from, 319, 325, 410, 568; (temporal), for, in (tô wîdan feore, in eternity, 211, 1321; tô sôðe, s. sôð; tô hwan, to what [purpose], 1158; with inflected inf. [Lat. gerund], tô gecŷðanne, 533; tô gecêosanne, 607; tô gelæstenne, 1166). (2) with gen., tô þæs, = to such a degree, so; tô þæs heard, so intolerable, 704 (cf. tô þan, = so, 703).

tô, adv., too; tô lyt, 63; tô swîðe, 663; tô late, 708; (adv. of direction), þær hie tô sægon, while they looked on (cf. Ger. zusehen), 1105.

tôgênes, adv., in return, in reply, 167, 536.

tôglîdan, sv. I., fall apart; swâ lago tôglîdeð, as the sea separates, 1269; nihthelm tôglâd, the helmet of night fell apart (i.e. darkness vanished), 78.

tohte, f., fight, battle; tohtan sêcaþ, such battle, 1180.

torht, bright, luminous; super. tâcna torhtost, the brightest of signs, 164.

torht, n., brightness, clearness; torht ontŷnde, 1149.

torn, offence, anger, grief; nalles for torne, by no means on account of grief, 1134.

torngenîðla, m., wrath-provoking enemy; torngenîðlan, 568, 1306.

tôsomne, adv., together, 1202.

tôweorpan, sv. III., throw apart, break in pieces, destroy; p.p. tôworpen, 430.

tôwrecan, sv. V., drive apart, scatter; wurdon heardingas wîde tôwrecene, the heroes were driven wide asunder, 131.

trâg, evil; swâ tiles, swâ trâges, 955.

trâg, f., evil; wênde him trâge hnâgre, he feared the deplorable evil, 668.

tredan, sv. V., tread; trydeð, traverses, 612; pret. mearh moldan træd, the horse trod the earth, 55.

trêo, n., tree (lifes trêo, tree of life [in Paradise], 757); tree, tree of the cross (rôde trêo, 147, 206, 856), cross, 89, 107, 128, 165, 214, (trîo), 429, 442, 534, 701, 706, 828, 841, 867, 1027; trêow, 664; gen. trêowes, 1252.

Trôiâna, pl., Trojans, 645.

trymman, wv. I., strengthen, encourage; hine god trymede, him did God make strong, 14; fêðan trymedon eoredcestum, 35(?) (s. note, 35).

tû, s. twegen.

tûhund, two hundred, 2; .cc., 634.

turfhaga, m., turf-covering, turf sod; under turfhagen, 830.

twâ, s. twêgen.

twegen, m., two, 854; f. twâ, 880, 955, 1180; n. tû, 605 (cf. 754); dat. twâm, þâm twâm dælum, to these two parts, 1306.

twentig, twenty; .xx., 830.

twêo, m., doubt (*twoness*), 171; twêon swîðost, very much in doubt, 668.

tweogan, twêon, wv. II., doubt, [668].

tyht, m., motion; on tyhte, in motion, 53.

þ.

þâ, adv., there, then, 7, 25, 42, 69, 94, etc.; rel. conj., inasmuch as, as, since, when, 1, 172, 294, 389, 709, etc.

þa, s. sê.

þafian, wv. II., consent to, allow, suffer to come to pass, 608.

þâm, s. sê.

þan, adv., tô þan, = so; tô þan strang, so severe, 703; [wiððan, 926]; (cf. ǽrþan, forþan, siððan).

þanc, m., thought, grace, thanks; sîe ðê . . . þanc bûtan ende, to Thee be thanks without end, 811 (cf. 893).

þancian, wv. II., thank; gode þancode, she thanked God, 962, 1139.

þane, s. sê.

þanon, adv., thence, 143, 148; from that time, 348.

þǽr, adv., there, 41, 84, 114, etc.; where (rel.), 329, etc.; þǽr hê on corðre swæf, *as* he slept *there* in the crowd, 70; þǽr hie tô sǽgon, as they looked on, 1105; þǽr . . . ne, unless, 839, [979].

þâra, þǽra, þǽre, s. sê.

þâs, s. þes.

þæs, s. sê.

þæt, s. sê.

þæt, conj., that, 9, 144, 170, 175, etc.; þǽt þe, that, 59 (?); that, in order that, 324, 375, 409, 428, 552, 677, 679, 1055; that, so that, 15, 36 (?), 209, 501, 580, 830, 933.

þê, rel. prn., (*alone*) who, which (noun and acc.), 160, 163, 183, 298, 319, etc.; (*with dem.*), s. sê; (*with pers. prn.*), þê þis his bêacen wæs, whose sign this was, 162; þû ðê âhst doma geweald, Thou, who hast power over wills, 726; conj., that, 985; ðê dryhten ǽr âhangen wæs, where the Lord was hanged, 717.

þê, s. sê and þû.

þêah, conj., yet, 500; although, 48, 82, 174, 362, 393, 479, 509, 513, 707, 824, 1118, [1122], 1259.

þeaht, f., thought; on môdes þeaht, in the mind's thought, 1242.

þeahtian, wv. II., think, deliberate, reflect; þeahtedon, 547.

þearf, f., need; nû is þearf mycel, now there is much need (that), etc., 426; is êow rǽdes þearf, (there is need to you), you have need of foresight, 553.

þearf, s. þurfan.

þearl, strong, severe, violent; þreanŷd . . . þearl, violent, terrible necessity, 704.

þêaw, m., custom, habit, usage; dat. pl. cristenum þêawum, Christian usages, 1211.

þec, s. þû.

þegn, m., servant, man, warrior; þegn ôðerne, 540; þegna þrêate, 151; þegna hêap, 549; disciple, (ond his þegnum hine . . . seolfne geŷwde, and showed himself to his disciples, 487).

þegnung, f., service, ministration; tô þegnunge þinre, 739; þâ þegnunge, 745.

þencan, wv. I., think; pret. pl. þôhton, 549; consider, intend, wish, (lýsan þòlite of hæftnêde, wished to release (you) from bondage, 296).

þêod, f., people, nation, 468; dat. on þysse þêode, 539; ofer þæt Ebrêa þêod, 448; pl., men, people, gen. þêoda, 185, 421, 659, 781.

þêodan, wv. I., add, commit, [403]. [ple, 1156.

þêodcwên, f., queen of the peoþêoden, m., king (of Christ), 487, 563, 777, 858; (of Constantine), þêodnes, 267.

þeodenbealu (acc. to Wülker), added injury, extraordinary injury, 403. [þêodscipe, 1167.

þêodscipe, m., discipline; þurh þêon, wv. (S. 408, 8), commit; þêodon, [403].

þêos, s. þes.

þêostor, þýstor, n., or þêostru, þýstru, f., darkness; lêoht wið þýstrum, light with darkness, 307; þêostrum forþylmed, shrouded in darkness, 767.

þêostorcofa, m., dark space; in þêostorcofan, 833.

þêostorloca, m., dark lock-up, dark prison; under þêostorlocan, 485.

þêostre, dark; þêostrum geþancum, with dark thoughts, 312.

þêowdôm, m., service; in godes þêowdôm, 201.

þêownêd, f., servitude, slavery; - þêownêd þolian, en   'e the slave's necessity, 770.

þerscan, sv. III., thrash, beat; ~ þirsceð, 358.

þes, prn. (adj. and subs.), this; m. þes, 703, 704; f. þêos, 468, 533, 551, etc.; n. þis, 162, 435, 903, etc.; dat. (m), n. þissum, 576; f. þysse, 402, 539, 643; acc. m. þysne, 312; n. þis, 630, 659; instr (m.), n. þýs, 92; pl. nom. and acc. þâs, 749,

1173; gen. þyssa, 858; dat. þyssum, 700.

þicgan, sv. V., receive; pret. sg. þege, 1259.

þîn, pers. prn., thy, thine, 489, 510, 597, etc.; s. þû.

þincan, s. þyncan.

þing, n., thing; þinga gehwylc, 409, (cf. 1156); tô þinge, as a fact (?), 608.

þinggemearc, n., characterization of a thing, determination of time, time; gen. (adv.) þinggemearces, according to time (as one counts time), 3.

þingian, wv. II., intercede for (with dat.); ac his eald fêondum þingode þrohtherd, but patiently he made intercession for his embittered enemies, 494; speak, made a speech, (him . . . wið þingode, spoke to him, 77); Judas hire ongên þingode, Judas replied to her, 609, 667.

þis, þis-, s. þes.

þolian, wv. II., suffer, endure, 770.

þone, s. sê.

þonne, adv., then, 446, 489, 526, 931, 1286; conj., when, if, 50, 473, 618, 1178, 1179, 1185, 1273, 1280; than, (after comp.) læsse . . . þonne, 48; ænlîcra þonne, 74; furðurþonne, 388; (with implied comp.), þæt wæs fær mycel, open ealdgewin þonne þêos æðele gewyrd, that was a great danger, the known battle of olden times, (older, or greater?) than this noble event, 647.

þracu, f., onrush, storm, conflict, battle; þræce, to the contest, 45; wið þêoda þræce, against the attack of the people, 185.

þrâg, f., time; þrâgum, at times, sometimes, 1239, [668].

þræcheard, strong in battle, valiant in combat, 123.

þrǣgan, wv. I., run; þrǣgde, 1263.

þrêa, m. f., threat, oppression, might; þrêam forþrycced, with might oppressed, 1277.

þrêalic, terrible, horrible; þæt wæs þrêalic geþôht, that was a horrible conception, 426.

þrêagan, wv. III., reprove, punish; p.p. in ðâm midle þrêad, punished in the middle, 1296.

þrêanêd, f., dire necessity; þrêanŷd, 704; þrêanêdum, 884.

þrêat, m., crowd, troop, multitude; dat. (instr.), þreate, 51, 326, 329; þegna þrêate, 151; folca þ., 215; wigena þ., 217; gumena þ., 254, 1096; secga þ., 271; wera þ., 537; beorna þ., 873; for þyslîcne þrêat, before such a crowd, 546.

þrêo, three, 2, 285, 483, 869, 1286; .iii., 833, 847; gen. þrêora, 858.

þreodian, wv. II., think over, reflect upon, consider; pret. sg. þreodude, 1239; pret. pl. þrydedon, 549.

þridda, third, 855, 1298; sio þridde, 884; þŷ þriddan dæge, 185 (cf. 485).

þringan, sv. III., throng, press, hasten; pret. pl. þrungon, 123, 329.

þrîste, bold, determined, confident, 267; audacious, 1286.

þrîste, adv., boldly, confidently, 409, (1167).

þrîtig, þrittig, thirty; .xxx., 3.

þroht, m., torture, 704.

þrohtherd, strong in enduring torture, patient, 494.

þrosm, m., smoke; þrosme beþehte, covered with smoke, 1298.

þrôwian, wv. II., suffer, endure, 769; þrôwode, 421.

þrŷðbord, n., strong shield, 151.

þrydian, s. þreodian.

þrym, m., glory, majesty (of God), the Most Glorious; eallra þrymma þrym, the Glory of all glories, 486, 519; allra cyninga þrym, the Most Glorious of all kings, 816, (cf. 1090); þrymmes hyrde, Guardian of glory, 348, 859; þrymme, with glory (= glorious), 745; in þrynesse þrymme, in the majesty of the trinity, 177; on þrymme, in majesty, 329.

þrymcyning, m., glorious king, king of glory, 494.

þrymlîce, adv., gloriously, 781.

þrymsittende, throned in glory; ðe . . . þrymsittendum, to Thee throned in glory, etc., 811.

þrŷnes, f., threeness, trinity; in þrynesse þrymme, 177.

þû, pers. prn., thou, 81, 83, 84, etc.; þû þe, Thou who, 726; þû (alone) (Thou) who, 727, 730, 732; gen. þin, sê ôhteð þîn, who will persecute thee, 928; dat. þê, 79, 81, 82, 441, etc.; acc. þec 403, 447, 539, 676, 823, 931; þê, 522, 789, 814, etc.

þûf, m., banner, 123.

þurfan, pret. pres., need; ne þearft ðû . . . sâr nîwigan, thou needst not renew the sorrow, 940; need, may, dare (?), ic þâ rôde ne þearf hleahtre herigean, this cross I dare not despise with the laughter of scorn, 919 (?); cf. þorfte, 1104.

þurh, prep. with acc., through, causal (occasion, agent, means, instrument), 120, 147, 153, 165, 172, 183, 199, 281, 289, etc., 459, 626, 646, 808, 1106; at, because of, on account of, 86, 98, 400, 1167, 1301;

(manner), in, with, 6, 685; by, for the sake of (þurg þæt beorhte gesceap, etc., by that bright object [I will pray], 790; ic þæt geswerige þurh sunu meotodes, that I swear by the Son of the Creator, 686; ic éow healsie þurh heofona god, I adjure you by the God of heaven, 699).

þurhdrîfan, sv. I., shove through, penetrate, imbue; mid dysige þurhdrifen, imbued with folly, 707.

þurhgéotan, sv. II., pour through, fill, imbue, saturate; gléawnesse þurhgoten, impregnated with knowledge, 962.

þurhwadan, sv. VI., go through, bore, pierce; þe ... fêt þurhwôdon, (of the nails) which pierced the feet, etc., 1066.

þus, adv., thus, so, 189, 400, 528, 1120, 1237.

þûsend, n., thousand; m., 285, 326.

þŷ, s. sê.

þyder, adv., thither, on that side, 548.

þyncan, wv. I., seem, appear; pret. sg. þuhte, 72; sêlost þûhte, 1165; opt. pres. sêlest þince, 532; seem good, dô swâ þê þynce, do as seems good to thee, 541.

þys, s. þes.

þyslic, thuslike, such a; for þyslicne þreat, before such a crowd, 546; (adv.), in this manner, thus, 540.

þysne, þyssa, þysse, þyssum, s. þes.

þŷst, s. þêost.

U.

ûðweota, m., wise man, philosopher, scribe; ûðweotan, 473.

ûhta, m., or ûhte, n. (S. 280. 1), dawn of morning; on ûhtan, at dawn, 105.

ûhtsang, m., song at dawn, [29].

unâsecgendlîc, unutterable, 466.

unbræce, indestructible, everlasting; æðelum unbræce, in its properties endless, (1029).

unclæne, unclean; fram unclænum ... gâstum, 301.

uncûð, unknown; uncûðe wyrd, unknown occurrence, 1102.

uncŷðig, ignorant, 961; elnes oncŷðig, unacquainted with power, powerless, 725.

undearninga, adv., openly, unreservedly, 405; undearnunga, 620.

under, prep. (with dat.), under, 13, 46, 75, 147, 245, 507, etc.; under (deep in), 218, 485, 625, 653, 695, 832, 843, 1092; (with acc.), under, 44, 764.

ungelîce, adv., unlike, differently, unequally, 1307.

unhwîlen, without limit of time, eternal; drêam unhwîlen, 1232.

unlifgende, lifeless, 879.

unlŷtel, not a little, much, great; mægen unlŷtel, not a little crowd, 283; folc unlŷtel, not a little folk, 872.

[**unne**, f., permission, favor, [1246].]

unoferswîðeð, unvanquished, invincible, 1188.

unriht, wrong, false; unrihte æ, unrighteous law, 1042.

unriht, n., wrong, injustice, sin; unrihtes, 472, 516; on unriht, 582.

unrîme, numberless, unnumbered; unrîme mægen, 61.

unscyldig (Ger. unschuldig), guiltless, innocent; unscyldigne, (423), 496.

unscynde, not injuring, blameless, glorious; dôm unscyndne, 365; gife unscynde, 1201, 1247.

[unsêoc,unsick,1247; Ettmüller.] unslâw, unslow, stirring, active, 202.

unsnyttro, f., unwisdom, folly; unsnyttro, in folly, 1285; unsnyttrum, foolishly, 947.

unsôfte, adv., unsoftly, with difficulty; sume unsôfte aldor generedon, some saved life with difficulty, 132.

untrâglîce,adv.,without reserve, — without hesitation, 410.

untwêonde, undoubting, unwavering; hyht untwêondne, unwavering hope, 798.

unweaxen,not grown up,young; mec ... unweaxenne, 529.

unwîslîce, adv., unwisely, 293.

ûp, adv. (direction), up, upwards, 87, 95, 353, 700, 712, 714, 717, 736, 794, 803, 879, 1107, 1226.

uppan, prep. (with dat. or acc. postpositive), over; him ûppan, over him, 886.

uppe, adv., up, above; uppe = on high, 52; [im schwange, 1266, according to Dietrich].

ûprador, m., upper heaven, firmament, 731.

ûpweard, adv., upward, toward heaven, 806.

ûr, m., aurochs, name of the rune for u.

ûrigfeðra, dewy-winged, 29; ûrigfeðra earu, 111.

ûs, pers. prn., dat. us, 400, 637; acc. ûsic, us, 533.

ûsse, pl., our; fæderas ûsse, 425, 458.

ût, adv., out; beran ût þræce rincas under roderum, to lead out to combat the heroes under heaven, 45.

W.

wâ, adv., woe; ond gehwædres wâ, and in either event woe (?), 628.

wadan, sv. VI., wade, go, advance; wadan wægflotan, wave floaters press on, 246.

wæðan, wv. I., hunt, roam around; wæðed be wolcnum, darts — over (past) the clouds, 1274.

wædl, f., poverty, want; gewende tô wædle, betakes himself to want, 617.

wæg, m., wave; wæges welm, the wave's motion, 230.

wægflota, m., wave-float, ship; pl. wægflotan, 246.

wæghengest, m., wave-horse, ship (Ger. hengst); wæghengestas, 236.

wald, s. weald.

wælfel, greedy for corpses, ghoulish, 53.

wælhlence, f., battle-link, coat of mail; pl. wælhlencan, 24.

wælhrêow, wild in battle, unrestrained, cruel; wælhrêowra wîg, the battle of the cruel, 112.

wælrest, f., death-rest, bed of slaughter, grave's quiet; wunode — wælreste, rested in the quiet of the grave.

wælrûm, f., battle-secret; wælrûne ne mâð, he did not conceal the battle-secret, 28.

wan, wan, wanting color, dark, black (of the raven), 53.

wang, m., field; nê þæs wanges wiht, nor anything of this field, 684.

wangstede, m., point of the field, locality, field; of ðâm wangstede, 794; on ðâm wangstede, 1104.

wannhâl, unhealthy, weak; wraðu wannhâlum, help for the sick, 1030.

wansælig, unhappy, miserable; weras wonsælige, 478; werum wansæligum, 978.

wæpen, n., weapon, 1189; wæpen âhôf, took up arms, 17; wæpnum, 48.

wæpenþracu, f., storm of weapons, conflict; acc. wæpenþræce, 106.

wær, fidelity (wær wið þec, fidelity toward Thee, 823); favor, protection (wære bêodan, announce protection, 80).

wærlic, cautious, prudent; worda wærlicra, of prudent words, 544.

wæstm, m. f. n., growth, fruit; wæstmum gêacnod, fructified with fruit, 341.

wât, s. witan.

wæter, n., water; ymb þæs wæteres wylm, around this water's stream, 39 (cf. 60).

wê, pers. prn., we, 364, 397, 399, 401, 402, etc.

wêadæd, f., woful deed, evil deed, 495.

weald, m. (Ger. wald), forest· on wealde, 28.

wealdan, red. vb., rule, possess; with instr. duguðum wealdan, 450; with gen. þæs ðu ... wealdest, this Thou controllest, 761; walde ... wuldres on heofenum, possesses glory in heaven, 801.

wealdend, wielder, guider, ruler, lord, king (of God), 4, 80, 391, 512; (waldend), 732, 752, 773, 781, 789(?), 851, 892, 1043, 1085, 1090(?); (of Christ) (waldend), 206, 337, 347; (waldend), 421, 482, 1067.

weallan, red. vb., well up, boil, move (of waves), agitate; weallende

gewitt þurh wigan snyttro, mind agitated (lit. moving) by the warrior's wisdom, 938.

weard, m., warden, watch, guardian, protector; (of God), 84, 197, 1022, 1101, 1316; (of Christ), 338, 445, 718; (of Constantine), 153; ceastre weardas, the guardians of the city, 384.

weardian, wv. II;, guard, protect, take possession of, inhabit; stede weardedon ymb Danûbie, they took possession of the region around the Danube, 135; hreðer weardode, inhabited the bosom, 1145.

wearhtreafu, n. pl., home of the damned, hell; of ðâm wearhtreafum, 927.

weaxan, sv. VI., wax, grow, increase; pret. sg. wêox, 12, 914, [547].

webbian, wv. II., weave, project; inwitþancum wrôht webbedan, with wicked thoughts wove crime, 309.

weccan, wv. I., wake, [106].

wed, n., pledge, security, extenuation; wed gesyllan, to give pledge (?), 1284.

wêdan, wv. I., rage; wêdende, 1274.

wefan, sv. V., weave; wordcræft wæf, I wove skill of words, 1238.

weg, m., way; weg to wuldre, way to heaven, 1150.

wegan, sv. V., carry, bear; môdsorge wæg ... cyning, the king experienced sorrow of heart, 61; gnornsorge wæg, he bore sorrow, 655.

welm, s. wylm.

wêmend, adviser, discloser; rihtes wêmend, revealer of right, 880.

wên, f., hope, name of the rune *w*; wên is geswiðrad, hope is departed, 1264.

wêna, m., expectation; dêaðes on wênan, in expectation of death, 584.

wênan, wv. I. (with gen.), hope for, expect; wênan, 1104; pret. sg. wende, 62, [348]; wendon, 478, [880]; wende him trûge hnâgre, he feared the deplorable evil, 668.

wendan, wv. I., wend, turn; þæt hîe hit for worulde wendan ne meahton, that they might not avert this before the world, 979; pret. sg. wende (348); wende hine of worulde, he turned himself from the world, 440.²

wendelsǽ, m., boundary sea; boundary of the sea; æt wendelsǽ, 231.

weorc, n., work; hrefn weorces gefeah, the raven rejoiced at the work, 110; cwên weorces gefeah, 849; synna weorc, 1318; weorcum fâh, besmirched by deeds, 1243.

weorðan, sv. III., with p.p. (forming passive or circumlocution for pret.), 581, 688; pret. sg. weard, 5, 9, 69, 102, 178, 183, 638, 776, 804, 989, 1035, 1050; pret. sg. opt. wurde, 336, 429, 961, 976; (without p.p.), be, become, happen, occur (weorðan, 220, 1049, 1177; wyrðeð, 575; weorðen, 428; wearð, 15, 41, 501, 1036, 1042; wurdon, 130, 584, 1278; wurde, 401).

weorðian, wv. II., hold worthy, honor; pret. sg. weorðode, 1137; pret. pl. weorðodon, 831; pret. pl. opt. weorðeden, 1222; p.p. weorðod, 1196.

weorpan, sv. III., throw, cast; p.p. worpene, 1304.

weorod, troop, legion, band, folk, multitude, 158; dat. sg. weorode, 844; gen. pl. weoroda, 752, 815, 897; dat. pl. weorodum, 351, 782, 867 (cf. weorud, 1117; weorude, 1281; weoruda, 223, 681); wereda, 1085; werod, 19, 48, 53, 60, 94; werodes, 38; werode, [217], 230; weroda, 789, 1150 (?).

weoruld, s. woruld.

wer, m., man, person, 508; weres, 72, 341, 959, 967, 1038; wer, 785; weras, 22, 287, 314, 478, 547, 559; wera, 304, 475, 537, 543, 596; werum, 236, 978, 1222.

wered, s. weorod.

wergan, wv. I., condemn, curse, despise; þâ gê wergdon þane, for you despised him, 294.

wergð(u), f., curse, condemnation, punishment, 309; of wergðe, 295; wergðu drêogan, suffer punishment, 211, 952.

wêrig, weary, unhappy, miserable; sîo wêrge sceolu, the miserable throng, 763; þâ wêregan nêat, 357; wêrge wræcmæcggas, unhappy men of misfortune, 387.

werod, s. weorod.

werodlêst, f., want of men; for werodlêste, for want of men, 63.

werþêod, f., men-folk, folk, people; on þysse werþêode, 649; geond þâ werþêode, 969; werþêodum, 17.

wesan, sv. V., be; wæs, 1, 7, 11, 13, etc.; wâron, 22, 25, 46, etc.

westan, adv., from the west, 1016.

wêsteu, m. n., waste, desert, wilderness; on wêstenne, 611.

wîc, n., dwelling; wîc gewunode, inhabited the dwelling, 1038 (cf. wîc beheold, 1144).

wicg, n., horse; sê þæt wicg byrð, who directs (?) that horse, 1196.

wîcian, wv. II., dwell, encamp; pret. sg. here wicode, the army encamped, 65 (cf. wîcedon).

wîd, wide, broad, expanded; tô wîdan feore, for extended time, = in eternity, forever, 211, 1321; on wîdan feore, in extended time (i.e. during the long period of the world's existence); wîdan fyrhð, during long life, = eternally, 761 (cf. 801).

wîde, widely, 131, 969; side ond wîde, far and wide, 277.

wîð, prep. (with gen.). (1) against; wið hungres hlêo, protection against hunger, 616. (2) (with dat.), against, 18, 64, 165, 185, 416, 525, 837, [926], 1182, 1188 (him . . . wið þingode, he spoke to him, 77); with, 307, 308. (3) (with acc.), against, toward, 403, 513 (wære wið þec, fidelity toward thee, 823, 927?).

wiðercyr, m. (Ger. wiederkehr), return, 926.

wiðerhycgende, hostile-minded, hostile, 952.

wiðersæc, n (?)., hostility, opposition; wiðersæc fremedon, they offered contradiction, 569.

wiðhycgan, wv. I., scorn; beteran wiðhycge, (that) he scorn the better, 618.

wiðrêotan, sv. II., contend against, resist; gê þâm ryhte wiðroten hæfdon, you had withstood the right, 369.

wiðsacan, sv. VI., oppose, contend against, renounce, scorn, abandon; (with dat), wiðsæcest sôðe ond rihte, 663; pret. sg. þînum wiðsôc aldordôme, 767; þâm wyrsan wiðsôc, 1040; pret. pl. wiðsôcon sôðe ond rihte, 390; (with acc.), wiðsæcest þone âhangan cyning, 933; pres.

opt. þâ wiste wiðsæce, 617; pret. pl. þæt wê wiðsocun ær, 1122 (?).

wiðweorpan, sv. III., reject; wiðwurpon, 294.

wîf, n., wife, woman, 223, 286, 508; wîfes, 1132; werum ond wîfum, 236, 1222.

wîg, m. n., war, battle, 131; wîges wôma, noise of war, 19; acc. wig, 112; wîgges lêan, 825; dat. (instr.) wîgge, 48, 150, 1182, 1189, 1196.

wîga, m., warrior; gen. sg. þurh wigan snyttro, 938; pl. wigan, 246; gen. pl. wigena, 63, 150, 153, 217, (wigona), 344, 1090.

wîgend, m., warrior, 106; wiggende, 984.

wîgg, s. wîg.

wîgspêd, f., success of war, victory, 165.

wîgþracu, f., storm of war, attack; æfter wîgþræce, after the battle-storm, 430; þâ wiggþræce, 658.

wiht, f. n., wight, whit, anything; nê þæs wanges wiht, nor anything of this field, 684.

wilfægen, of elated will, glad, 828.

wilgifa, m., granter of desires, giver of joy; (of Constantine), þæs wilgifan word, 221; (of Christ), weoroda willgifa, 815; (of God), hira willgifan wundor, 1112.

willa, m., will, wish, desire, joy, 773, 789, 963, 1136, 1160; dryhtne tô willan, for the Lord's sake, 193 (cf. 678, 1011); acc. willan, 267, 681, 1071, 1085, 1132, 1153; willum gefylled, filled with joy, 452 (cf. 1252).

willan, anv. (S. 428), will, wish (often forming future, but with idea of volition); 1st p. sg. wille,

574, 790, 814; 2d p. sg. opt. wille, 608, 621; 3d p. sg. opt. wile, 420; pret. sg. wolde, 219, 469; pret. pl. woldon, 40, 361, 394, 971; wolde ic, þæt ðu funde, I would that thou wouldst find (them), 1080; hû wolde þæt geweorðan, how could this happen! 456.

willgifa, s. **wilgifa**.

willhrêðig, glad-hearted (because of a fulfilled wish), exultant, 1117.

willsîð, m., desired journey; on willsîð, for the longed-for journey, 223.

willspel, n., desired news, good tidings, glad message; æt þâm willspelle, at this good news, 994; wilspella mǽst, this greatest coveted news, 984.

wind, m., wind; winde gelîccost, 1272.

winemæg, m., friendly man, friend; winemagas, 1016.

winnan, sv. III., fight, contend 1181 (s. note, 1181).

winter, m., winter (year); .xxx. . . . wintra, thirty (of) winters, 4; wintra gangum, in the course of years, 633.

wintergerîm, n., number of years, 654.

wîr, m., wire; ofer wîra gespon, 1135; wîrum gewlenced, 1264.

wîs, wise, learned, 592; super. þâ wîsestan, 153, 169, 323.

wîsdôm, m., wisdom, 1243; gen. sg. wîsdômes, 357, 543, 596, 939, 1144, 1191; acc. 334, 674.

wîse, f., wise, manner, circumstance; þâ wîsan, 684.

wîsfæst, very wise; weras wîsfæste, 314.

wist, f., substance, food, 617.

wiste, s. **witan**.

wita, m., wise man, councillor; witan snyttro, wisdom of a wise man, 544.

witan, pret. pres., know (wit, wot); ic wât, 419, 815; pl. witon, 644; pret. sg. wiste, 860, 1203; pret. pl. wiston, 459; imperative, wite, 946.

wîtan, sv. I., reproach; þe him sîo cwên wite, (with) which the queen reproached them, 416.

wîte, n., punishment, torture (of hell), hell; láðlîc wîte, 520; in wîta forwyrd, 765 (cf. 1030); heardum wîtum, 180; in wîtum, 771.

wîtebrôga, m., torturing terror; þâ wyrrestan wîtebrôgan, the worst torturing terrors, 932.

wîtedôm, m., prophecy, prediction, 1153.

wîtga, m., prophet, 351, 1189; gen. sg. wîtan sunu, the son of a prophet, 592; pl. wîtgan, 561; gen. wîtgena, 289, 334, 394.

wlanc, proud, stately; wlanc manig, many a proud one, 231.

wlîtan, sv. I., see, look; wlât ofer ealle, he glanced over all, 385.

wlite, m., appearance, form, beautiful form, beauty; on wlite, 1319.

wliteg, s. **wlitig**.

wlitêscŷne, beautiful in appearance, 72.

wlitig, beautiful, 77; þæt wlitige treo, 165; super. wlitegaste, 749; wlitî wuldres trêo, 89.

wôð, f., voice, tone, song; wôða wlitegaste, the most beautiful of songs, 749.

wolcen, n. (welkin), cloud; pl. ofer wolcna hrôf, upon the roof of the clouds, 89; under wolcnum, 1272; be wolcnum, 1274.

wolde, s. willan.

wom, m. n., spot, blemish, sin; under womma sceatum, 583 (cf. 1310).

womful, full of blemishes, sinful; womfulle synwyrcende sceaðan, the bespotted, sin-committing enemies, 761.

womsceaða, sin-besmirched enemy, 1299.

wôma, m., noise; wiges wôma, 19; swefnes wôma, noise of a dream, vision, 71.

wonhŷdig, heedless, foolish; wonhŷdige, 763.

wonsǽlig, s. wan.

wôp, m., weeping; wôpes hring, sound of weeping, 1132.

word, n., word; gen. sg. wordes, 314, 419; instr. worde, 946; acc. word, 221, 334, (338), 344, 394, 440, 547, 582, 724, 749, 771, 939, 990, 1003, 1072, 1168, 1191; gen. pl. worda, 544, 569, 1284; dat. (instr.) wordum, 169, 287, 351, 385, 529, 537, 559, 589, 893, 1319; wordum ond bordum, 24.

wordcræft, m., wordcraft, art of speech; wordcræftes wîs, 592; poetic art (wordcræft, 1238).

wordcwide, m., speech; wrixledan wordcwidum weras, the men exchanged thoughts in speech, 547.

wordgerŷne, n., verbal secret, secret (hidden in words); þurh witgena wordgerŷno, through the prophets' secret in words, 289, (cf. 323).

world, s. woruld.

worn, m., multitude, number, (304?), 633.

worpian, wv. II., throw, throw

at, pelt; stânum worpod, pelted with stones, 492; stângreopum worpod, 825.

woruld, f., world; world, 1277; on worulde, 561; of . . ., 440; in . . ., 994, 1153, (worlde) 1252; fram . . ., 1142; acc. on woruld, into the world, 508; in woruld weorulda, in the world of worlds (i.e. in eternity), 452; for worulde, before the world, (i.e. before humanity), 4, [304], 979.

woruldgedâl, n., separation from the world, death; tô woruldgedâle, 581.

woruldrîce, n., kingdom of the world; on woruldrîce, 456, (cf. 779); in worldrîce, 1049.

woruldstund, f., life in the world; æfter woruldstundum, throughout my sojourn upon earth, 363.

wræc (?), s. wracu.

wræcmæcgg, m., miserable man, man of misfortune; wérge wræcmæcggas, unhappy men of misfortune, 387.

wracu (or **wræc?**), f., revenge, punishment; tô wræce, a vengeance, 17, (cf. 495).

wrâð, perverse, perverted; þurh wrâð gewitt, 459; wroth, angry, hostile (wið wrâðum, against the hostile, 165; wrâð wið wrâðum, hostile against hostile, 1182).

wrâðe, adv., perversely, 294.

wraðu, f., support, help, 1030; þær ðû wraðe findest, where thou wilt find help, 84, [294].

wrætlîce, adv., wonderfully, splendidly, artistically; super. wrætlîcost, 1020.

wrecan, sv. V., drive, press forward; stundum wræcon, they pressed forward a while, 121, 232.

wreccan, wv. I., awake, 106.

wrêon, sv. I. and II., cover, conceal; pret. pl. wrigon, 583.

wrîðan, sv. I., wreathe, twist; wriðene wælhlencan netted (?), coats of mail, 24.

wrixlan, wv. I., exchange, change, (547), 759.

wrôht, m. f., accusation, crime, 309.

wrôhtstæf, m., crime; þurh wrôhtstafas, through crimes, 926.

wuldor, n., glory; wuldres, 752, 801; wuldre, 1135; wuldor, 813; wuldres miht, might of glory, glorious might, 295, 727; wuldres trêo (of cross), tree of glory, 89, 828, 867 (cf. 217, 844, 1252); with gen. pl. most glorious (cyninga wuldor, 5, 178, cf. 186); glory, heavenly glory, heaven (wuldres, 77, 84, 738, 1040, 1090; in wuldre, 747, 782, 823; tô wuldre, 1047, 1150); glory (glorification), 893, 1117, 1124.

wuldorcyning, m., King of Glory (of God); wuldorcyninges, 1321; wuldorcyninge, 291, 963, 1304.

wuldorfæst, glorious, (as fast as heaven?); wuldorfæste gife, 967.

wuldorgeofa, m., bestower of glory; weoruda wuldorgeofa (God), the men's Bestower of Glory, 681.

wuldorgifu, f., glorious gift, grace; onwrige wuldorgifum, might reveal it by grace, 1072.

wulf, m., wolf, 28, 112.

wund, f., wound; synna wunde, the wound of sins, 514.

wundor, n., wonder, miracle, 868, 1112, 1122, 1254; pl. wundor, 827, 897; feala . . . wundra, many (of) miracles, 363, 777; wundrum, wonderfully, 1238.

wundorwyrd, f., wonderful event; ymb wundorwyrd, 1071.

wundrian, wv. II., marvel, wonder; wundrade ymb þæs weres snytro, she marvelled at the wisdom of this man, 959.

wunîgan, wv. II., dwell, be, 821, (remain), 908; pres. opt. wunige, 624; pret. sg. wunodest, 950; wunode, 724, 1028.

wylm, m., wave, motion (of wave), current, stream; wæges welm, wave's motion, (230); ymb þæs wæteres wylm, beside this water's stream, 39; (of fire), in þæs wylmes grund, 1299; in wylme, 765, 1310; in hâtne wylm, 1297.

wyn, f., joy, bliss; wuldres wynne, bliss of heaven, 1040.

wynbêam, m., tree of delight; (of cross), wuldres wynbêam, 844.

wynsum, winsome; of ðâm wangstede wynsumne, from this winsome spot, 794.

wyrcan, wv. I., work; þâ hê worhte, which he wrought, 827 (cf. 897); work, build, 1020 (nales sceame worhte gâste mînum, in no wise wrought I this shame to my spirit, 470).

wyrd, f., Weird, fate (hûru, wyrd gescrâf, forsooth, Fate decreed, 1047); fate, event, transaction, object (acc. wyrd, 541, 583, 1064, 1102; wyrda, 80, 589, 813, 978, 1124, 1256).

wyrdan, wv. I., destroy; mînne . . . folgað wyrdeð, destroyeth my following, 904.

wyrðe, worth, worthy, dear, 291.

wyrresta, the worst; þâ wyrrestan wîtebrôgan, the worst of the torturing terrors, 932.

wyrsa, worse; þâm wyrsan wiðsôc, opposed the worse, 1040.

Y.

ẎỮ, f., wave; ẏ̃ða swengas, strokes of waves, 239.

Ẏ̃ðhof, n., wave-dwelling, ship; ald ẏ̃ðhofu, old ships, (252).

yfel, n., evil; ne geald hê yfel yfele, he did not return evil for evil, 493; yfela gemyndig, mindful of evils, 902.

yfemest, adv., uppermost; yfemest in þâm âde, 1290.

ylde, s. elde.

yldra, s. eald.

ymb, prep. (with acc.), (loc.), around, about, 50, 66, 260, 869; about, on, near, 39, 136; on, 60, 227; (temporal), after, 272, 383; ymb sige, for victory, 1181; about, concerning, in regard to, 214, 442, 534, 541, 560, 664, 959, 1064, 1071, 1255.

ymbhwyrft, m., sphere of earth; ealne ymbhwyrft, 731.

ymbsellan, wv. I., surround, envelop; þâ ymbsealde synt mid syxum eac fiðrum, which are also surrounded with six wings, 742.

ymbsittend, besieger; Hûna ... ymbsittendra âwêr, of the Huns . . . encamped somewhere round about, 33.

Ẏppe, evident, known, 435.

Ẏr, bow, name of the rune for y; (according to Rieger) gold, 1260.

yrfe, n., inheritance, heritage; yrfes brûcaþ, enjoy the heritage, 1320.

yrming, unfortunate man, [1290].

yrmðu, s. ermðu.

yrre, (wrong, erring), angry, 573; eorre, 401; þurh eorne hyge, in her angry soul, 685.